THE LITERARY ORIGIN OF THE GOSPEL OF JOHN

by HOWARD M. TEEPLE

Religion and Ethics Institute, Inc.
Evanston
1974

Library of Congress Catalog Card Number: 73-87487

Price $6.00

Published by
Religion and Ethics Institute, Inc.
P.O. Box 664
Evanston, Illinois, U.S.A. 60204

Printed in the United States of America by
Adams Press, Chicago, Illinois

TO

GLADYS

THE INSTITUTE

The Religion and Ethics Institute was incorporated under the laws of the state of Illinois as a nonprofit organization 29 November 1972. The purpose of the Institute, as stated in its charter, is "to promote the discovery and distribution of sound historical and scientific knowledge in the fields of religion and ethics." The Institute proposes to do this through both discovery on the research level and distribution on the popular level. The present volume, on the research level, is the Institute's first publication.

PREFACE

The present writer's interest in the question of the literary origin of the Gospel of John began in 1961 when I disagreed with Sidney Temple's article "A Key to the Composition of the Fourth Gospel." In response to it I read a paper entitled "Grundschrift in the Fourth Gospel?" at the annual meeting of the Society of Biblical Literature in St. Louis in December. In connection with the research for the paper I studied Rudolf Bultmann's theory in his commentary on the gospel and attempted to solve the problem myself. After a month's effort I concluded that the gospel is much too complex to unravel, and I abandoned the project as hopeless.

Fortunately, in 1965 John Reumann, then New Testament Book Review Editor of the Journal of Biblical Literature, invited me to review The Composition and Order of the Fourth Gospel by Dwight Moody Smith, Jr. Smith's summary and discussion of the theories of Bultmann's critics revived my hope that solution of the literary problem is possible. My review ended with this statement: "We are confident that the book will not only foster understanding of Bultmann's theories but will have a stimulating effect upon future Johannine study." One of the persons stimulated by Smith's work has turned out to be the present writer. Since the summer of 1965 all my available spare time has been given to the study of the problem.

In chapters 4 to 8 of the present book the theories of others are surveyed chronologically within each chapter in the order of publication. If the information was available to me, the position or vocation of a writer is given in connection with the main description of his theory. Unless indicated otherwise, the position listed is that held at the time the particular work was published. The date the theory was published is given in parenthesis, while the title of the work is given in the bibliography. In the bibliography, if possible, an author's full name is given as listed in the National Union Catalog of the United States Library of Congress. Thus the reader will find a book listed in the public catalog of his library under the same entry as that given in the bibliography. Although the general practice in writing and publishing is to give only each author's surname and initials in the bibliography, printing the full name enlarges the reader's knowledge and aids him in finding the author's works. In conformity with the Library of Congress catalog, commentaries on the Bible are listed under "Bible," with a cross-reference from the commentator's name. If a work in the bibliography is mentioned in the notes, the title is cited in an abbreviated form in the notes; this short form is given in brackets in the bibliography.

The text of the Gospel of John in this book is my translation of the Greek text in Novum Testamentum Graece by Nestle and Aland (25th ed., 1963). I made the translation in order to obtain a more literal version which will display in English more of the distinctions in vocabulary and syntax in the Greek text. Some distinctions, however, are not apparent even in a literal translation; for example, there are two different Greek verbs for "love." When significant for detecting the literary strata, such distinctions are inserted in brackets in the translation. A further reason for making the new translation is to provide an English rendering of an up-to-date text, in which the selection of textual variants takes into account the characteristics of the individual writers within the gospel. The translation necessarily is awkward to read, for it is intended as a literal reflection of the Greek, not as a polished version in modern English idiom.

Credit belongs to the following libraries for the use of their resources: Chicago State University, The University of Chicago, Garrett Theological Seminary, Northwestern University, and Seabury-Western Theological Seminary.

I gratefully acknowledge the competent assistance of Kathleen McCullough, Nell Lewis, and my wife, Gladys, in preparing the manuscript. Ms. Lewis accepted the responsibility for the final editing and typing of the first ten chapters. I am indebted to Gladys for her encouragement and assistance throughout the entire eight years of work.

Evanston, Illinois
October 1973

CONTENTS

ABBREVIATIONS

ATANT	Abhandlungen zur Theologie des Alten und Neuen Testaments
ATR	*Anglican Theological Review*
BA	*Biblical Archaeologist*
BEvT	Beiträge zur evangelischen Theologie
BJRL	John Rylands Library. *Bulletin*
BL	*Bibel und Leben*
BWANT	Beiträge zur Wissenschaft vom Alten und Neuen Testament
BZ	*Biblische Zeitschrift*
BZNW	Beihefte zur die Zeitschrift für die neutestamentliche Wissenschaft
CBQ	*Catholic Biblical Quarterly*
CJT	*Canadian Journal of Theology*
EvT	*Evangelische Theologie*
Exp	*The Expositor*
ExpT	*Expository Times*
FRLANT	Forschungen zur Religion und Literatur des Alten und Neuen Testaments
HNT	Handbuch zum Neuen Testament
HTKNT	Herder's Theologischer Kommentar zum Neuen Testament
HTR	*Harvard Theological Review*
ICC	International Critical Commentary
JAAR	American Academy of Religion. *Journal*
JBL	*Journal of Biblical Literature*
JBR	*Journal of Bible and Religion*
JTS	*Journal of Theological Studies*
Meyer	Meyer, Kritisch-exegetischer Kommentar über das Neue Testament
NovT	*Novum Testamentum*
NovTSup	Novum Testamentum, Supplements
NTA	*New Testament Abstracts*
NTS	*New Testament Studies*
RB	*Revue Biblique*
RGG	*Die Religion in Geschichte und Gegenwart*
RSR	*Recherches de science religieuse*
SBS	Stuttgarter Bibelstudien

SBT	Studies in Biblical Theology
SNTSMS	Society for New Testament Studies Monograph Series
TB	Theologische Blätter
ThRu	Theologische Rundschau
TLZ	Theologische Literaturzeitung
TSK	Theologische Studien und Kritiken
TZ	Theologische Zeitschrift
WMANT	Wissenschaftliche Monographien zum Alten und Neuen Testament
ZKT	Zeitschrift für katholische Theologie
ZNW	Zeitschrift für die neutestamentliche Wissenschaft
ZTK	Zeitschrift für Theologie und Kirche
ZWT	Zeitschrift für wissenschaftliche Theologie

CHAPTER 1

THE LITERARY PUZZLE

Ever alluring, yet seemingly insoluble, is the puzzle of the literary origin of the Gospel of John. Did one writer compose it? Did he use written sources? Did a redactor rework it later? From 1796 to the present day biblical scholars have tried to solve the puzzle, but no "solution" has won general acceptance. Some writers have contributed valuable insights, however, and a few have solved certain aspects. Yet most laymen are unaware of the difficulty, for even after repeated reading of the gospel, they have not noticed the evidence of disunity and of composite writing.

The Prologue, the first eighteen verses, of the Gospel of John hails Jesus as an incarnate god, the Word and the Light; but this line of thinking is interrupted twice by verses which have as their theme the idea that John the Baptist was a witness to Jesus (verses 6-8 and 15). When these verses are removed, the surrounding verses fit together very well; verse 9 continues the thesis in verse 5 that Jesus is the Light, and verse16 continues the notion of fullness of grace in verse 14. Did the author of the gospel think and write in such a manner? Or did he use a written source and insert into it the verses about the Baptist? Or has a later redactor made the insertions?

Chapter 13 closes with Jesus talking to Peter and predicting the latter's denial. Chapters 14-17, however, suddenly drop the narrative and ascribe to Jesus speeches with subject matter that is quite unrelated to Peter's denial and that are abuptly addressed to a plural audience instead of Peter. In chapter 18 the narrative is resumed. Why is the narrative interrupted by four chapters of speeches?

In these examples a block of material breaks the line of thought in the context. When the block of material is removed, the verse that precedes it and the verse that immediately follows it join together so well that this appears to be their original location. The present arrangement of the material forms what may be called the "ABA pattern": topic A is abruptly dropped for topic B, followed by a sudden return to topic A. In ancient literature the ABA pattern tends to be a characteristic of composite literature rather than of the composition of a single author. The pattern was produced when someone made a later insertion into written material. The inserted matter could come from a source, or it could be composed by the person making the insertion.

Another aspect of the literary puzzle of the Gospel of John is the presence of inconsistencies. Tradition-minded biblical scholars have always been reluctant to admit it, but today most scholars who have studied the gospel agree that there are contradictions. For example, did Jesus baptize or not? In verse 26 of chapter 3 we read that John's disciples report to him that Jesus "is baptizing and everyone is coming to him." This statement is supported in 4:1 with the remark that the Pharisees had heard that Jesus was making and baptizing more disciples than John. To our surprise, we find these statements negated in the very next verse: "and yet Jesus himself did not baptize, but his disciples (did)"! Why does this contradiction occur?

In 5:26-29 we read that the dead will be raised and judged and that the Father has given the Son the authority to execute judgment because he, Jesus, is the Son of Man. The basis of judgment will be whether one has "done good things" or has "committed wicked things." Conversely in 12:44-50, where Jesus is not identified with the Son of Man, he has not come to judge the world, and it is not he but the words which he has already spoken that will judge men on the last day. The basis of judgment will not be whether man has done good deeds or bad, but whether he has rejected Jesus and his words. Can these two passages be harmonized or are they the work of two different writers?

In 6:50-58 "life eternal," immortality, is made absolutely dependent upon eating the flesh of the Son of Man; the Spirit is not even mentioned. Nevertheless, in verse 63 of this chapter there is a statement which indicates the opposite: "The Spirit is the thing making alive; the flesh profits nothing." Would the same writer make these conflicting statements? If not, why are they there?

In 7:8 Jesus says that he is not going to the feast. Yet two verses later we read that he went. What is the explanation of this contradiction?

Vocabulary differences among certain sections of the book constitute a feature that needs to be explained. In the Prologue Jesus is called "the Logos," a Greek term which in this passage is usually translated as "the Word." Why is he never "the Logos" in the rest of the book? The terms "fullness" (Greek: plērōma) and "grace" (Greek: charis) occur in the Prologue, but never in any other verses of the gospel. Only in the Prologue is Jesus referred to as the "only-begotten god," who has been declared by the Father (1:18). The distinctive vocabulary of the Prologue will be described more fully in chapter 10 below. Why do these terms not occur in the remainder of the book?

In some passages Jesus' significant deeds are called "signs"; in others they are referred to as "works." Why?

Julius Wellhausen in 1908 called attention to certain temporal and geographical problems in the Gospel of John.[1] According to verses 3 and 4 of chapter 7 Jesus until then had not manifested his works in Judea, but this is contradicted by his trips to Jerusalem in chapters 2 and 5. Martha went back to the house to send Mary to Jesus, and only Mary then went to him (11:28-29), yet ten verses later the sister who is standing with Jesus at the grave of Lazarus is Martha, not Mary. In 12:36 Jesus goes away and hides himself from the people, and the commentary in the next seven verses shows clearly that the writer regards Jesus' public career as having come to an end, yet in 12:44-50 Jesus abruptly and loudly proclaims his message again. In chapter 19 Pilate twice leads Jesus out of the praetorium to present him to the Jews as their king, without any mention of Jesus' re-entering the praetorium. Wellhausen recognized here doublets (two forms of the same basic story) of the public presentation of the prisoner. What is the correct solution to these problems?

Mention may be made of a few more of the many literary difficulties in the gospel that biblical scholars have observed. In 3:25 the writer begins to tell a story about a dispute over purifying. The story which is told, however, and the sayings connected with it, deal not with purification but with other subjects: namely, certain characteristics of the Son and the superiority of Jesus to John the Baptist. Why is the purification dispute mentioned when it has nothing to do with the context and is left hanging in the air? Has a different story been substituted for the original?

Verse 23 in chapter 2 refers to "signs" (miracles) which

Jesus did in Jerusalem, but in this gospel he does not perform any wondrous acts in that city until later (in chapter 5). Would the original author be so careless?

At the end of chapter 5 Jesus is still in Jerusalem, but chapter 6 begins with his crossing the sea of Galilee, an action which clearly presupposes that he is in Galilee instead of Jerusalem. H. E. Edwards has commented:

> It is as if you were reading a letter from a friend in which he was telling you about salmon fishing in Scotland, and then, as you turn the page, the letter went on: 'After this I went over London Bridge.' . . . You would be sure something was missing.[2]

In John 8:31 Jesus is speaking to Jews who had "believed him," yet only six verses later he tells the same audience that "you seek to kill me because my word has no place in you." The latter description does not fit Jesus' followers, and in this gospel the charge "you seek to kill me" is characteristically directed against the Jews who do not believe on Jesus. What has caused this mix-up concerning the identity of Jesus' audience?

The second verse of chapter 11 identifies Mary of Bethany as the Mary who had anointed Jesus, as though the event had already happened. Yet this incident does not occur until later, in chapter 12.

At the end of chapter 14 Jesus closes a speech with the words "Arise, let us go from here." Instead of going anywhere, however, he delivers another long speech in the same place. A change of location does not occur until two chapters later. Geographical discrepancy is especially surprising, for in this gospel considerable attention is given to travel and to locations.

In chapter 18 Annas is the high priest of the Jews in verses 13a and 15-23, but Caiaphas is the high priest in verses 13b and 24. Couldn't the writer make up his mind, or is there a better explanation?

The Gospel of John draws to a close at the end of chapter 20 with the explanation of why "these things" have been written. Nevertheless, another chapter follows. The content and the point of view in this appendix show marked differences from the rest of the book. Was chapter 21 written by a different author? Did he make insertions and retouches in the rest of the gospel as some biblical scholars maintain? If he did, is that the explanation of the literary roughness?

The long discourses in chapters 14-17 stand apart from the rest of the gospel. They not only abruptly interrupt the narrative context, but their content has some distinctive terms and ideas. Most of the discourse material in the gospel is interwoven with the narratives, but these long speeches are quite unrelated to any story. Are they derived from a special source?

Such is a sample of the problems which form the literary puzzle of the Gospel of John. Some biblical scholars have applied comprehensive terms to them. Wellhausen, writing in German, applied to them the word Anstösse, "offenses."[3] Morton Enslin called them "rough spots."[4] Probably the best term for them is "aporias." Eduard Schwartz used the term in his study of the gospel's literary problems,[5] and Robert Fortna employs the word in his recent source theory.[6] Although in the English language the term is associated with "doubts," in its original language, Greek, an aporia is a "difficulty." Fortna defines aporias as "inconsistencies, disjunctures and hard connections, even contradictions." In short, as we use this word in Johannine studies, aporias are literary difficulties.

What do the aporias, the ABA pattern, and the inconsistencies in the Gospel of John tell us about the literary origin of the book? Do they indicate that the author had a peculiar manner of writing? Or that an editor used written sources? Or that a redactor revised it later? Or that leaves in the original manuscript were accidentally displaced? Or a combination of causes?

CHAPTER 2

HINDRANCES TO SOLUTION

The traditional Christian view of the gospel's authorship has long been a hindrance to the solution of the literary problem. The possibility of sources or revision was difficult to recognize while it was generally believed that the author was John the apostle and that he composed the present gospel by writing down his recollections of Jesus' words and deeds. This fact was noted in 1910 by Hans Wendt, professor of theology at Jena: "So long as the authorship of this Gospel by the Apostle John is accepted, it is clear that the question of its sources cannot enter."[1] Fortna states that "much of the early literary criticism of the gospel is hampered by the intrusion of the historical question"; therefore in his dissertation "no attitude toward apostolicity is assumed at all. And there is no attempt here to find a historical 'kernel' or a 'reliable' tradition lying behind Jn."[2] My own procedure was first to investigate the question of authorship and settle it at least in my own mind, and then move on to the literary problem. If the Gospel of John is composite, but investigations presuppose single apostolic authorship, how can we ever find the proper solution to the literary problem? Such a presupposition automatically blinds us to the significance of much of the evidence.

The tradition that the apostle John wrote the gospel had its origin in the zeal of early Christians to support their beliefs by claiming apostolic authority for them and the books which contained them. By about A. D. 85 a general statement of apostolic authority was anachronistically ascribed to Jesus: "He who hears you hears me, and he who rejects you rejects me, and he who rejects me rejects him (God) who sent me" (Luke 10:16). Clement, a bishop of a church in Rome, asserted in 96 that the beliefs of his church were received from the apostles, who in turn had received them from Jesus himself: "The apostles preached to us the gospel from the Lord Jesus Christ" (1 Clement 42).

The next stage in the development of the theory of apostolic authority was reached when the "gospel" received from the apostles was interpreted no longer as merely oral preaching but as a written book. Papias took this step around 130 when he asserted that Matthew wrote a gospel.[3] In support of their doctrines the Christian Gnostics claimed that their beliefs were founded on revelation from Jesus and that some of their writings were composed by apostles such as Thomas, Philip, and John. In an effort to combat the Gnostics' claim to knowledge superior to that of other Christians, Irenaeus (ca. 180) asserted a similar authority for the four gospels of the present canon. The most explicit of Irenaeus' statements concerning the authorship of the Gospel of John runs as follows: "John, the disciple of the Lord, who even reclined on his breast, produced a gospel while he was living at Ephesus in Asia" (Adv. Haer. iii. 1). The context in which this passage occurs reveals the motive behind the assertion, for here Irenaeus is attempting to counteract gnostic heresies by means of the authority of the apostles. His claim is based not on a historical tradition (as the internal evidence demonstrates), but on zeal to defend a less unorthodox faith from the rapidly growing heresies. At about the same time Theophilus of Antioch, while defending Christians from pagan charges, cited the gospel as the writing of "John" (Ad Autolycum ii. 22). The claim of apostolic authorship for the writings of the church provided authority and defense against criticism, whether from Jews, pagans, or Christian Gnostics.

But through the centuries the tradition that John, a companion of Jesus, wrote the book was a belief which automatically excluded the idea that any written sources are involved. Since churchmen assumed that the present text of the gospel is essentially the same as the text John wrote, the possibility of later revision was also taboo. If the literary problem was noticed at all, the simple solution offered was that John wrote in that manner.

Doubts concerning the apostolic authorship of the Fourth Gospel began with critical examination of the internal evidence in the gospel itself. Later this was supported by investigation of the external evidence, church tradition.

One element in the internal evidence is the disagreement of the Gospel of John with the other canonical gospels. This significant evidence was observed early in the evolution of modern historical scholarship of the New Testament. Hermann Reimarus, professor of Hebrew and Oriental languages at Hamburg ~~University~~, made a historical study of the purposes of Jesus and his disciples. His written conclusions, at odds with orthodox theology, circulated only among friends and students, but in 1778, ten years after his death, they were edited and published by Gotthold Lessing. Reimarus' opinion of the authorship of the Gospel of John is reflected by the fact that when he reconstructed Jesus' life, he relied primarily on the synoptic gospels.

About 1780 Johann Herder, general superintendent of the Protestant Church at Weimar, called attention to the divergence of John from the other gospels and concluded that all efforts to harmonize them are futile.[4] In 1792 appeared The Dissonance of the Four Generally Received Evangelists, a small book written by Edward Evanson, a former clergyman. In it Evanson notes the discrepancies among the four gospels, accepts the authenticity of Luke, and rejects the other three. Although his work is less scholarly than that of Reimarus and Herder, it is significant as a pioneer British step away from the traditional ecclesiastical view of the Gospel of John. Early in the nineteenth century Johannine authorship was rejected by Vogel (1801), Heinrich Ch. Ballenstedt (1802), and H. H. Cludius (1808).[5]

In 1820 Karl Bretschneider, the general superintendent of the Protestant Church at Gotha, published in Latin his work originally written in German, entitled (title translated into English) Probabilities Concerning the Nature and Origin of the Gospel and Epistles of the Apostle John. In it he, too, rejects the historicity of the Gospel of John on the basis of its divergence from the synoptic gospels. He presents his unorthodox conclusions cautiously as only "probabilities." Among these is the probability that the author of the gospel "was neither the apostle John nor any other companion of Jesus" and the further probability that he "was neither a Palestinian nor a Jew." His book has been hailed by W. F. Howard as an "epoch-making work"[6] and by Benjamin W. Bacon as "the first serious critical argument against the traditional authorship."[7] It promptly stirred up a hornet's nest of denunciations. Tradition-minded theologians were fond of John and were zealous to defend the authority of its theology. Also, some rationalists preferred it to the synoptic gospels for its departure from Jewish eschatology. Friedrich Schleiermacher lent his weight to the defense of Johannine authorship. Confronted with attacks from all sides, Bretschneider retracted and announced his change of opinion on the matter.

In his two-volume work on the life of Jesus (1835-36), David Strauss, too, rejects the historicity of the Gospel of John because it is so different from the synoptic gospels. After examining the whole gospel point by point, he declares that the author of John selected and created incidents to serve his dogmatic and apologetic purposes. Strauss at that time was lecturer on Hegelian philosophy at Tübingen University.

These men were pioneers in recognizing that the tremendous differences between John and the synoptic gospels indicate that many gospel traditions must not be genuine (they erred, however, in placing too much trust in the synoptics). The two canonical gospels which church tradition has ascribed to disciples of Jesus are Matthew and John, yet they are the two which agree the least! Matthew is pro-Jews, pro-Jewish law, and anti-Gentiles. John is anti-Jews, anti-Jewish law, and pro-Gentiles. The two gospels are a world apart in the points of view and vocabulary they ascribe to Jesus. It is incredible that Jesus would think and speak in one manner before one disciple and in a completely different manner before another disciple. Therefore recognition of the disagreement of the Gospel of John with the other three was sufficient in itself to challenge the merit of the tradition of apostolic authorship. The differences do not prove that the synoptic gospels are historical; they do prove that at least some of the church traditions of apostolic authorship are false.

There are other new books in the New Testament besides the gospels which supply evidence on the question. Historians now realize that Paul's letter to the Galatians and the Book of Acts indicate that the attitude of the disciple Peter toward Gentiles and toward obedience to the Jewish law was much nearer to the attitude in Matthew than in John. This evidence was certain to lead eventually to skepticism about the tradition that John was written by an eyewitness, for Peter had heard Jesus speak and would hardly have misunderstood Jesus' attitude toward matters regarded as vital by Jews.

In 1840 E. C. J. Lützelberger noted another kind of internal evidence against the tradition of apostolic authorship. In his book he observes that in the supplementary chapter 21 the statement "and we know that his testimony is true" indicates that the gospel proper (chapters 1-20) was not written by John, for the authority of the book must not have been very great if a later writer had to certify to the readers that the author of the gospel had not written any untruth. If the gospel had actually been written by a disciple of Jesus, it would not have needed such support.[8]

Another fundamental element in the internal evidence is the nature of the material in John. The content simply is not the type of matter that would be recorded by a Palestinian Jew in the first century A.D. who was reporting actual sayings and deeds of another Palestinian Jew. If the record were authentic, its report of the teaching of a Jew in Palestine would probably be compatible with the Jewish thought of that place and time --another insight contributed by Reimarus. In 1797 Herder applied this principle when he grasped the non-Palestinian nature of much of John. He concluded that the author deliberately rejected the Jewish messianism of the other gospels to present Jesus to the Gentiles as the savior of the world.[9] Nearly forty years later Strauss, in his famous study of the life of Jesus, presented his decision that all four gospels are too mythological in nature to have been written by eyewitnesses. As a consequence of his denial of the historicity of the gospel myths, he was dismissed from Tübingen University. More recently, C. H. Dodd has remarked that it would be surprising if John were written by a Galilean disciple, considering that the gospel's outlook is "metropolitan" rather than Galilean.[10] Pierson Parker has disproved the traditional theory by showing in detail that the gospel simply does not fit what is known of the life of John, the son of Zebedee.[11]

Some critics have observed the semi-gnostic aspect of the gospel and noted that this is non-Palestinian in nature. Other writers have attacked that conclusion by pointing out that Jerusalem and Galilee were not immune to gentile influence. The weakness of the latter argument is the fact that no Palestinian Jewish material, either literary or archaeological, of that period goes nearly so far in a gnostic direction as does John. On the other hand, some Alexandrian Jewish writings (especially Philo's) and some Alexandrian pagan literature (especially the _Poimandres_ produced by the Hermetic cult) afford some rather close parallels. Philo wrote in the first half of the first century of the Christian era, and Dodd dates _Poimandres_ "not later than about A.D. 125-30."[12] It is very probable that the ideas in _Poimandres_ existed in the Hermetic cult earlier than the writing of that tractate, and thus could have influenced the Gospel of John.

Eagerness to find in Palestine the Johannine type of thought caused some biblical interpreters to exaggerate the parallelism between the gospel and the Scrolls from Qumran. Strenuous efforts were made to show close similarity between the thought and terminology in the gospel and in the Scrolls.[13] W. F. Albright was a leader in claiming that parallelism between John and the Scrolls indicates that both the narratives and sayings in John date from oral tradition in Palestine before 70, and therefore "we may be assured that it [John] contains the memories of the Apostle John."[14] Other scholars have rightly opposed such claims, observing that they are unjustified.[15] The claims must be rejected for the following reasons:

1. The parallelism in terminology is only coincidental, for the terms were widely used in the ancient world. The terms "light," "darkness," "knowledge," and "spirit of truth." The common use of such expressions resulted from their prevalence in the religious thought of the time, and not from origin in the same background, either geographical or ideological.

2. The alleged parallelism in thought simply does not exist. The theology and ideology in general in the gospel are utterly different from that in the Scrolls. When the same terms are used, they are given very different meanings in the respective bodies of literature. Significant too is the fact that the difference in definition of terms invariably involves a major difference in beliefs which each body of literature regards as basic in religion. The gospel and the Scrolls alike make acceptance of the "light" instead of "darkness" basic for salvation, but at Qumran this is ethical dualism, whereas in John it is metaphysical dualism as in Gnosticism. In both, "knowing" or "knowledge" of what God reveals is essential for salvation, but how different is the content of the knowledge! In John it is knowledge of God and the Son; in the Scrolls it is knowledge of the Jewish law and the proper interpretation of it. In contrast to the Scrolls, in John the Jewish law is rejected; it is "your law" and contrary to what one must know to be saved. Further, it is important to recognize that, when in the alleged parallels the thought is different, the difference in John is not in the direction of primitive Christian thought. This indicates that the main background of the gospel is not Jewish.

The beliefs in the Scrolls and in the gospel are antithetical not only in respect to Jewish law but nearly so in respect to Jewish eschatology. At Qumran the emphasis upon imminent eschatology was strong to the point of fanaticism. In the Gospel of John eschatology is rejected in many passages, while the passages that do exhibit it usually connect it with the Son of Man. Son of Man eschatology is definitely not the type at Qumran.

The wide distance between their religious views is demonstrated further by the fact that the Gospel of John possesses, and the Scrolls lack, two features basic in Gnosticism: salvation depends upon knowing the Father (and the Son); "the world" and "the flesh" are inherently evil.

3. Even if the alleged parallelism existed, it would not necessarily indicate that the gospel or even the traditions in it originated in Palestine. John is filled with semi-gnostic and pagan ideas which are paralleled in literature written outside of Palestine and are not paralleled in any literature known to have originated in Palestine. It contains much that is contrary to many basic Palestinian-Jewish tenets (including those at Qumran). How could a gospel with a Palestinian-Jewish background have so many ideas mixed into it that were characteristic of paganism and Hellenistic mysticism? No one has given a satisfactory explanation! It is far more probable that the gospel would contain those ideas if it originated in an environment in which they were present.

Some writers have attempted to explain the gulf between the Palestinian theory and the non-Palestinian evidence by claiming that the gospel is based upon Palestinian traditions, either oral or written, and the non-Palestinian ideas were imposed on it later. This claim is refuted by the fact that when the gospel is tested for sources or strata, no layer approaching Qumran's views emerges.

4. The existence of the alleged parallelism would not necessarily show that the gospel or its traditions originated in the first century, because some Jewish influence continued to be exerted on Christianity in the second century. Also, John cannot be early because it contains material about problems which originated late in the church; for example, the exclusion of Christians from the synagogues (which occurred about 90) and Docetism in the church.

One is astonished that, in spite of the evidence to the contrary, the theory that the Qumran Scrolls indicate a Palestinian background for the Gospel of John was so widely advocated in the 1950s! F. C. Grant correctly put his finger on the cause when he stated that the theory is "an example of the wish fathering the thought."[16] The misuse of the Dead Sea Scrolls as a basis for the claim that the gospel had a Palestinian background is one of the most serious errors in modern biblical scholarship. The claim leads to complete misunderstanding of the nature and origin of the Gospel of John.

We have surveyed the internal evidence first, because doubts concerning the apostolic authorship of the gospel first arose from it. Later the external evidence, the church tradition, was examined by biblical scholars and found to be unreliable. Bacon's The Fourth Gospel in Research and Debate, published in 1910, is a classic refutation of the church tradition. Recently Dodd has mentioned some of the weaknesses of the external evidence.[17]

One serious weakness is the fact that the gospel was not generally used in the church until after 150. Through the first half of the second century the only Christians known to have accepted and used the Gospel of John were the gnostic heretics, especially the Valentinians.[18] Polycarp (135) displays knowledge of the Gospels of Matthew and Luke, but not of John. Although Justin, writing around 150-160, seems to know the Gospel of John, he includes only the synoptic gospels under the label "the Memoirs of the Apostles." If a disciple wrote it, surely it would have been accepted earlier.

The second weakness of the external evidence, however, is the most devastating to its claim to validity. Historians now recognize that the cause of the origin of the church tradition was not historical knowledge but the prevalent zeal to give apostolic authority to early Christian books.

The old tradition of apostolic authorship had many conservative supporters who fought back tenaciously. Theologians who believed that the incarnation is a vital Christian doctrine were especially reluctant to relinquish the authority of the gospel. This attitude is reflected in Bishop William Temple's statement: "I regard as self-condemned any theory which fails to find a very close connection between the Gospel and the son of Zebedee."[19] Under that opinion, any new theory to the contrary is already prejudged, before its supporting evidence is examined!

Many articles and books were written to defend Johannine authorship. In his book published in 1876 Willibald Beyschlag, professor of pastoral theology at Halle, claims that the gospel is a historical eyewitness account, and he defends this view by attacking the "historical-critical school" of biblical interpretation, which he traces to F. C. Baur. He condemns that school of thought for its rejection of the validity of the Johannine miracle stories, and he especially attacks the contemporary books of Theodor Keim and Adolf Hilgenfeld.[20] Keim was professor of theology at Giessen, and Hilgenfeld was professor of theology at Jena. Around the turn of the century there appeared a rash of partition theories, which viewed only a portion of the gospel as authentic. In reaction against the partition theories of Wellhausen, Schwartz, Friedrich Spitta, and Wilhelm Soltau, Heinrich Appel wrote a book published in 1915, defending the unity of John and trying to prove that the whole book is genuine, written by the apostle. Marie-Joseph Lagrange, founder of the École Pratique d'Études Bibliques in Jerusalem, upheld a similar view in his commentary on the gospel (1925). Recent efforts to defend Johannine authorship have been made by H. P. B. Nunn, F.-M. Braun, D. Crossan, and L. Morris. We have already observed Albright's effort to use the Qumran documents as a basis for upholding Johannine authorship.

Even after the old belief in Johannine authorship was discredited, the tradition continued to hamper the efforts to solve the literary problem by misguiding the investigators, chiefly in two ways. One way was that indirectly it induced some biblical scholars to accomodate their proposed solutions to the "mediating view" that the gospel was written through an intermediary, a disciple of John the apostle. This view contrasts with the tradition in the Muratorian Fragment (ca. 200) that John composed the gospel by writing down what was revealed to his disciples and bishops during a three-day fast. In the mediating view a disciple wrote mainly what he had received from John, but in the Muratorian tradition (which is equally worthless for factual history) John wrote what he received from his disciples and bishops.

We should review how the theory of authorship by a disciple of John began. Jacob Eckermann set forth this view in 1796, but later withdrew it. His theory will be described briefly in chapter 4. Heinrich Paulus, professor of exegesis and ecclesiastical history at Heidelberg, in 1821 proposed that the evangelist, who may have studied gnostic philosophy, was John's disciple; after John's death he composed all of the gospel on the basis of his recollections of John's preaching.[21] In the latter part of the nineteenth century many biblical scholars were torn between the traditional view of Johannine authorship on the one hand and the complete rejection of it by the historical-critical school of thought. They sought a compromise that would preserve some sort of connection between the gospel and the apostle John. The theory that the gospel was written by a disciple of John appealed to many because it served to explain the gospel's divergence from the other gospels and yet maintain its essential authority. One form of the view was that the disciple was a presbyter, or elder, who lived in Ephesus and was also named John. Early in the second century Papias made an uncertain reference to two Johns, at least one of whom he called "John the Presbyter."[22] Irenaeus identified the two Johns (or rather, tried to) and said that John the apostle lived in Asia. J. Estlin Carpenter remarked that the church fathers often mistakenly identified two different persons with each other; Irenaeus even identified James, the brother of John, with James, the brother of Jesus.[23] The mention of two Johns provided the basis for Michel Nicolas' suggestion in 1862. He proposed that the gospel was written by John the Presbyter in Ephesus, who wrote also 2 John and 3 John and was a disciple of the apostle John. Adolf Harnack adopted this theory in 1897,[24] and in the next three decades a large group of biblical scholars accepted some form of it.[25] William Sanday labeled as "mediating theories" those with the view that the author of the gospel was John the Presbyter in Asia (regardless of whether he was viewed as a disciple of John the disciple of Jesus).[26] All forms of the theory of authorship by a Johannine disciple clearly rested on wishful thinking; there is no evidence whatever that the gospel was written by a disciple of John, yet the view was very popular with biblical scholars! Furthermore, neither Papias nor Irenaeus mentions two different Johns as being involved in the writing of the gospel, and the Nicolas-Harnack theory is not supported by valid evidence. Recently Rudolf Schnackenburg (1970) has argued that the origin of the gospel is that the beloved disciple was a historical disciple of Jesus who mediated the traditions to the Johannine circle that wrote the book.

The second way in which the tradition of Johannine authorship misguided the efforts to solve the literary problem of the gospel was that the tradition often shaped the form of partition theories. The desire to make at least a portion of the gospel conform to the tradition of Johannine authorship was the inspiration for many of the earlier source and redaction theories. The portion selected as Johannine was the portion best suited to the biblical scholar's own theology or point of view. Wilhelm Bousset, Albert Schweitzer, and W. F. Howard recognized that this motive lay behind the theories of Christian Weisse, Alexander Schweizer, Wendt, and Spitta.[27] Paul Schmiedel, professor of theology at Zurich, remarked that the nineteenth century efforts to partition the first twenty chapters of John rested usually "upon the supposition that one half is due to a trustworthy historian and an eyewitness, the other to a badly informed contributor."[28] Concerning the flood of partition hypotheses which appeared early in the twentieth century, Dodd remarked that they "can be seen in retrospect to have been largely inspired by the wish to recover some kind of Grundschrift to which the critic might feel justified in assigning the credibility which he could no longer attribute to the work as a whole."[29] Conservative biblical scholars tended to preserve as historical the passages which contained the miracles and incarnation. The liberal theologians of the day modernized Jesus by saying that he had "spiritualized" Jewish eschatology by reinterpreting it. Therefore the liberals tended to preserve the passages which removed the terms "kingdom of God," "the Christ," and "the judgment" from the traditional Jewish framework.[30] The underlying motivation (to assign authority to the passages the biblical scholar liked) explains why many writers ascribed a "source" in the gospel to the apostle John, even though none of the alleged sources contain any evidence that it comes from him.

In this chapter we have seen that the tradition of Johannine authorship is an obstacle to finding the solution of the literary puzzle of the Gospel of John. Certain other factors have been hindrances too and must be mentioned.

The complexity of the material in the gospel has certainly been a deterrent to the attempts to unravel the tangled threads. The variety and even inconsistency in thought render difficult the understanding of the relationship of the parts to each other. Above all, the complexity confuses the critic who tries to make a literary analysis. The abrupt changes and interruptions in the line of thought, the inconsistencies, and the vocabulary changes indicate the use of sources or later revision, but finding consistent patterns has been difficult. Also, the historian who searches for the gospel's background finds his task difficult because of the complexity. Some aspects of the book suggest a Jewish-Christian background, while other features indicate a gentile-Christian environment. The gnostic tone of parts of the gospel has led to debate. The general complexity of the material is partly responsible for the wide variation in the proposed solutions.

Another factor which has hindered the discovery of the solution has been an inadequate knowledge of the environment of the gospel. We need to know as fully as possible the events and the ideas in Judaism, paganism, and Christianity in the era in which the book was written. Gradually more knowledge of these three backgrounds has been found and is being applied to the interpretation of the gospel.

Finally, a survey of the history of the attempts to solve the literary puzzle reveals that the greatest hindrance of all is bias. How few of the efforts to solve the literary problem have been objective investigations which really proceeded from the literary and historical evidence! Recognition of the powerful effect of the psychological factor in shaping views of the authorship of the gospel should warn us of the danger of bias and persuade us to strive to be thoroughly objective in our own procedure.

CHAPTER 3

THE QUESTION OF UNITY

How much unity exists in the Gospel of John? Does the book have the same literary style throughout? Are there significant differences in vocabulary in different sections of the gospel? Does a definite plan, or design, run through it? How consistent is the theology? If the gospel lacks unity, what is the cause (or causes)?

Obviously the question of unity could have a close relation to the literary puzzle. If the gospel is a unity, it may have been written by, and therefore its aporias probably produced by, a single author or by an editor who gave unity to the source materials. Or perhaps a redactor came along later and gave unity to the source materials an editor had compiled. On the other hand, if the gospel is not a unity, the disparity should provide clues for detecting the literary origin of the book.

In the traditional Christian view the unity of the gospel was usually assumed, for after all it was believed to be the work of one man who was none other than a disciple of Jesus reporting what he had seen and heard. After the unity of the book was questioned, it was stoutly defended by conservative theologians because the authority of the book and its distinctive ideas seemed to depend upon its unity. For if the gospel is not a unity, it may contain not the teaching of Jesus but later streams of church tradition which are very unlike Jesus' thoughts.

Ever since Bretschneider questioned the gospel's solidarity, in 1820 the issue of the unity of the book has continued to be debated. Strauss in 1858 opposed the view that the gospel is a "seamless robe" by declaring that it has been "patched together out of miscellaneous shreds of diverse materials"[1] (the metaphor "seamless robe" was suggested by John 19:23). Both Bretschneider and Strauss encountered tremendous storms of opposition.

It remained for the partition theories, however, to bring the issue into sharp focus. Around 1840 Weisse, Daniel Schenkel, and A. Schweizer set forth their individual theories that the gospel incorporates source materials. Their theories met such strong hostility that few other writers produced theories of this type for nearly half a century. Then in the two decades from

1890 to 1910 a considerable number of German biblical scholars bloomed forth with a variety of partition theories: source, redaction, and combinations of the two. These theories are included in the survey in the next four chapters. In reaction against those upsetting interpretations, conservative biblical exegetes rushed in to defend the harmony and consistency of the gospel. The Germans Theodor Zahn, Bernhard Weiss, and Appel, and the American New Testament textual critic living in Germany, Caspar René Gregory, denounced the partition theories and argued that John is a unitary work.

The desire to protect the authority of the gospel was not the only cause of the defense of its unity. Even Schmiedel (ca. 1900), who rejected Johannine authorship and the historical value of the book, opposed the partition theories of his day. Eduard Meyer (1921), too, insisted on John's unity, even though he abandoned Johannine authorship.[2] These two men, as well as some others, were led by internal evidence to conclude in favor of unity.

One important kind of internal evidence is the linguistic style, that is, the grammar and syntax of the Greek text. Some writers have observed that certain Greek constructions are characteristic of the book and are scattered through it; therefore they concluded that the gospel is a unity. C. K. Barrett in his commentary lists nine stylistic usages as typical of the gospel.[3] He regards them as evidence that the book as a whole is "so uniform" that the discourses cannot be assigned to one source and the narratives to another. It was the apparent stylistic unity which once caused me to abandon my effort to solve the problem.

Eduard Schweizer (1939, at Nesslau in St. Gallen; in 1949 became professor of New Testament at Zurich University) concludes that, though sources may have been used, the general uniformity of style which has been imposed on the work as a whole by the evangelist prevents us from definitely separating the sources.[4] He does believe, however, that the characteristics of style indicate a general division between the discourses and the narratives and that John 2:1-10, 13-19; 4:46-53; 12:1-8, 12-15 stand out as source material, although modified by the author of the gospel. He bases his conclusions upon his list of thirty-three stylistic features he selects as characteristic of the gospel, but not common in the rest of the New Testament. He examines the occurrences of the features to determine if they fall into a pattern that indicates sources. He considers only the instances in which the same features occur close together at least twice. If he had found several separate groups of characteristics, the pattern would have been evidence (in his opinion) that there are separate sources or strata in the book. He fails to find such a pattern, except that the features associated with the narrative style are more interrelated than are the characteristics of the discourse style. Further, he tests the partition theories of Spitta, Wendt, and Emanuel Hirsch against his list and finds that the pattern of the sylistic characteristics does not fit their theories. He recognizes that there are inconsistencies in the gospel, but like some other critics, he eliminates the difficulty by attributing them to textual displacement. Hirsch (1950) rightly points out that Schweizer's method proves nothing in respect to sources. Sources, too, could vary from the rest of the New Testament; some of the characteristics were common in Hellenistic Greek even if not so in the New Testament; and the evangelist could have imitated the style of his source material.

Eugen Ruckstuhl (1951), professor of New Testament at the Priesterseminar in Lucerne, has expanded Schweizer's list to fifty stylistic characteristics.[5] He places them in three categories: nineteen that are the most important, twelve that are next in importance, and nineteen of least significance. He investigates whether they occur at random throughout the gospel, or whether they fall into groups in which they appear only with one another. His presupposition is that random occurrence would indicate that there are no sources, whereas occurrence in groups would be evidence of source material. He concludes that the stylistic features do not fall into such groups and therefore the evangelist did not employ sources.

The bases of Ruckstuhl's selection of the stylistic characteristics are threefold: (1) the feature rarely occurs in the rest of the New Testament; (2) it occurs frequently in John; (3) it would hardly be imitated by another writer. Actually, the frequency of a characteristic in the rest of the New Testament has no bearing whatever on the question of the unity of the gospel. Also, by restricting the characteristics to the most frequent in John, both Schweizer and Ruckstuhl omitted the most significant evidence! The features which occur frequently are generally those used by several writers, whereas the characteristics which are peculiar to a particular writer--and thus are the most important for detecting his work--tend to be those which occur less often. Basing a study on the characteristics of several or all of the authors in the gospel dooms to failure any effort to uncover the literary origins. This is a fatal error in method.

Ruckstuhl's purpose is to prove that the gospel is a literary unity and that Bultmann's theory is wrong. Ruckstuhl is open to the criticism that this is his working presupposition rather than his conclusion from evidence.[6] He does point out errors in Bultmann's method, nevertheless. Then he jumps to the conclusion that it is futile to search for sources, but D. Moody Smith rightly observes that this is "an exaggerated claim."[7] The errors in Bultmann's theory do not disprove all other source theories.

Writers do not agree on the extent of the stylistic unity in John. In Ruckstuhl's opinion there is an overall unity, and the few variations in style are merely a result of the different materials involved: discourses, narratives, and dialogues. He, however, has a strong bias in favor of unity. Bultmann, on the other hand, sees considerable stylistic variation and regards it as part of the evidence of sources. Joachim Jeremias (as well as E. Schweizer) believes that there are stylistic differences between the narratives and the discourses.[8] Ernst Haenchen has stated emphatically that the Fourth Gospel is not a stylistic unity.[9]

Even if there is some stylistic unity, Johannine scholars disagree on its cause. Walter Bauer and Ruckstuhl claim that the stylistic features are so uniform that they indicate that the book was written by one author. We observe that there are four other possible causes of stylistic unity, however. The evangelist may have used sources, rewriting the material in his own style (E. Schweizer's view). Or he may have used sources and imitated their style when he composed his own portions of the gospel (Bultmann's view). Schenkel in 1840 noted both possibilities.[10] Another possible cause of stylistic unity is that a redactor may have revised the gospel later and impressed his own style on the book. Finally, a redactor may have adjusted his own style to that of the gospel, as Bacon concluded.[11] Hirsch and Siegfried Mendner, too, concluded that a redactor produced the stylistic unity by imitating the evangelist's style.[12] A major weakness of the last theory is that if a reviser tried to follow the style of the gospel so closely, surely he would not have disrupted the original so ruthlessly and left such glaring substantive difficulties.[13]

Excessive reliance on style is a real danger in literary study. Some erroneous conclusions have been the result. Many critics have decided that style supports the traditional belief that one author wrote the whole book. The stylistic unity of chapter 21 and the rest of the gospel caused Howard to discard his opinion that the appendix was written by a different writer.[14] A. E. Brooke and B. F. Streeter,[15] among others, concluded on the basis of stylistic similarity that one writer composed the gospel and all three Johannine epistles. Stylistic criteria should not be used exclusively, for other types of evidence (vocabulary, aporias, thought content) need to be considered too. Haenchen, Hirsch, Fortna, and Werner Kümmel conclude that stylistic criteria cannot be the only ones employed. The evidence is cumulative. But if stylistic criteria should not be used exclusively, neither should they be neglected, for they tend to be the most objective and reliable of guides, when properly used.

Misuse of stylistic criteria must be guarded against too. Selection of wrong characteristics has led scholars astray: for example, E. Schweizer and Ruckstuhl. Choosing the traits which occur most frequently rather than the ones distinctive of each writer gives a false appearance of unity to the gospel. Smith has observed the looseness of the manner in which stylistic evidence has been used; it can be made to point in different directions, depending upon its selection and the presuppositions governing its use and interpretation.[16]

Other kinds of unity besides stylistic have been claimed for the Gospel of John. Some writers assert that there is a unity of vocabulary and that the differences that exist simply result from the nature of the material. But some of the variation in vocabulary cannot really be explained as merely the result of the literary type or subject matter of the passages in which they occur. For example, there is no sound reason why the term logos, the "Word," could not be applied to Jesus outside of the Prologue. How can context explain the choice of the names "Simon," "Peter," and "Simon Peter"? Diction can indicate disunity when a certain verb is used in one passage, and a synonymous verb is used in another.

Unity of design is another kind of uniformity claimed for

the gospel. A common purpose runs throughout, it is said, and in the opinion of some writers this demonstrates that the book was composed by a single author. Here is a typical comment, applied to the first twenty chapters: "But the general unity of plan and spirit forbids the idea either of partition into sources or of extensive revision."[17] In the early 1920s Meyer stated that, although the final chapter and a few additions are the work of an editor, the book, even in the Prologue, displays the evangelist's unity of design and thought. At the same time Hans Windisch took a similar position, seeing in the gospel a dramatic structure put together by one author. R. H. Lightfoot maintained that the gospel presents a unity of structure and purpose in that it is in six sections which fit together to form a compact whole; the plan of the book is that each section is connected to a Jewish sacred festival. More recently John L. McKenzie has observed that scholars agree that John is carefully planned, but they do not agree on what the plan is. Belief that the gospel conforms to a design has not been universal, however; as early as 1838 Weisse stated that the book has no plan.[18]

A considerable number of New Testament scholars have concluded that, although the gospel has an overall plan, the evangelist used sources nevertheless. Wilhelm Heitmüller in 1907 decided that the author probably used written material, yet he imposed a unity of design on the book as a whole (except the later glosses and chapter 21). A similar view appears in some of the source theories described briefly in the next two chapters. Wilhelm Wilkens claims that the evangelist himself revised the gospel according to a definite plan.

Finally, some New Testament critics have claimed that the Gospel of John is a unity in thought. In the first two editions of his work The Fourth Gospel; Its Significance and Environment, R. H. Strachan held the theory that the gospel has been revised. But in the third edition he states that "further reflection on the style and thought of the Evangelist" has caused him to abandon that theory. Strachan arrived at his later conclusion because he became convinced that the book is a unity in both thought and style. Lightfoot stated that the gospel is "a unity of structure."[19]

Thus a prevalent view in the past has been that the Gospel of John is uniform in one or more of these respects: style, vocabulary, plan, and thought. This view has led some biblical exegetes to state that it is impossible to separate layers in the gospel. James Moffatt wrote: ". . . the Fourth gospel has been composed in such a way that any earlier documents can no longer be disentangled without recourse to highly arbitrary canons of literary procedure and speculative reconstructions of the text."[20] Streeter felt that, if the sources of the gospel have undergone the amount of adaptation and rearrangement that some theories have postulated, it is impossible to unravel the process by which the book was constructed: "As well hope to start with a string of sausages and reconstruct the pig."[21] E. Schweizer, as we have observed, concluded that the sources have been reworked too much to permit us to distinguish them.

Currently, however, the trend among Johannine scholars is toward the view that the gospel is not a literary unity and that strata by different writers can be distinguished. Throughout the twentieth century the number who acknowledged at least some disunity gradually increased. As adherence to the tradition of the apostolic authority of the book has declined, so has decreased the defense of the gospel's unity among the prominent Johannine scholars.

Simple Explanations of the Disunity

The biblical scholars who see divergence and aporias in the gospel, however, are sharply divided on the causes of the disunity. The more complex theories which have been offered to explain the disunity will be described in the next five chapters; here we will sketch some comparatively simple explanations.

The easiest and most traditional solution is the view that the evangelist merely wrote in that manner. In 1854 K. F. Schneider explained the aporias as the result of the boring work of a scatterbrain.[22] Alfred Resch in 1896 asserted that John must have composed the gospel in such a state of ecstasy that he was incapable of distinguishing between his memories and his visions.[23] Wilhelm Wrede concluded that John was a confused author, not entirely of sound mind.[24] Meyer thought that the evangelist was clumsy, Bauer regarded him as deficient in writing ability, and Martin Albertz chose senility of the evangelist as the explanation. Ernest Renan explained the "bad connections" in the narrative sections as the result of "the recollections of an old man."[25] Moffatt contended that the author was more concerned with religious ideas than with chronological sequence in the gospel, and therefore the danger of partition and dislocation theories is that they assign literary interest to the author which he never had.[26] In his commentary Strachan explains away the discrepancies in the locale of Jesus' journeys in the gospel by stating: "This Evangelist is not interested in itineraries." He attributes the breaks in thought to the author's way of writing: "The Evangelist has a habit of interrupting the immediate flow of his thought. Note the two sudden references to the Baptist in the Prologue."[27] Barrett adopts a similar view: ". . . his theological thought does not habitually move in straight lines. It is rather his custom to regard a question from one point of view, and then adopt adopt another, sometimes taking up a somewhat different subject between the two treatments."[28] One form of the explanation of the inconsistencies in John is the claim that they are merely the result of the author's carelessness; this was Schmiedel's explanation.[29]

Schnackenburg argues that the tensions, contradictions, and aporias could be the result of the way the author wrote; that is, he could have made fresh starts, shifted the perspective and introduced new traits. Nevertheless, he regards chapters 15-17 and 21 and some other passages as the work of later hands. He resorts to transposition to restore the evangelist's order before the editors made changes.

The variation in the vocabulary and literary style has been ascribed to the evangelist too. Ernst Käsemann argues that the variety in the gospel, indicated by Bultmann's criteria, merely shows that the evangelist was capable of expressing his thought in several ways. In his article published in 1964 Edwin Freed has collected many of the variations in the gospel in the treatment of names, Old Testament quotations, and leading and conflicting ideas. He also briefly compares the gospel with 1 and 2 John. Although Freed does not definitely reject the possibility of the use of sources or revision, throughout his article he favors the view that the differences within the gospel, and even between the gospel proper (chapters 1-20) on the one hand and chapter 21 and the Johannine epistles on the other, are merely the result of a single author's zeal for variation in his writing. Price believes that the key to the gospel is a "peculiar combination of simplicity and profundity, product of the Evangelist's mind and experience rather than the complex literary history of his Gospel," and that this combination renders "inadequate most--if not all--of the restatements of John's theology."[30]

The argument that the author merely wrote that way is a very weak explanation. The claim that geographical and chronological inconsistencies are the result of the evangelist's lack of interest in such matters is not reasonable; in the gospel much care is given to providing geographical and chronological details. If there is only one author who was primarily interested in religious details, why are there inconsistencies in the religious thought? The book is not consistent on questions then regarded as basic in Christianity, including such issues as the physical resurrection of the dead, Jesus' function as a judge, and the role of the Spirit. The inconsistencies and shifts in point of view on vital issues constitute strong evidence that more than one writer is involved.

Examination of other ancient writings of the Hellenistic and Roman periods discloses that sharp breaks in thought, shifts in view, and inconsistencies are characteristic of composite literature, at times produced with the use of sources, and in other instances the result of insertions by a redactor or a copyist. Sometimes parallels in ancient literature are cited to support the claim that a single author could be inconsistent and make sharp breaks in his thought. Careful study of these parallels, however, usually reveals that they, too, are composite. This is the situation with the two references in the Prologue to the Baptist which Strachan noted; the references are evidence against, not for, single authorship. An example of a sharp break which formerly was regarded as a characteristic of Paul is 1 Corinthians 13. Eric Titus has correctly identified this "love chapter" as an insertion by a later hand for the purpose of changing the tone of Paul's letter.[31]

The fact that it is impossible to restate adequately the gospel's theology is not evidence of the author's combination of simplicity and profundity, but rather points sharply in the opposite direction: to the complexity of composite literature. In any age several persons are more liable to be inconsistent than is one person, unless he is insane. Recognition of the composite origin of the book renders unnecessary the conjectures that the evangelist was incompetent, ecstatic, or senile.

Another explanation of the disunity in the Gospel of John is the conjecture that the author wrote over a considerable period and changed some of his thinking as time passed. This has been suggested by Bauer, who thinks that one man wrote the book, not continuously but between interruptions.[32] Although Howard relies chiefly on a different explanation, he suggests that one reason for the inconsistencies of thought could be that the sections of the gospel "may have been written at considerable intervals, under varying influences and in different moods."[33] F. C. Grant conjectures that the strands in the gospel are "blocks of material which may have been written down by the author himself, prior to his writing of the gospel."[34] Barrett accepts lapse of time as an explanation along with the theories that shifting the theological point of view was part of the author's method and that the material was drawn from several sources.[35]

There is no valid evidence for the conjecture that one author wrote the book over a period of time. The inconsistencies appear within individual chapters and not merely between them or between the first part and the last part of the gospel. If composition by one writer occurred over a period of time, then he inserted his later views among earlier ones, creating inconsistencies and rough literary connections. If he reworked his writing later, why did he not rewrite it and produce a smooth, consistent book? It is also questionable whether one person would have changed his views sufficiently to cover the range of thought in the Gospel of John.

A third simple explanation of the disunity is the theory that the gospel may have been written by a group, a "school"; the various writers presumably held similar but not identical views. At the beginning of the present century Bousset favored this solution; Heitmüller in 1914 and Anton Fridrichsen in 1939 accepted it.[36] In the nineteenth century Renan stated that though John wrote the narrative, a school of his disciples wrote the discourses and present form of the gospel.[37] Joseph Estlin Carpenter, a Unitarian clergyman and formerly lecturer at Oxford, in his book The Johannine Writings suggests that probably every local church had its group of teachers, who might differ from each other in modes of thought and expression. As the body of utterances grew, the desire to record them would naturally arise. Therefore the group would collect several kinds of materials and construct a narrative framework for them "founded on a common conception of Jesus' word and work." Then the task of actually writing the new gospel was entrusted to one writer. In the case of the Gospel of John the material the writer used was probably partly oral, partly written, produced by an Elder (probably at Ephesus) who may have been named John. Later the book was enlarged and revised by inserting some fresh products of meditation or some traditions not previously recognized. Thus Carpenter's theory combines "cooperative authorship" and redaction.

The theory that a group of teachers or disciples were instrumental in producing the gospel is sheer speculation. There is no evidence for it unless we ascribe some historical value to the tradition in the Muratorian Fragment. If sections of the book disagree on major issues and doctrines, it is improbable that it was composed by a group holding the same general Christian beliefs. Price (and most others today) rejects the idea of a "school."[38] The theory of a school of writers originated not directly from internal evidence but from the gradual and reluctant breaking away from the old tradition of Johannine authorship which the evidence compelled. Many biblical scholars tried to retain as much as possible some connection between the apostle and the gospel. First, there was the tradition that John himself wrote the book; next, the theory that a disciple of his wrote it; next, since there is internal evidence that there were several writers, that theory was expanded to the view that it was a "school" of John's followers who wrote it.

Another explanation given for the disunity is that the original author rewrote the gospel by retouching it and by inserting more material. This idea is rather similar to the explanation that the evangelist wrote over a period of time. Parker has proposed that the evangelist produced two different editions of his gospel. Wilkens and Raymond E. Brown carry the idea several steps farther. Their theories are described in Chapter 7. As will be remarked there, revision by the original author is very improbable as an explanation of the literary phenomena in the gospel.

Finally, another proposed simple solution is the conjecture that the author never finished writing the gospel. Alexander Faure offered this suggestion in 1922.[39] Howard adopted the notion, stating that in John we may have an unfinished book "in varying states of revision, . . . imperfectly arranged, and awaiting his [the evangelist's] final revision."[40] The theory was favored by Strachan, and more recently has been accepted by Wilkens and Walter Grundmann, and regarded as probable by Smith.[41] Smith admits that it is difficult either to demonstrate or to refute this theory. Actually, this is one of the weakest explanations of the literary difficulties in John. The inconsistencies, the sharp breaks in thought, and the variations in vocabulary and style read like a composite work produced by several writers, not like a single author's draft. The book is finished in that it comes to a definite close at the end of chapter 20. Has anyone found in ancient literature a rough draft known to have been written by one author which has aporias like the Gospel of John? The theory of an unfinished gospel should be rejected.

Far more thorough and complex explanations of the disunity and aporias have been offered, mainly source, redaction, and accidental displacement theories. There are also combinations of two or more of these, and there are some special source theories which are not typical. We turn now to a survey of the chief examples.

CHAPTER 4

SOURCE THEORIES

Partition theories attempt to explain the literary structure of the gospel as the result of the work of two or more writers. There are two general types: source theories and redaction theories. A sharp line between the two is not easily maintained. In a typical source theory the evangelist was an editor who used one or more written sources, perhaps adding his own material. In a typical redaction theory a redactor has revised the original gospel, which was basically similar to the book as we now have it. If the original document was not a gospel, or if it formed only a minor part of the present gospel, the original was only a source. As a further guide we may ask, Is the use of source material, or is later revision, the primary explanation of the aporias in the book? Even with these criteria it is sometimes difficult to classify a theory.

Various factors caused men to produce source theories. Reimarus in the late eighteenth century prepared the way by questioning the historical accuracy of the Gospel of John because he observed the discrepancies between it and the synoptic gospels.

An early influence was Strauss' rejection of the historicity of the miracle stories. His opinion was a response to the philosophic rationalism of the late eighteenth and early nineteenth centuries. The rationalists believed that only that which conforms to reason is valid in religion, and therefore they became increasingly suspicious of the gospel miracle stories, for their supernaturalism is contrary to reason and natural law. Consequently the rationalistic accounts of the life of Jesus explained the miracle stories as having natural causes or reinterpreted them in some other way to make them probable as historical events. An outstanding example is the two-volume life of Jesus written by Paulus.[1] Strauss, who wrote a few years later, was not a true rationalist, for he rightly regarded the miracle stories as myths and rejected them instead of rationalizing them.[2] Strauss' upsetting conclusions caused a preference for the discourses and less miraculous narratives in John. As a result early biblical scholars who proposed source theories limited the source either to discourse material or to the narratives which seemed plausible. In reaction against the criticism that discredited the gospel, some conservative biblical scholars turned to source theories. Since it was no longer reasonable to claim that the whole gospel is historical, the traditionalists hoped by means of a source theory to save a portion of the book as an authentic report by a disciple of Jesus.

Recognition of internal disharmony in the gospel was a direct cause of source theories that appeared a little later and developed gradually. The disharmony included both the literary problems and the inconsistencies in thought.

Jacob Eckermann, professor of theology at Kiel University, in 1796 was a pioneer in offering a source theory; through Weisse it had enormous influence for over a century. Eckermann asserted that the disciple John wrote down Jesus' discourses after hearing them, and after John's death a disciple of his added to them the narratives and the chronological framework. When Eckermann assigned all the speeches to a written source, he apparently was the first to try to identify a source on the basis of literary type. In 1807, however, he retracted his opinion.[3] In 1811 Christoph F. Ammon, professor of theology at Erlangen University, published his own theory, which was essentially the same as Eckermann's.

In 1838 Christian Weisse, a professor of philosophy at Leipzig University, took up the theory of a Johannine written source and developed it. According to Alexander Schweizer, Weisse was influenced by Schleiermacher's theory of the composition of the Gospel of Matthew; namely, that Matthew consists partly of genuine speeches of Jesus and partly of traditional stories about him.[4] Weisse's hypothesis is that the source consisted of speeches composed by the apostle John, but based on his recollections of the teaching of Jesus and the Baptist. The central idea in John's memoirs was the concept of the divine Logos. After the apostle's death, his pupils wished to preserve his writing, so one of them used it to compose didactic speeches that he ascribed to Jesus, but that actually included the apostle's own ideas presented from the subjective standpoint of John's disciples. This editor constructed a life story of Jesus by combining his own speech compositions with material from written narratives, which probably were not the synoptic gospels. He tried to adapt the narrative part to the didactic parts, but he was not altogether successful because his written sources, already fused, could not be adapted in the same degree.[5]

Weisse thus asserts that two kinds of sources are incorporated in the gospel: narratives and didactic speeches. He concludes that in the didactic part the editor must have added his own composition to the authentic teaching of Jesus, for much does not correspond to the form and content of Jesus' way of speaking as we know it in other sources. Conversely, in the narrative parts there are indications of a report by an eyewitness to the narrated events. These indications include the fullness of detailed features and the vividness of the narratives. Weisse recognizes, however, that, as in the Gospel of Mark, details and vividness do not necessarily mean the writing is the work of an eyewitness. He remarks that the gospel has neither an overall view nor a unified idea of Jesus' teaching.

Weisse's work was a significant step, for he attempted to determine source material not merely on the basis of general literary genres (speeches vs. narratives), but also on the grounds of details within a literary genre. Consequently according to his theory there are both authentic and unauthentic materials within each of these two literary categories.

Daniel Schenkel, who later became professor of theology at the Universities of Basel and Heidelberg, followed Weisse in 1840 by "attempting to prove Weisse's hypothesis," as Alexander Schweizer expressed it. Schenkel reconstructs two blocks of speech material (Redestock) written by the apostle John. One of these is employed as a source in the speeches in the first twelve chapters of the gospel, and the second speech composition consists of the farewell speeches in chapters 14-17. Schenkel's theory begins with his observations of chapter 21, of the contrast between the first and second halves of chapter 6, of the incongruence that the Greeks in chapter 12 drop out of the book, and of the breaks in the composition at 12:44 and 14:31. He maintains that the editor made an arbitrary and often awkward dismemberment of the first block of speech material when he inserted portions of it among the various narratives. Later Schenkel rejected belief in the Johannine authorship of any of the gospel.[6]

Alexander Schweizer was a professor of theology at Zurich. His theory (1841) rejects Schenkel's and Weisse's method of separating gospel source material on the basis of speeches vs.

stories. Unlike Schenkel, he believes that the speeches cannot be separated from the conversations, for example, the conversations resulting from the questions of the disciples. He divides the narratives into two categories, Judean and Galilean, and claims that the Judean narratives came from the pen of an eyewitness (the apostle John), whereas the speeches were written later by another hand from a Hellenistic-dogmatic standpoint. Thus Schweizer reverses Eckermann's and Weisse's evaluation of the speeches, contending that the authentic material is to be found not in them but in the Judean narratives. He bases this on his opinion that the stories are joined together more definitely than the speeches and that some stories (e.g., the foot washing) are "unusually true and clear."[7] He believes that Weisse's hypothesis leads to the conclusion that the whole gospel is not genuine for these reasons: (1) If the editor fitted the Johannine speech-writing into many places in the narratives, the fitting process was subjective and arbitrary and would change the character of the material. (2) The editor probably altered the speeches to blend them with his own style and reworked the narratives into a unity, rearranging them. Therefore the material is no longer in the form in which the editor found it, and the whole book is unauthentic. Schweizer does not want to accept that conclusion, so he expressly repudiates Weisse's hypothesis.

Yet Schweizer insists that two different hands were involved in writing the gospel. "John, or whoever the original author was," wrote the Urschrift, or Urbericht, consisting of Judean narratives; it was "doubtlessly a selection determined by the subjectivity of the author," intended to supplement the Galilean tradition.[8] Thus the Urschrift did not have the implausible Galilean miracle stories. Apparently Schweizer was the first to attempt to determine sources on a geographical basis (Judean vs. Galilean setting).

Both Wilhelm Bousset and Albert Schweitzer charged that Schweizer was motivated by the intention of saving the authenticity of a portion of the gospel.[9] Schweizer's apologetics in the third section of his book make it clear that the charge is justified, for he is very much concerned with proving that the Grundschrift is "authentic," written by an eyewitness. As Bousset observed, Schweizer was eager to prove this by removing the Galilean miracle stories and the literary difficulties, both of which raised doubts about the genuineness of the gospel. Nevertheless, in an article published in 1864, Schweizer discarded his hypothesis.[10]

Weisse expanded and revised his own theory in his book published in 1856. Here he followed Schenkel in claiming that there are two Johannine speech sources, one used in the first part of the gospel and the other in the remainder. Traces of one in which John spoke in his own person rather than in the person of Jesus are in the Prologue, 3:13-21, 3:31-36, and 5:19-27. The second speech source is a connected fragment that consists of chapters 14-17, except such statements of direct dialogue as "Arise, let us go hence" in 14:31. Weisse accepts Johannine origin for the speeches in chapters 5 (except verses 28-29), 8, and 10.[11]

After this burst of source theories around the middle of the nineteenth century, few attempts to separate the gospel into components were made for two generations. Bousset[12] attributed this to the opposition that greeted the theories, especially from the esteemed conservative New Testament scholar Friedrich Lücke.

In this same period, however, one major source theory did appear: Ernest Renan presented his famous interpretation of the gospel. He was professor of Hebrew at the Collège de France, but in 1864 he was removed from office because of his unorthodox view that Jesus was not divine. His theory (1863, with revisions to 1896) begins with the view that John the Elder in his old age wrote the narrative sections (except chapter 21), which sketched the life of Jesus. He wrote it because he perceived inaccuracies in the gospel accounts then current and because he was annoyed that he himself was not accorded an important enough place in the other gospels. Renan was impressed by the details in the narrative, and concluded that the sketch is a better life of Jesus than the synoptic gospels, although its author was not an eyewitness. A school of John's disciples in Asia Minor wrote the discourses and compiled the present form of the gospel. The discourses are not words of Jesus, for they are unlike the synoptic gospels, and in them breathes a new spirit of mysticism and Gnosticism. They were written to give the authority of Jesus to the author's fond doctrines.

Source theories began to emerge again when Hans Wendt,

professor of systematic theology at Heidelberg, and later at Jena, set forth his hypothesis (1886-1911). It was a development of the kind of theory advocated by Eckermann and Weisse. In Wendt's view the Prologue and the longer discourses are from a source written by the apostle John which consisted of the historically valid tradition of Jesus' teaching. In the source the discourses were uttered by Jesus near the close of his earthly career, but the evangelist arranged them throughout Jesus' ministry. The evangelist composed the narratives.

The following kinds of evidence led Wendt to adopt the theory of a written discourse source: (1) There are editorial interpolations that sever connected passages in the discourses. (2) The "cast of ideas" in the discourses differs from that in the historical framework in two ways. First, the narrative parts based the proof of Jesus' messiahship upon "signs," whereas in the discourses the proof consists of "works," "words," or "works and words." Second, the explanatory remarks appended to certain sayings of Jesus are not in harmony with the original sense of those sayings but show affinity with the view in the narrative parts of the gospel. (3) The accounts given in the narrative passages of the ministry of the Baptist and of Jesus "disagree in several respects with what is recorded in our other oldest sources, viz. the Logia of Matthew and the Gospel of Mark." This is in spite of "clear traces" that the evangelist knew the synoptic gospels. On the other hand, the longer discourses show no trace of literary dependence on the other gospels. Further, there exists "a wonderful agreement between the thoughts expressed in these Johannine sayings of Jesus and the cast of thought evident in the Logia of Matthew and the Gospel of Mark."[13]

This last statement of Wendt's is surprising. How could anyone who observed many differences in ideas within the Gospel of John be blind to the more obvious differences in "cast of thought" between the discourses in John and the thought in the Gospel of Mark and the Logia in Matthew? Wendt was not the last to try to test the historicity of parts of John by comparing them with the synoptic gospels; James Drummond and Strachan, for example, interpreted synoptic parallels as evidence of the authenticity of the Johannine discourses.[14]

In 1890 Hugo Delff, a teacher of philosophy and theology in Husum, Germany, tried to show that the authentic Johannine core of the gospel consists of the Jerusalem tradition in the book. In this tradition Jesus, who was a Jewish rabbi, spoke like the rabbis of his time. Further, in this tradition Jesus was not the preexistent Logos and god, but a God-sent prophet and absolute man. The evangelist, the disciple John, was identical with the Presbyter John mentioned by Papias. The evangelist, who wrote the core, was a student of the rabbis, and he wrote to win the priestly circles to the belief that Jesus was the Messiah.

According to Delff an interpolator later inserted material from an apocryphal gospel that belonged to the Galilean circle of tradition. This material includes the Galilean miracles, synoptic materials, metaphysical passages (including the main part of the Prologue) that are based on Alexandrian philosophy, and the final chapter of the present gospel. Delff claims that the interpolator also transposed some passages and that his overall purpose was to bring the gospel into line with Alexandrian metaphysical philosophy and the millenarianism of his own day. This claim weakens Delff's theory exceedingly, for Alexandrian metaphysics and Christian millenarianism were very different schools of thought, and it is extremely improbable that Alexandrian metaphysics was a component of Galilean tradition.

James M. Thompson, an English clergyman and writer on the French Revolution, set forth his source theory in a series of two articles (1915, 1916). Here he analyzes the conclusion in John 20:30-31 and observes that it is concerned with three key terms: "sign," "the Christ," and "life." Then he examines the rest of the gospel to determine where and in what sense these words are used. Thompson concludes that the occurrence only in the narrative portions of chapters 1-12 and in 20:30-31 of the terms "sign" and "Christ" (except "Jesus Christ" in 17:3) and the apocalyptic sense of the term "life" indicate the use of a narrative-gospel source. He observes that the messianic point of view in chapters 13-21 has shifted from the earlier apoclyptic to the later mystical Christology. The view of the source was, roughly speaking, synoptic, but it was edited later from a specifically Johannine point of view when the present gospel was produced. John 20:30-31 originally was the conclusion of this source, and it should be moved to its original location at the end of chapter 12.

Thompson deserved more credit than he has received. He was one of the pioneers in examining the narrative portions of John on a scientific, objective basis, and his theory is a forerunner of modern theories of a Gospel of Signs source. He analyzed the narrative portions, not on a geographical basis (Judean vs. Galilean), but on a linguistic basis, and remarked that 20:30-31 was the conclusion of the source. Although Howard in the bibliography in his The Fourth Gospel in Recent Criticism and Interpretation lists Thompson's articles, he does not even mention his source theory in the text, where he leaves the impression that Thompson's chief concern was textual dislocation!

Wilhelm Soltau in 1916 set forth the latest and most developed form of his own theory of the growth of the Gospel of John. He taught history at the gymnasium at Saverne, France. According to him some writer soon after 80 combined "legends" (L) that were oral narratives derived from the apostle John with some passages (S) obtained from the synoptic gospels. This document was the Grundschrift (G), the original gospel. About 130 the evangelist produced essentially the present gospel by adding to the Grundschrift more narratives and sayings including "antisynoptic" traditions and brief explanatory insertions. About a decade later someone inserted the lengthy discourses (R) from a written source. After 150 a "Continuator" added chapter 21 and an "Interpolator" made two or three insertions. Soltau's view is a combined source and redaction theory.

Robert H. Strachan was a Scottish clergyman who later taught New Testament in various universities, and finally was professor of New Testament language and literature at Westminster College, Cambridge. In the early stage of his thinking (1917, 1925), he believed that an editor added a chronological framework to the disciple John's preaching notes to construct a drama somewhat like the synoptic gospels. A redactor later inserted more material. In 1941, however, Strachan abandoned this view and concluded that with the exception of a few scattered retouches and the addition of chapter 21 by a later hand, the book was written by one--but nonapostolic--author.

Eduard Meyer, professor of ancient history at the University of Berlin, asserted in 1921 that the evangelist employed with great freedom sources including the synoptic gospels and a source of major historical value that appears in the Passion story. Later the primitive gospel that the evangelist wrote passed through the hands of an editor who added chapters 15-17 and 21 and various pieces such as 19:35 and the story of Peter and the anonymous disciple at the empty tomb (20:2-9).

Alfred Loisy, professor of church history at the Collège de France, did not hold a partition theory when he discussed the origins of the Fourth Gospel in his commentary published in 1903, but later (1921, 1936) he concluded that around the end of the first century or the beginning of the second a gnostic prophet wrote hymns and meditations. About 135-40 someone in Asia Minor collected them and used them as a basis for constructing the gospel, which was intended as a manual of initiation into Christianity. This editor borrowed material from the synoptic gospels and wove the whole into a chronological framework. Nevertheless, he produced his book in opposition to the synoptic gospels and their views. About 150-60 a redactor revised the body of the gospel and added chapter 21, borrowing from the synoptic gospels; his anti-Marcionite motives led him to stress a physical resurrection of Jesus and to represent the gospel as the work of a disciple of Jesus.

In 1922 Alexander Faure in Seebach bei Thal wrote an article on Old Testament quotations in the Fourth Gospel in relation to the hypothesis of sources. In this essay he asserts that previous attempts to separate sources from later material in the gospel lack a solid foundation or "starting point" (Ausgangspunkt). He believes, however, that he has found the necessary starting point for distinguishing a source: the two kinds of formulas with which quotations from the Old Testament are introduced in John. In the first part of the gospel the introductory formula, with some variants, is "it is written"; beginning with 12:38 the formula is "that it may be fulfilled." These facts, states Faure, "shake" the thesis of the literary unity of the gospel; they indicate two separate interpretations of the Old Testament or at least two different uses of it. The location of the two series of formulas indicate that there is a real division between 12:16 and 12:38 and that on each side of the division stands a separate work. He remarks that the Old Testament quotations in 12:39-40 and 19:37 differ from the Old Testament quotations that immediately precede them in that they are introduced with "again" and the verb "say" and they vary from the Septuagint. Consequently he concludes that there are two authors in the second half of the gospel.

Faure does not wish to construct his source hypothesis on the Old Testament quotations alone, so he also uses other distinctive linguistic features. Finding that some occur in both the first and second parts of the gospel, he concludes that the Gospel of John does not consist of two separate works simply attached to each other, but rather that a source was used in the first part. This source accounts for the distinctive features of the first part, and the work of the evangelist explains the similarities of the two parts. Although the source document (*Quellenschrift*) was revised in process, traces of it remain. The source was a book of miracle stories and may have been called a *Book of the Signs of Jesus*. Faure appears to be the first to assign this title to a source in the gospel. He states that the purpose of the source document was to prove by means of Jesus' miracles and the testimony of John the Baptist and his disciples that Jesus was the Jewish Messiah, the Christ. The "thought world" of the evangelist who wrote the gospel, however, was quite different. For the evangelist, faith is not the belief that Jesus is the Christ but belief that Jesus is sent from God, and the basis of faith consists of hearing the word of Jesus and of seeing Jesus.

Faure's final, overall explanation of the origin of the gospel is this: The Evangelist collected various materials and models including "thought" sections (*Gedanken*) as well as the *Book of Signs*. With this matter he formed a rough "sketch" of a gospel and revised it again and again by adding, transposing, inserting. But he never finished the gospel--"perhaps death took the pen out of his hand." Later an ecclesiastical reviser tried to bring the gospel nearer to the prevailing beliefs and rituals of the church by inserting support for eschatology, physical baptism, and the Lord's Supper. The reviser also removed matter that was offensive to his dogmatic views.

Chronologically, Faure's interpretation is the next essentially objective source theory after Thompson's. Faure's article is full of important evidence, and no student of source theories should fail to examine it, but Howard overlooked it in his *The Fourth Gospel in Recent Criticism and Interpretation*. Unfortunately, his mistaken conclusion that the gospel is an unfinished book has had wide influence upon subsequent interpretation.

Maurice Goguel, professor of Protestant theology at the University of Paris, published his theory in 1923. He begins with the presupposition that unlike some books of the Old Testament, simple compilation of source materials never occurred in the composition of the books of the New Testament. The Fourth Gospel is quite complex, Goguel maintains, because the evangelist used sources, composed some passages, and later revised the gospel himself, and then an editor and some redactors made additions. Consequently it is useless to try to reconstruct the sources in John (or any other New Testament book).[15] The evangelist employed noncanonical sources which contained synoptic tradition and nonsynoptic tradition. His synoptic tradition was more primitive, or earlier in form, than the tradition in the synoptic gospels; this is indicated by the topographical details not added for theological reasons, by the discussion with the Jews in the story of the cleansing of the temple, and by two features in chapter 6: the enthusiasm of the crowd for Jesus, and his retreat from it to a mountain. In 1:19-35 the evangelist used a source which contained nonsynoptic elements; he knew and used two recensions of the source, as the doublets in the passage show. In addition he employed the synoptic account, mainly the Gospel of Luke, in the Passion story.

In Goguel's opinion the evangelist often revised his source material; he omitted parts, inserted additions, and altered the location of passages. Occasionally a source had already been altered by a redactor before the evangelist found it, for example, 7:3-5.[16] The evangelist composed also material to express his theological views and to reflect on Jewish disbelief in Jesus. Long after he had finished the gospel, he added chapters 15-17 and a few brief passages. Still later, a redactor added chapter 21 and passages about the Beloved Disciple. Finally, later redactors inserted the glosses 1:15 and 5:28-29.

One of the most speculative theories is that of E. S. Hoernle in his book The Record of the Loved Disciple (1931). In this hypothesis there once was a Gospel according to St. Philip [not to be identified with the gnostic Gospel of Philip which has since been found in Egypt], which Hoernle labels P and which described miracles through which Jesus declared his divinity.

There was also a Record of the Loved Disciple, St. John, which Hoernle calls R. R was in two volumes: RD, spiritual discourses presenting the doctrine of the Father and the Son, and RN, the narrative of the disciple whom Jesus loved. RN itself was in two parts, the ministry of Jesus and the passion of Jesus, and consisted of poetical stanzas.

Hoernle claims that there were two stages in the formation of the Gospel of John. In the first stage some of the words of Jesus in RD were incorporated in P to illustrate each work of Jesus. In the second stage the rest of RD and most of RN were inserted. This highly conjectural proposal stands in sharp contrast to the relatively inductive approach in Faure's theory nine years earlier.

Benjamin W. Bacon, professor of New Testament exegesis at Yale Divinity School, presented the culmination of his study of the question in his book The Gospel of the Hellenists, published in 1933. Here he envisions three steps in the formation of the present gospel. The first stage was the composition of a series of didactic speeches, each speech introduced by an appropriate sign and constructed to associate a Jewish feast with a theme suggested by Jesus' teaching. For example, the healing of the blind man is the sign which introduces the discourse on the Light of the World which is associated with the Jewish Festival of Lights. In the second stage John, the Elder of 2 and 3 John, who was also the Elder at Ephesus, expanded the collection of discourses by adding narratives and thus produced a gospel, a life of Christ. He prefixed the Prologue and wrote a second draft (chapters 13-14) of the first Farewell Supper Discourse (chapters 15-16) amd substituted it for the first. Finally the redactor revised the gospel to accomodate it to the traditions in the synoptic gospels. He added 3:31-36, 5:28-29, and chapter 21. He inserted the first draft of the Farewell Supper Discourse behind the second draft and transposed chapters 5 and 6. Bacon tries to reconstruct the original gospel by printing the present gospel with the redactor's work in italics. In earlier work Bacon opposed the idea that any sources were used; he ascribed all changes to a redactor.[17]

Rudolf Bultmann, professor of New Testament at Marburg University, has given us the fullest presentation of his hypothesis in his commentary on the Gospel of John entitled Das Evangelium des Johannes. The first edition, published in fascicles, was completed in 1941, and the 17th edition was published in 1963. It is remarkable that a book which has appeared in so many editions and has been so widely discussed in the Western world has only recently (1971) been published in English. He summarizes his theory in the "Introduction" of his commentary and in his article "Johannesevangelium" in the encyclopedia Die Religion in Geschichte und Gegenwart, 1959 edition. Truly a combination theory, it is a mixture of source theory, redaction theory, and displacement theory.

Starting from the Prologue of the gospel, Bultmann postulates a gnostic source, the "Revelation Speeches" (Offenbarungsreden; also called RQ, Redequelle, discourse-source), a collection of poetry written in Aramaic, emanating from the circle of followers of John the Baptist. The milieu of this source was a type of Gnosticism similar to that of the Odes of Solomon and the Mandaean writings. The evangelist translated the Aramaic into Greek, transforming much of the poetry into prose.

The evangelist employed also a narrative account, the "Signs Source" (Semeiaquelle, sometimes designated SQ). Literary characteristics are used to detect the source, which was written in a Semitized Greek, that is, Greek influenced by traits borrowed from Semitic languages, chiefly Aramaic. The Signs Source has elements in common with the synoptic gospels, but its heightening of the miraculous reveals that it represents a later stage of Christian tradition than do the synoptics.

In addition the evangelist incorporated a "Passion Source," also written in Semitized Greek, and independent of the synoptic gospels. It cannot be separated from the rest of the gospel on stylistic grounds, for its style is essentially the same as that of the evangelist. Nevertheless, a source is present, for there is matter here which does not reflect the evangelist's theological interests, and certain passages are plainly insertions by the evangelist. In addition he is acquainted with synoptic tradition outside the Passion story, especially the Gospel of Mark.

Finally a redactor found the text out of order, with some pages broken into pieces. He arranged it in the present order, which is different from the evangelist's order. The redactor added chapter 21, some explanatory glosses, and some passages supporting ecclesiatical interests such as the Lord's Supper, baptism, and eschatology. He tries to make the author an eyewitness and to bring the book closer to the synoptic tradition.

Bultmann applies the term "editor" to the redactor instead of the evangelist.[18]

Dwight Moody Smith, Jr., while professor of New Testament at Methodist Theological School, Ohio (he is now at Duke University Divinity School), presents a full discussion of Bultmann's theory in his book The Composition and Order of the Fourth Gospel (1965). Using Bultmann's commentary as a basis, he reconstructs the Greek text of each of the sources and of the gospel before its disarrangement.[19]

Bultmann's method of determining the Revelation Speeches source has been strongly questioned, and rightly so. The stylistic criteria he sets up for finding the material which belongs to it occur outside of it as well as in it. This fact indicates that either the criteria are not valid or Bultmann has not included in the source all the material that belongs in it. His explanation is that the evangelist copied the style of his source; if that happened, Bultmann should not have included those stylistic characteristics which the evangelist copied, because we cannot be sure when they indicate source material.

Another vital objection to his method is that his assumption that the Revelation Speeches were all written as poetry is unwarranted. To reconstruct this source he begins with the Prologue and claims that the whole source was poetry because the Prologue and occasionally the discourses contain poetry. He errs, however, for the Prologue is distinct (as the vocabulary and thought show) and is not from the same source as the speeches; therefore poetry in the Prologue does not indicate that the speeches originally were poetry. Bultmann's mistaken assumption leads him to emend verses and even phrases to "restore" them to the poetic form he imagines they had originally. Käsemann notes that a weakness of Bultmann's premise is that the chain-type of poetic structure in the Prologue does not occur in the speeches.[20] Worst of all, by rewriting portions of the text Bultmann spoils the evidence and prevents us from accurately separating the work of the various writers. Another error is his presupposition that since the Revelation Speeches contain Semitic stylistic traits, they were written in Aramaic. The Greek of some writers contained Semitisms, however, so Semitisms do not necessarily indicate translation from Aramaic, as Ernest C. Colwell aptly demonstrated.[21] Bultmann errs also in connecting the source of these discourses with John the

Baptist. This mistake is the result of using the Mandaean literature as evidence because it, too, is semi-gnostic and honors the Baptist. That literature and the association of the Baptist with gnostic thought, however, originated long after the Gospel of John was written. In spite of these mistakes, Bultmann has many valid insights, and his recognition that the Fourth Gospel consists mainly of written sources, editorial work, and a redactor's later retouching is essentially sound. He rightly rejects the theory of accidental displacement of the leaves of the codex and the hypothesis that the evangelist never finished the gospel.

Burton Scott Easton (1946), professor of New Testament at General Theological Seminary, early examined and rejected Bultmann's theory of a pagan Revelation Speech source. He observed that there is no evidence of the existence of a pre-Christian Gnosticism which taught that the Revealer would be incarnated or that he would die to save others (10:11). Easton asks if the source as Bultmann reconstructs it is a unity. Like many writers since, Easton points out the weakness of Bultmann's uncertainty as to whether in some passages the evangelist is quoting from the source or is writing in the source's style.

Ernst Haenchen (1956), professor emeritus of New Testament at Münster in Westfalen, offers some suggestions but does not present a developed source theory. When he wrote, there was a trend toward the theory of oral tradition as the direct source of the Gospel of John. In opposition he suggests that the tradition employed by the evangelist probably came from the latter's own Christian community and may have been a written account based on oral tradition. Perhaps what Bultmann calls the "Signs Source" was really an enlarged edition of Mark, for the synoptic pieces in John could have come from the Gospel of Mark. The evangelist probably corrected his source material dogmatically and wrote his gospel in a small community. Its composition in a small community would not exclude the possibility that it was published later in a large city such as Antioch or Ephesus (but why does Haenchen think the gospel originated in a small community?). Haenchen accepts the possibility that the nonsynoptic material, too, may have come from a written source.

Wilhelm Hartke (1961), professor of the history of early Christianity at Humboldt University in Berlin, believes that the gospel consists of three literary layers which can be recognized clearly according to their theology and linguistics. In his theory the

Grundschrift, or Z, was dictated by the apostle John and written down by John Mark in Jerusalem in the year 43/44. It presented twelve "Signs of the Messiah Jesus."[22] It contained no accounts of Jesus' suffering, death, and resurrection, whereas "Urmarcus," an earlier book of signs, did. Next, John Mark added V, or "Ur=Johannes-Evangelium," which contained the Prologue and a Passion story of Jesus. John Mark was the Elder of Ephesus, "the disciple whom Jesus loved" in the gospel, and his mother was Mary Magdalene. Lastly, Judas Barabbas, the editor of the gospel and of the Johannine epistles and the author of the canonical Revelation of John, added the third layer, H, which consisted of material which was eschatological and predestinarian in content.

Hartke's very conjectural theory is especially to be faulted for his effort to identify the three authors of his strata. It is a serious mistake to assign an author to the gospel or any portion of it, because there is no reliable evidence whatever connecting any of the writing with any certain person, and there were many early Christians besides the few whose names we know who are equally probable as authors. All of Hartke's identification of authors in John rests on sheer speculation, as does his claim that Judas Barabbas wrote Revelation. Further, his reconstruction of sources rests on only superficial use of evidence.

G. H. C. Macgregor, professor of divinity and biblical criticism at the University of Glasgow, and A. Q. Morton (1961), a Church of Scotland clergyman, combine the literary interpretation of the former with the statistical analysis of the latter, and therefore in the exposition of their theory they refer to themselves as "the Commentator" and "the Analyst," respectively. They maintain that an editor produced John by fusing two sources, J_1 and J_2, while making a few changes and insertions of his own which they label R. They call the editor "the redactor." J_1 was the short original form of the gospel, and J_2 was a somewhat briefer document which in John is divided into five "panels" (at first construed by the authors as six). Morton believes that J_1 itself was composite.

The theory starts with the assumption that the autograph, the original manuscript, of the gospel was a codex and therefore the editor predetermined the length of the manuscript and forced his sources to fit into it. An autograph of 180 columns is postulated. Morton contends that the editor had to know in advance the relative sizes of his two sources and the new book he was writing. The editor must have learned this by copying from J_1 until a certain number of columns of the new book were filled, and then copying an equal or related number of columns from J_2. Thus he was able to maintain the proportion of his sources as he continued to copy them. One result of this procedure was that it caused him to transpose 7:15-24 from the end of chapter 5 to its present position, because otherwise the block of sixteen columns of J_1 material would not have finished at the close of the story of the feeding of the five thousand, which made an ideal introduction to the Bread of Life theme he copied from J_2. Macgregor comments that with one exception the J_2 panels occur at equal intervals in John. Both authors view this as confirmation that the editor followed a definite plan of conflation and that the J_2 panels had fixed limits.

Morton tests statistically his hypothesis that J_1 and J_2 are too unlike each other to come from the same source, and that the blocks of J_1 and J_2 material would fit a certain number of columns in the "Gospel model," the autograph as he conceives it. He concludes that the material passes these tests. The high proportion of long paragraphs in the gospel (nine, consisting of more than thirty lines each in Souter's Greek text, in contrast to one in Mark and Luke) is seen as evidence of conflation because the combining of source materials tends to increase the number of long passages.

In his commentary in the Moffatt series (1928) Macgregor ascribed to a later redactor the rearrangement of the text and the interpolation of new material. But now he is persuaded by Morton's analysis that both resulted from the evangelist's conflation of sources. He finds that each of the panels of J_2 begin or end at a point where he had suspected dislocation, whereas "no convincing cases of displacement" occur within the panels. This indicates that J_2 is a minor source that has been intruded into the major source, J_1. Further indication that J_1 was a continuous major source, he claims, is that when J_2 is removed, the sequence from one J_1 section to another is satisfactory.

Although Macgregor accepts Morton's theory in general, he has reservations: "The Commentator would not be willing to commit himself to agreement in detail with his colleague's analysis of the Gospel. He still finds it difficult to believe that a scribe's mind would work in just this way."[23]

Macgregor is fully justified in having doubts that the editor worked that way. A writer did not have to determine in advance the length of his codex, for leaves were added as needed until the book was finished. It is equally improbable that the scribe would feel that he had to end each section from a source at the bottom of a column in his manuscript so that he could start the next block from the other source at the top of his next column. Morton thinks that the editor operated this way in order to calculate precisely the length of his manuscript. But there was no need for such precise calculation! There is reason to doubt that ancient scribes--unlike modern analysts--were so mathematically inclined. Furthermore, other ancient conflated literature shows that editors were guided by vocabulary and thought content rather than by such a mechanical standard as always copying the same amount in each block of material from a source.

A more serious, and in my opinion fatal, objection is that the characteristics of J_1 and J_2 overlap too much for these two groups of material to have been separate sources. Certain passages in J_1 are more similar in nature to some passages in J_2 than they are to the rest of J_1, and vice versa. If sources were employed by the editor, Macgregor and Morton have failed to discover either their content or the editor's reasons for shifting from one source to another. Fortna describes the authors' claim that they have found an adequate method of analysis as "fantastic."[24]

In 1961 Sydney Temple, who has taught religion in Lexington and Amherst, Massachusetts, and at the University of Hawaii, approached the problem by investigating 6:24-71. In his article he divides the material into three layers: the Corė, the evangelist's writing, and the Homily. The Core is the oldest tradition, "which may be based on an eyewitness tradition."[25] It is characterized by Aramaisms and direct discourse between Jesus and the people or the disciples. It stresses the spiritual theme. Next, the evangelist wrote a theological treatise to convince readers that Jesus is the Jewish Messiah, as he states in 20:31. He incorporated the Core material in his composition and was concerned with the emerging problems of faith in the young church. He emphasizes "works" instead of "signs," has Jesus call himself "the Son," is concerned with "the last day," and writes smoother Greek. The Eucharistic Homily (verses 48-59) is a doublet of some of the Core and the evangelist's work, intended as an interpretation of the Eucharist. The Homily may have been inserted when chapter 21 was added.

At the annual meeting of the Society of Biblical Literature in St. Louis in December 1961, the present writer read a paper criticizing this hypothesis and the literary theories of Wilkens and Bultmann.[26] The criticism of Temple's article is repeated here. To determine the three strata he sets up criteria "based on differences of style, language, and content."[27] One of his main categories of criteria for detecting the Core consists of a list of eight alleged Aramaisms. In the passage which Temple is analyzing five of the Aramaisms do occur more in the Core than in the rest of the passage, but two of these occur only once each, which could be a coincidence. As for the other three Aramaisms, one occurs equally inside and outside the Core, and the other two occur more outside than within it. Clearly some of the Aramaisms do not support Temple's selection of Core material. Then why were Aramaisms chosen as characteristics of the Core? Temple has been influenced by the works of C. F. Burney, Charles Torrey, and Matthew Black, who all advocated the Aramaic origin of the Gospel of John. That influence combined with the writer's interest in finding an early Core "which may be based on an eyewitness tradition" supplies the answer. Other Greek linguistic criteria chosen by Temple also occur both inside and outside his Core. Further, when his theory is tested by applying to the rest of the gospel his linguistic and content criteria, it is inconsistent. The linguistic features and the ideas claimed to be characteristic of the Core are scattered throughout the body of the gospel and are not particularly associated with each other. Thus the criteria are not reliable means of determining a source, either in chapter 6 or in the gospel as a whole.

Temple's article published in 1962 has more merit. He calls attention to the distinctive nature of the two stories of miracles (2:1-11; 4:46-54) which alone in the text are numbered (the "first" and "second" signs of Jesus). Unlike the other Johannine narratives, these are not launching points for symbolic discussions. They are like the synoptic narratives in length, in type, and in the fact that editorial connections join them to the adjacent context. Distinctive characteristics of the two signs stories include the absence of "he answered and said" and the presence of the expressions "signs and wonders" and "manifested his glory." The two stories come from a different tradition than the evangelist's main source, the Core, in which sections are often introduced with the phrase "after this." The reason that the evangelist incorporated the two signs narratives, states Temple, is that in two places in its text the Core mentioned visits of Jesus to Galilee without reporting what happened there; the evangelist inserted the two signs stories at those places because their locale is Galilee and they served to fill out the account.

Temple rightly recognizes that the stories of the "first" and "second" signs are clearly from a source, and that the two stories constitute a fundamental starting point for an investigation of the existence of a signs source. Nevertheless, the possibility of editorial and redactional insertions in these stories needs to be raised. By concluding that the signs stories were not in the narrative Core source, Temple causes us to ask a crucial question: Was there another narrative source in the first half of John, or was there only one narrative source?

Rudolf Schnackenburg (1965), professor of New Testament and biblical theology at Würzburg, believes that a signs source is possible, but he emphatically rejects the idea that a written logia, or discourse, source was employed. If the evangelist relied on any written sources, he used them freely, the way he used the Old Testament books. This unsound idea of Schnackenburg's apparently is derived from Charles Goodwin's article.

Robert Tomson Fortna, professor of religion at Vassar College, in his doctoral dissertation (1965) and book (1970) based on it, searches for a signs source, a definite gospel, in the Gospel of John. He focuses his investigation on the narrative material and finds such a source, which he calls "The Gospel of Signs." He closes his works with a reconstruction of the Greek text of the source.

As he reconstructs it, the Gospel of Signs consists of an account of John the Baptist, the call of the disciples, seven miracle stories, the story of the Samaritan woman, and a passion narrative. Among the miracles he includes the large catch of fish in chapter 21, for he does not recognize a redactor as the author of that chapter. The purpose of the Gospel of Signs is to convince potential Jewish converts that Jesus is the Messiah. This source is not historically superior to other gospel material, and on the whole it shows "a relatively developed form" of the synoptic tradition.[28] Fortna states that the source had a consistent style and that in general the stylistic tests used by E. Schweizer and Ruckstuhl confirm the source as he has reconstructed it.

Fortna begins his study with the presupposition that source analysis should take priority over other methods of literary criticism of the Gospel of John. The basis of his presupposition is the reasoning that aporias indicate that there are at least two strata and that "one principal writer" produced the aporias by editing source material.[29] He dislikes redaction as a possible explanation because it would eliminate some of the material from the original Gospel of John and leave less evidence for source analysis. A weakness of Fortna's method is the exclusion of redaction. Aporias can be caused by redaction as well as by use of sources, and therefore both possibilities should be considered. There is also the possibility of a combination situation in which a redactor added source material. We may question also whether one should begin the study with the presupposition that the gospel is the work of one principal writer. Fortna has some valuable insights, however, and generally he is moving in the right direction.

Jürgen Becker (1970), professor of New Testament at Kiel, concludes that there is a signs source in John. Its miracles present Jesus as the theios anēr, "divine man," of the Hellenistic world, and as the Jewish Christ. The evangelist modified it in some passages to promote his own theology. He introduced the theme of the cross and resurrection, and he increased the number of the miracles. The evangelist attacks the source's Christology and minimizes its idea of revelation through miracles. Becker reconstructs the content of the signs source.

W. Nicol (1972) agrees with Fortna that John used a Gospel of Signs Source, "S". His "separation" (a term he prefers to "reconstruction") of S is similar to Fortna's, except that he does not include any of the Passion story or chapter 21. His four sets of "indications" of S material are form, style, aporias, and "ideological tensions." Less than a third of his book is devoted to source analysis, however; in the rest he discusses the background of S and the theological character of the work of John, the writer of the present gospel. He concludes that the background of S is more Jewish and Christian than Hellenistic, and that John interprets the miracles symbolically as demonstrations of Jesus' earthly glory, which corresponds to the mighty glory of the exalted Christ.

Nicol's "separation" of S is superior to Fortna's in that he does not include any of chapter 21, but Fortna's reconstruction is superior in that he recognizes that S extended into the Passion account. We should challenge Nicol's speculation that S was not a written source but the "gospel" which John, the author of the Gospel of John, had preached for years, a message of traditional miracle stories which he set down from memory when he wrote his book. In chapter 12 below we show that the manner in which the editor used S demonstrates that S was a written source.

In this chapter we have surveyed the general kind of source theory. Special categories of source theories will be described in the next two chapters.

NOTE: Edwin Broome's source theory (1944) was accidentally overlooked. He postulated seven sources: S_1, a collection of sayings beginning with "truly, truly"; S_2, sayings of a Greek nature without the formula "truly, truly"; S_3, sayings that are Aramaic in origin; S_4, the ego̅ eimi ("I am") sayings; S_5, the seven signs; S_6, stories about Jesus; S_7, a Passion source.

CHAPTER 5

HELLENISTIC-SPEECH THEORIES

One group of source theories springs from studies which point out similarities between the speeches in John and some religious speeches in the pagan background. Eduard Norden, a German classical philologist, was a pioneer in this field.

In his classic Agnostos Theos ("Unknown God"), published in 1913, Norden states that in the gnostic environment of Christianity there was "a soteriological speech-type," a kind of speech that proclaimed salvation and was characterized by the proclamation formulas "you are," "I am," and "this one is" (in Greek: su ei, egō eimi, and houtos estin). These formulas referred to the deity and proclaimed him or her as the savior of mankind. According to Norden, the use of the participle and the relative pronoun in the predicate to describe the deity was characteristic of the proclamation style. The soteriological speech-type was employed in missionary preaching to win converts and in prayers to invoke the deity. It was Hellenistic, not Hellenic; it originated among the Babylonians and Egyptians, spread to the Semitic prophets of Palestine and Syria, and was incorporated in "a mighty theosophical, gnostic, and mystical movement" which swept the Near East at the beginning of the Christian era. The Christian community as a consequence of its struggle with other salvation religions clothed the words of Jesus with form and content which stemmed from the phraseology of the proclamations of the Semitic "pseudoprophets." This is especially true with the speeches in the Gospel of John, but it occurs to some extent even in the synoptic gospels: "you are ["this is" in Matthew] my Son, the Beloved," at Jesus' baptism; "this is my body" at the Lord's Supper; and Jesus' "I am" before the High Priest.

Norden's work was developed somewhat by G. P. Wetter (1916), professor of theology at Uppsala. Wetter's thesis is that the self-proclamation style of the soteriological speech was requisite for the "Sons of God" who at that time abounded in the Near East. The same style is present in the Gospel of John. Neither Norden nor Wetter investigated the possibility that the Johannine speeches may come from a written source.

A study of Johannine speech material by W. H. Raney (in

Kingsville, Canada) was published in Germany in 1933. Raney notes briefly the prevalence of hymnody in the religions of ancient Egypt, Babylonia, and China, and in Hinduism, Judaism, and early Christianity. He views the following passages in John as "prose hymns" written by the evangelist to be sung or chanted by a cantor or choir: the Prologue; 3:14-21, 31-36; 10:1-18; chapters 14-17. He compares the Johannine prose hymns with other hymns with respect to the two basic characteristics: rhythmic thought (parallelism) and rhythmic tone (the accentual system) and concludes that in spite of some differences these passages in John are really hymns. He concedes that the passages are distinctive compared with the rest of the gospel and that they are involved in passages where it is difficult to trace the sequence, yet he holds the traditional view that the whole gospel must have been written by one author. He attempts to solve the problem of sequence by revising J. H. Bernard's theory of accidental displacement of the leaves of the manuscript. Raney speculates that the prose hymns must have been written on separate sheets readily detachable from the rest of the gospel and used by the choristers in the public worship. As the manuscript passed from one chorister to another and from one church to another, the hymns were not always returned to their proper positions. "Moreover, in this Gospel designed primarily for use in public worship, the same freedom of opinion or carelessness could not fail to have its effect also on some of the narrative portions."[1]

In his study Ego Eimi (1939) Eduard Schweizer focuses on the possible significance of the sentences containing the Greek formula egō eimi ("I am") and of the metaphorical speeches connected with them. He maintains that in the Semitic-Oriental environment of the New Testament there was an "I"-style of speech, which exhibited definite characteristics and usually was reserved for the speech of a god. The expression "egō eimi" played an important role in the "I"-style of speech as a formula for self-revelation by the deity. The expression is rather distinctive in that the personal ending of the verb (-mi) makes the personal pronoun (egō) unnecessary except for emphasis, yet the pronoun is used. Because it appears in other kinds of literature, however, the expression does not prove a connection between such speeches of a deity and those of the Johannine Christ--a correct judgment by Schweizer.

He finds that the Johannine speeches and the Mandaean writings have more in common than just the revelation formula ego eimi. The strong similarity of terminology and style, especially the repetition (Wiederaufnahme) of key words, indicates some relationship between the two groups of writings. The evangelist may have used a Christian speech source whose author had been a Mandaean, or he may have thoroughly rewritten a Mandaean document, or he may have composed both freely in the pattern of Mandaean texts known to him. Schweizer accepts as a working hypothesis, but not as a final result, the view that the evangelist used a written source, but judging from the unity of the present gospel, he must have rewritten the source thoroughly, giving it his own style and spirit.

Karl Kundsin (1939),[2] a professor at Riga, asserts that the speeches in the Gospel of John proceed not in a straight logical line but in a circular fashion with chains of statements which repeatedly go back to the starting point. Here and there a chain is condensed into prominent individual sayings. Turning to the non-Christian parallels to the "I am" sayings, he supplements the examples given by Norden. Kundsin claims that the Johannine speeches are distinctively Christian in their soteriological moment of decision in connection with the existential proclamation. He compares the Mandaean and the Johannine revelation speeches with respect to their style, then concludes that the Mandaean are direct imitations of those in the gospel when the soteriological concluding sentence repeats the preceding "I"-proclamation without logically growing out of it. Another continuation of the Johannine style in the Mandaean writings is the addition of a negative corollary to a positive salvation statement. Kundsin tries to solve the question of the origin of the "Johannine speech-type" on the basis of the Book of Revelation, an approach which Heinz Becker (rightly) specifically rejects.

Rudolf Bultmann, as we have seen, includes a collection of revelation speeches as a written source used in the Gospel of John. These speeches were not Christian writings, but the evangelist adapted them, using them because he and they came from a common milieu, the circle of John the Baptist.

Bultmann searches for parallels to the Johannine speeches and finds them both in content and in form--the latter especially in poetic structure--in gnostic works. To discover the nature of the speech source he leans heavily on the Odes of Solomon and the Mandaean writings, finding in them the closest parallels to the speeches in the gospel. He contends further that the revelation-speech source is related to a non-Christian source used in the First Epistle of John.

Despite the similarity of point of view of the evangelist and the speech source, Bultmann maintains that the two can be distinguished. He sees a difference in their use of the Old Testament, their treatment of Jesus, and the character of their language (more mythological in the source). He states that in the speech source Jesus speaks in the first person. Starting with the Prologue as a clue, Bultmann decides that the speech source consists of poetry whereas the rest of the gospel is prose; thus the revelation speeches can be detected through their poetic style, including rhythm and antithetical parallelism.

In 1941 Heinz Becker finished a doctoral dissertation under the direction of Bultmann at the University of Marburg. In the dissertation, published in 1956, he maintains that a speech source is incorporated in the gospel, but it cannot be discovered through such internal criteria as stylistic characteristics. It can be recovered, however, through the external approach of determining the Schema, or pattern, of the revelation speeches in Semitic and gnostic literature and searching for the same features in John. Becker concludes that the evangelist used a pre-Christian gnostic source. Although the evangelist expanded it by inserting notes, it can be reconstructed because the material still bears the characteristics of revelation speeches.

The pattern of a revelation speech consists of three basic elements, according to Becker. One is the self-proclamation in which the revealer announces his nature and origin, normally using a predicate nominative, as in "I am your Judge," "I am the Light." A second element is the invitation, or call to decision, in which mankind is asked to believe the message of the revealer. The third element is the "crisis saying," which contains one or both of two features: the promise of reward for believing the message and the threat of dire consequences of disbelief. The three elements occur in varying order, and not all are necessarily present. With its emphasis upon the inherently evil nature of the world from which man should be saved, the revelation speech is existential and gnostic in character.

Becker examines in detail the Johannine speeches, finding examples of all of the essentials of the revelation speech. Finally, he attempts a reconstruction of the Greek text of the speech source in the gospel.

His criteria for detecting the passages that belong to the source are (1) the presence of the basic elements of the pattern, e.g., 11:25-26 (the whole pattern does not occur in John in any one passage because the evangelist thoroughly split up his source); (2) the occurrence of rhythmic parallelism, both antithetical, e.g., 3:18a-b, and otherwise, e.g., 6:35b-c; and (3) the existence of apodictic formulations expressing absolute truth or certainty, e.g., 5:19b. On the other hand, certain features are excluded from the source because they are not characteristic of a revelation speech but are characteristic of the evangelist: dialogue, insertions, explanations, Old Testament quotations, reflection style (i.e., the writer reflects on what has been stated earlier, as in 6:36), "third colons" (i.e., third clauses or statements added to the two that form a parallelism, as in 6:27c), and unsymmetrical parallelisms.

Siegfried Schulz in 1960 incorporated elements of the Hellenistic speech theories in his "theme-history method" (see chapter 6 below). He views the egō eimi speeches as a unit with a common soteriological theme.

Have the speech-source theories established that the so-called revelation speech really existed as a literary type in the Hellenistic world? The numerous examples presented by Norden, Schweizer, Kundsin, and Becker from ancient Egypt, India, Babylonia, Assyria, and the Hellenistic Near East do demonstrate sufficiently that there was a general type of self-proclamation speech ascribed to various deities and deified kings. Norden was a leader in correctly recognizing that a soteriological speech-type existed, was Semitic in origin, and was adopted by the general gnostic mystical movement in the early Roman period. Recognition of the existence ofa general type of revelation speech is an aid to understanding the significance of this kind of material in the gospel.

Nevertheless, more care should be exercised in the selection of material used for evidence of the Hellenistic revelation speech as background. Of the gnostic materials, only the earlier traditions go back to the time that the evangelist compiled the present gospel; this probably includes Poimandres. Schweizer, Bultmann, and Becker emphasize the Mandaean background but actually the Mandaean literature was written too late to supply information concerning the origin of the gospel. In chapter 4 we objected on this ground to Bultmann's interpretation of the discourse source. The extant Mandaean writings date from about A.D. 700. They contain allusions to Muhammed and the spread of Islam, so at least a portion of their traditions originated after 600. The earliest known mention of the sect was made in 792 by Theodore bar Khonai.[3] Mandaean thought and literature originated long after the Gospel of John was produced, as Dodd rightly recognizes.[4] Therefore Mandaean writings must be rejected as guides to the understanding of the gospel. John the Baptist is the hero of the sect in Mandaean tradition, and heavy reliance upon Mandaean literature led Bultmann into the fallacy of deducing that both the revelation speeches and the evangelist himself came from the circle of the Baptist.

Although there was a self-revelation type of speech in the Hellenistic world and it tended to have a pattern of the three parts Becker describes, the three are not always in the same order and all three are not always present. The pattern and specific content of the speeches varied greatly and were not fixed so precisely that we can rely on them to reconstruct the original text of the speech source in John. We must remember, too, that the call to decision, the promise of reward, and the threat of punishment are features that are not confined to revelation speeches; they occur, for example, in the synoptic gospels.

Both Becker and Bultmann go too far in rearranging the material. On the other hand, they have proposed certain valid criteria for detecting matter added by the evangelist which should be excluded from the source or sources. One such criterion is that the explanations of the sayings are the evangelist's own compositions.

One of the permanent contributions of the speech-source theories is the recognition that the Gospel of John is not as unified as some biblical critics have claimed. There are certain characteristics in the speeches which are not in the rest of the gospel, and some of these traits are not necessarily the result of the subject matter. They indicate the presence of source material.

With the exception of Bultmann's, the theories examined assume that there was only one speech source. Considering the variation within the material, several sources may be involved. Bultmann's theory that the speeches in John come from a collection of speeches is a possibility. It is also possible that the evangelist did the collecting, and perhaps he used homiletic speech material (e.g., 3:16 ?) as well as speeches ascribed to Jesus.

The opinion that the speech source was pre-Christian is an error on the part of Bultmann, followed by his student Becker. The author (or authors) of the speeches borrowed some major ideas from the non-Christian world, but it was he and not the evangelist who Christianized the material. This is demonstrated by the fact that the Christian ideas in the speeches are not always the same kind of thought as those in the matter added by the evangelist.

CHAPTER 6

JOHN AND SYNOPTIC TRADITION

Until modern times it was generally believed that each of the four canonical gospels was written independently, without any literary influence from the others, but today only extremely conservative biblical interpreters hold that opinion. Now New Testament scholars recognize some kind of literary relationship among Matthew, Mark, and Luke; many realize that there probably is some kind of relationship behind the parallelism between John and one or more of the other three. The explanation of the similarities (and differences) between John and the synoptic gospels, however, is the subject of much lively debate.

Since 1920 there has appeared a large variety of explanations of the similarities between John and the synoptics. These range from theories of the dependence of John directly on the synoptics to theories of a common oral tradition behind all the gospels; an intermediate view is that John used written synoptic-like tradition as a source.

Blinzler has surveyed the views of biblical scholars on this question,[1] and he rightly appraises the influence of apologetic motivation as a factor in the opposition to suggestions of any Johannine dependence on the synoptic gospels. He observes that the desire to maintain the historical importance of John was behind the opposition to synoptic influence of Gardner-Smith, Mollat, J. A. T. Robinson, S. Schulz, and Gyllenberg. He suggests that the apologetic aspect may have been the cause of the widespread popularity of Gardner-Smith's thesis in the English-speaking world.[2] Blinzler objects to the erroneous claim, based on the same apologetic motive, that since Gardner-Smith the trend among biblical scholars has been strongly away from acceptance of any literary connection between John and the synoptics. By surveying the works on the subject, he disproves the apologetic claim. He reports Harrison's observation (1964) that among the newer writers there is a reaction against the position of Gardner-Smith, for example, Barrett. Blinzler lists 26 biblical scholars in the period 1946-1964 who reject direct literary relationship and 31 who accept it (my count); instead of a trend away from belief in literary connection this is actually a majority for it. Three of the 31 think the influence was from John to Luke (Mollat,

Feuillet, and Boismard), and Osty believes that the influence between the two flowed both ways. The 26 include both exponents of oral tradition and the advocates of written synoptic-like tradition.

The Synoptic Gospels

The first kind of theory offered to explain the similarities between John and the synoptic gospels was the view that the evangelist knew and used the synoptics. This explanation began to appear in the nineteenth century: J. L. Hug in 1826,[3] Baur in 1847, H. J. Holtzmann in 1869, and Harnack in 1897. In the first quarter of the twentieth century it was the prevailing view. Further study led to more precise formulations in the 1920s as Stanton decided that John used only Mark, while Streeter and Macgregor concluded that he used Mark and Luke. In chapter 4 we observed that the following biblical scholars have included one or more of the synoptic gospels as sources used by the evangelist or by a redactor: Wendt, Meyer, Loisy, Bacon, Bultmann, and Haenchen. The view is shared by other men we have mentioned, including Windisch, Bernard, Howard, Strathmann, and Barrett. The following summaries are limited to some of the recent theories of this kind.

In 1956 E. Kenneth Lee, in Horsforth, Leeds, found close parallels with Mark in John's stories of the feeding of the five thousand, the anointing, crucifixion, and resurrection. In addition Lee lists some 25 detached sayings and incidents in John which seem to reveal a knowledge of Mark. The literary parallels are close enough and numerous enough to convince him that the author of John used the Gospel of Mark. When Mark does not suit his purposes, he leaves it for another source and at times deliberately contradicts Mark. Whatever the source, the evangelist reinterprets the material according to his own faith.

Edwin D. Freed (1961), professor of Bible at The Lutheran Theological Seminary in Gettysburg, made a study of the Johannine story of Jesus' entry into Jerusalem. Focusing his attention on the Old Testament quotations, he maintains that in this story the evangelist was indebted to the synoptic gospels, especially Matthew, even for the quotations, and that he used elements from the synoptic accounts to strengthen his theme of Jesus' kingship. The quotation from the Psalms in 12:13 contains the term "Hosanna," which is lacking in the Septuagint. Since it occurs in the corresponding story in Matthew and Mark, the evangelist must have obtained it from one of these gospels. Like the synoptics, John presents the quotation without an introductory formula. John's changes in the synoptic account are often the result of his emphasis on the idea that Jesus is the king of the Jews, states Freed.

D. Moody Smith, Jr. (1963) vigorously attacks Freed's article. He comments that in comparison with the synoptics the story in John differs in context and in language, Johannine motifs are added, and many of the differences are "relatively insignificant" and display "no purpose or pattern." As for the lack of introductory formula with the Old Testament quotation, he claims it is omitted merely because it would be awkward there.

John A. Bailey (1963), at St. Paul's United College, Limuru, Kenya, in his doctoral dissertation written under the direction of Oscar Cullmann, studies in detail the traditions that are common to Luke and John but not to Mark. Bailey's work is comprehensive in that he lists fully these common traditions. He concludes that the Gospel of Mark and especially the Gospel of Luke are the major sources for the Johannine accounts of the anointing and the Passion story. His evidence is largely identity of language and narrative content.

In 1965 Freed expanded his investigation to include all the Old Testament quotations in John. Again he concludes that John is dependent upon the synoptic gospels but that some quotations are drawn directly from the Old Testament. He rejects <u>testimonia</u> (collections of Old Testament verses used as proof texts) and in general the Hebrew text of the Old Testament as sources used in John.

Werner Kümmel, professor of theology at Marburg, in his 1965 revision of the Feine-Behm introduction to the New Testament, is convinced fully that the literary contact of John with Mark and Luke is unmistakable. The evidence consists of identity of sequence, linguistic similarities, names, and individual features. He doubts that John is connected with Matthew.

Josef Blinzler (1965), professor of New Testament at the Academy of Philosophy and Theology in Passau, Germany, lists the parallels with the synoptic gospels and concludes that although it is questionable that John knew the Gospel of Matthew, he certainly knew the Gospel of Mark and may have known the Gospel of Luke. He probably did not have a copy of Mark in front of him, but he knew its content and worked parts of it into his presentation. The three most important kinds of evidence for this conclusion are (1) the many places in John where the evangelist presents things as already known to his readers (if his source were only oral tradition, he could not be so certain that his readers knew them); (2) many scenes in John are in the same order as in Mark (Blinzler agrees with Barrett in rejecting Gardner-Smith's theory that the pericopes were handed down in a definite order in oral tradition); (3) many times John has linguistic reminiscences of Mark. Blinzler rejects a Grundschrift as the source of synoptic tradition on the grounds that John is a unified work (following E. Schweizer and Ruckstuhl), not a "patchwork."

Francis E. Williams (1967), at St. Michael's School in Tucson, observes that some Johannine material is a variation of synoptic tradition, and he states that two factors worked to produce this result. One factor was the dramatization of sayings and parables into narrative, as in the Johannine story of the footwashing, which apparently grew out of the saying in Luke 22:27, "I am among you as one who serves." The second factor was the tendency for details to be moved from one narrative to another with a similar theme, as in the unnecessary mention of Martha waiting on table in John 12:2 (from Luke 10:40).

Williams concentrates on two Johannine stories, the wedding at Cana (2:1-11) and the dialogue between the Baptist and the Jewish delegation (1:19-28). He finds that they have "a particular affinity" with Lukan narratives. He concludes that, although his investigation is too limited in scope to provide generalizations concerning the relationship between Johannine and synoptic traditions, these stories indicate that we should look for possible connections between John and the synoptic tradition before we look for special sources or independent traditions.

Georg Richter (1969) at the Englisches Institut concludes that the evangelist reworked material from the synoptic gospels to refute Jewish charges against the Christians. Many of these charges are repeated by Jews in Origen's Against Celsus and Justin's Dialogue with Trypho the Jew. An example is the accusation that when Jesus was about to be arrested, he hid himself until he was captured. The evangelist counteracts the charge by depicting Jesus as stepping forward willingly and allowing the soldiers to arrest him. If Richter is right in his analysis, we must enlarge greatly the scope of the possible interests of the writers in John. Certainly the question of the use of the synoptic gospels cannot be settled only on the basis of the "theological" interests of the evangelist, as many writers have tried to do.

A modification of the view that the evangelist had the synoptic books before him is the theory that he was familiar with them and drew upon his memory for some of their pericopes. This theory is one explanation of John's divergence in details from synoptic stories. Charles Goodwin concludes that the evangelist quoted the Old Testament from memory and probably used the synoptics in a similar manner. A difficulty with the memory theory is that there is no evidence for it; it is only conjecture.

If the evangelist used the synoptic gospels, why does the Johannine form of a synoptic story differ so much in detail from the form in the other gospels? Biblical scholars have offered a variety of explanations besides the theory of an inadequate memory. Baur maintained that the evangelist was not interested in reporting history and that he wrote as he did to present his ideal "of a Christian community made up equally of Gentiles and Jews."[4] Zahn and Goguel believed that John was written to supplement the synoptic gospels. Scott asserted that the evangelist drew upon the synoptic sources to interpret them, to give the real inward meaning of Jesus' message. Bacon and Colwell held that John's purpose is to correct the synoptics, to turn the gospel in a more spiritual direction. Windisch concluded that the evangelist knew and rejected the other canonical gospels and wrote to displace them from circulation in the church. More recently, Titus has stated that John used the synoptics to appropriate material suited to his special theological interest.

One argument for Johannine use of the synoptic gospels appeared in the older discussions but is seldom advocated today: Mark must have been known to the author of John because it, Mark, was written several decades earlier. This is a non sequitur, for other early Christian literature demonstrates that the gospels were not universally known in the church before the middle of the second century.

Nevertheless, certain arguments for the Johannine use of Mark and Luke seem quite decisive. Presentation of some incidents in the same order in both Mark and John is strong evidence for the use of Mark (or possibly Matthew when Matthew has the same order). For example, the following events occur in the same sequence in John 6 as in Mark 6 and 8: feeding the multitude, walking on the lake, and Peter's confession. It seems incredible that this agreement is accidental, and improbable that this combination was already fixed in oral tradition. Further evidence consists of verbal parallels to Mark, especially in John 6 and the anointing in John 12. Certain details indicate that the evangelist used Luke too. Only Luke and John mention Annas, Lazarus, and the sisters Mary and Martha. In several incidents in these three gospels, John agrees with Luke, not Mark, in some ways.[5]

Oral Tradition

Conservative biblical scholars have never approved of the idea that the other canonical gospels could have been a source for John, for that would decrease its authority. After the belief in the independence and apostolic authorship of each gospel became untenable, many of these scholars turned to authentic oral tradition as the primary source behind the gospels. It was the German form criticism movement, Formgeschichte, which paved the way for oral tradition theories.

Percival Gardner-Smith was a lecturer in divinity at Jesus College, Cambridge University. In his small book Saint John and the Synoptic Gospels (1938), he launches a large-scale attack on the theory that the synoptics influenced John. He accuses the biblical scholars who accepted the theory--specifically Bacon, Streeter, and V. H. Stanton--of concentrating solely on the points of agreement between John and the synoptics until after they have decided that the fourth evangelist used the latter. Only after they have thus decided the matter, charges Gardner-Smith, do these critics consider the divergences between John and the other three [an unfair charge] . He claims that in contrast his method is "to take the Gospel as it stands, and, by noting simultaneously both the similarities and the dissimilarities, seek to determine on which side the balance of probability inclines."[6] He says his procedure is to consider "whether it is easier to account for the similarities between St John and the Synoptists without a theory of literary dependence, or to explain the discrepancies if such a theory has been accepted."[7]

Gardner-Smith's actual procedure is to attempt to answer the three chief arguments advocated in his day for the dependence of John on the synoptic gospels. To the argument that the similar general gospel framework indicates dependence, he replies that the evangelist must have obtained the general arrangement from the oral tradition, which was arranged according to the needs and conventions of apostolic preaching. To the argument that the presentation of certain incidents in the same order shows that John used Mark, he answers that by the time the gospels were written the broad gospel outline must have been developed so that "in the local churches many sections of the tradition had probably fallen into an accepted order."[8] To the argument that linguistic parallels and similar details are proof of dependence, Gardner-Smith again sets up oral tradition as the source of the similarities.

He supports his thesis by pointing to the divergence of John from the synoptic gospels in the traditions common to them. He maintains that John's divergences are not in accord with his theology, so he must not have originated them but derived them from a source, which Gardner-Smith characteristically assumes to be oral tradition. Further, he believes the major divergences show that the evangelist did not know the synoptics, which were too standard in the churches for John to disagree with deliberately. Christians believed that those gospels rested on the testimony of the Lord himself, and departure from the synoptic scheme would require an explanation.

How valid is Gardner-Smith's case? There is but slight merit to his observation (made earlier by Streeter) that John differs from the synoptics on points which have no theological significance for the evangelist. There are many other possible causes of the "pointless" contradictions in the synoptic-like material besides the theology of the evangelist, all of which Gardner-Smith overlooked. Possible causes of deviation from the synoptics include the evangelist's personal preference in vocabulary and style, his desire to add details, his interests other than theological, and the presence of the features in written sources he used. The "pointless" divergences are not necessarily more primitive than the synoptics, for some of them spring from apologetic motivation. Many recent writers have noted an anti-Judaism motive for transplanting the temple-cleansing incident to the beginning of Jesus' career. There is also anti-Jewish polemic behind the shift in application of the proverb about a prophet not honored in his homeland; the shift is from Christian explanation of the rejection of Jesus by the people to Christian explanation of his rejection by Jews in general.

Throughout his book Gardner-Smith weighs the similarities against the dissimilarities between John and the synoptics and observes that the dissimilarities are more numerous. This method is quite unreliable. More dissimilarities than similarities do not prove that the author did not use the other gospels, for an ancient writer could use a source much or little and in many ways: he could copy it exactly, or alter it, or merely allude to certain features. Gardner-Smith assumes that the evangelist would follow the synoptics closely if he knew them, an assumption that rests on the erroneous claim that the synoptics were well known and accepted as "standard works" throughout Christianity. The claim is disproved by the divergence from synoptic ideas in other books of the New Testament and in the Apostolic Fathers, and by the lack of citation of Jesus in these works.

As we have observed, Gardner-Smith describes his method as an examination of the gospel to see whether it is easier to account for the similarities without a theory of literary dependence, or to explain the discrepancies if such a theory is accepted. Actually, his approach is quite one-sided; he does not make an earnest effort to explain the discrepancies if the evangelist used the synoptic gospels.

A major inconsistency appears in his book: the synoptic gospels were too well accepted for John to disagree with them, yet John did not even know them! The fallacy of this attempt to have it both ways should be quite apparent. If John did not know the synoptics, then they were not standard in early Christianity at the time the evangelist wrote; if they were standard, then John would have known them and they are at least as probable a source as oral tradition.

Gardner-Smith expects too much of oral tradition. He contends that even the linguistic details and the order of pericopes were fixed in it and therefore the evangelist drew even these from it. But his claim that the oral tradition was fixed is inconsistent with the divergence between John and the synoptic gospels. If a fixed oral tradition is the source behind all four canonical gospels, why do they vary so much?

Although he mentions in passing the possibility that John may have been influenced by writings now lost,[9] he does not consider it seriously. He overlooks the various source theories of his day and the evidence of the aporias in the gospel.

Finally, Gardner-Smith manifests the customary bias for an early date for the gospel and the preservation of some of the book's authority.[10] He believes that freeing John from indebtedness to the other gospels permits an earlier date and hence "a new possibility of regarding the Fourth Gospel as an independent authority." He adds: "So long as it was believed that John knew Mark, and altered his account in an arbitrary and irresponsible manner, interest in him as a historian could never be great. But if in the Fourth Gospel we have a survival of first century Christianity which owed nothing to synoptic developments, and which originated in quite a different intellectual atmosphere, its historical value may be very great indeed."[11] Although this statement appears in his conclusion, it reveals the motivation underlying his book.

Many biblical scholars regard Gardner-Smith's book as the major influence turning the tide away from the theory of Johannine dependence upon the synoptic gospels. Indeed, for the next two decades it did set the trend in American and British discussions of the issue. The book's influence is still felt, and Stephen Neill is not convinced that Gardner-Smith's arguments "have ever been effectively answered."[12] Dodd, who has developed further Gardner-Smith's thesis, remarks that the latter's book "has exerted an influence out of proportion to its size."[13] We should add a corollary. Considering the shallowness of Gardner-Smith's method and the bias underlying it, the book has exerted an influence out of proportion to its merit! The reason is that it said what many wanted to hear. Haenchen remarked that his thesis was "revolutionary--or should one say reactionary?"[14]

For many years C. H. Dodd was professor of divinity at Cambridge University. In his book The Apostolic Preaching and Its Developments, published two years before Gardner-Smith's work, Dodd recognizes that the kerygma, the apostolic preaching, was not uniform and detailed except on a few points.[15] Thus he does not claim that the kerygma is the source of the similarities between John and the other canonical gospels. He states that the Johannine interpretation of the kerygma "in form and expression, as probably in date, stands farthest from the original tradition of the teaching," although he believes it supplies "the most penetrating exposition of its central meaning."[16]

After Gardner-Smith wrote his book, however, Dodd followed his lead. In his The Interpretation of the Fourth Gospel (1953) Dodd claims that oral tradition has displaced literary dependence as the explanation of the similarity of portions of the Gospel of John to the synoptic gospels.[17] He develops this theme more fully in his Historical Tradition in the Fourth Gospel (1963).

Dodd declares his goal by asking: "Can we in any measure recover and describe a strain of tradition lying behind the Fourth Gospel, distinctive of it, and independent of other strains of tradition known to us? This will inevitably raise afresh the much debated question of the relation of the Fourth Gospel to the Synoptics."[18] The independent tradition for which he is searching is oral tradition, but he is not concerned with whether the evangelist obtained it directly in oral form or from oral tradition recorded in documents.[19]

He argues that there is an oral, precanonical tradition behind John that dates from the beginnings of the Christian transmission of Jesus' sayings and the stories about him. His evidence includes Aramaic terms and Semitisms, certain Jewish or Jewish-Christian features, and some geographical names in John. As further evidence he believes he finds a relation between the pre-Johannine tradition and the tradition behind the synoptic gospels. He maintains that both traditions contain the literary forms which form critics see in the synoptics, that there are Johannine series of units which supplement or complement synoptic series, and that there are places where the Johannine tradition appears to supplement the synoptic tradition "in the sense of clarifying points left obscure."[20] Dodd rightly rejects the presupposition that nothing in John can be early tradition of Jesus unless corroborated in the synoptics.

Is Dodd's approach to the problem reliable? Far from it, in spite of the popularity and influence of his two books on the subject. He, too, operates with a bias. He, too, is determined to show that somewhere in John is authentic tradition of the life of Jesus. He begins with a protest against the German "revolt against historicism" which appeared in the second decade of the twentieth century and has had wide influence in recent years. The "revolt" found little or no historical tradition in the gospels, and Dodd objects to its general effect, which has been to discourage the attempt to find in the gospels historical facts, especially about Jesus. Like Gardner-Smith, Dodd believes that form criticism has revolutionized the approach to the gospels, and consequently he turns his back on documentary criticism in favor of the theory of oral tradition.

Dodd, as well as Gardner-Smith, demands much evidence to indicate the use of the synoptic gospels, and little evidence to indicate the influence of oral tradition. He explains all similarities of words and sequence between John and the synoptics as a result of the general (oral) tradition of the church. The fallacy of the explanation is that there is no evidence of the existence of an oral tradition uniform enough or detailed enough to explain the similarities. Dodd thinks that the dissimilarities inconsistent with the evangelist's views and traits must come from oral tradition. The weakness of this often-used argument is that it ignores other possible causes of the dissimilarities: for example, the evangelist could have changed the synoptic material for reasons unknown to us, or he could have used a source with different traits and views that drew upon the synoptics, or a redactor with different traits and views could have inserted synoptic material. Advocates of oral tradition invariably neglect to consider all the literary possibilities.

Another major part of Dodd's method is his search for features which could be early and thus could be interpreted as evidence of pre-canonical oral tradition. One feature is the presence of Aramaic terms and Semitisms in passages which are parallel to synoptic passages. This feature, however, entered Christian tradition at a late date as readily as in the primitive period. Christian converts brought in Semitisms from their personal background, from Hellenistic Greek language, and from the Septuagint. Some converts knew the Aramaic language and used Aramaic terms in their writing (e.g., Paul and the author of Mark). The whole school of thought which has used Aramaic features, real and alleged, in the gospels to try to prove that gospels were originally written in Aramaic or contain authentic oral tradition from Jesus, has conveniently and persistently ignored the historical fact that Semitic linguistic influence could and did enter Christian tradition later.

Another indication of early tradition, in the opinion of Dodd and others, is that John contains native place names lacking in the other gospels and that the evangelist seems to be well informed the topography of Jerusalem and southern Palestine. On the contrary, this feature does not necessarily indicate earliness, for details of Palestinian topography could come just as readily from a later writer as from an early writer or from oral tradition.

It is quite disillusioning to discover the frequency with which "biblical scholars" during the last hundred years have followed a procedure similar to Dodd's. In their eagerness to prove that Christian traditions or Christian documents are authentic, they searched for features which could be early, then assumed that they necessarily are early!

Bent Noack (1954), professor of New Testament exegesis at the University of Copenhagen, goes beyond Dodd by contending that all the material in the gospel came directly from oral tradition as the evangelist wrote it down from memory. To Noack the semi-gnostic saying in Matthew 11:27 and Luke 10:22 shows that the gnosticizing of Christianity, which occurs in John, was already present in the oral tradition. He views the synoptic-like material in John as an additional indication of common oral tradition as the source. He asserts that in John the Old Testament is loosely quoted from memory, and he uses this also to support his theory. A weakness of this argument is that loose quotation of Scripture or other material is not necessarily from memory or oral tradition; the church Fathers, for example, often intentionally quoted loosely to support their arguments. Goodwin, in his article published the same year, recognizes that if the evangelist quoted the Old Testament loosely, he could have quoted the synoptics loosely too.

Noack points out some flaws in Bultmann's theory, and in his reply Bultmann objects to Noack's breaking up the gospel into small fragments, thereby begging the question in favor of his own theory. Noack does so by interpreting the fragments as small units of oral tradition which the evangelist placed together in the gospel.[21] Noack juggles his interpretation of evidence to fit his theory; he ascribes the distinctive character of the Johannine tradition to the oral sources, but he assigns the aporias to post-Johannine redaction. Fortna observes the weakness of this and suggests that the evangelist's redaction of sources would explain both the aporias and the distinctive character of the Johannine tradition.[22]

Pierson Parker, professor of New Testament literature and interpretation at General Theological Seminary, in his study of the relationship between Luke and John (1963) remarks that the contacts between the two gospels are "largely allusive" in that something in one reminds us of something in the other, but there is no topical connection. He observes the differences between their versions of a story and, most importantly, "the completely different mentality of the two writers." Since John is related more closely to Luke than to the other gospels in these traditions, it is improbable that ordinary oral tradition is the source. Therefore Parker postulates that the two evangelists worked in the same areas and heard the same words about Jesus, and each wrote his gospel as he remembered and digested the discussions of Jesus' sayings.

A weakness of Parker's theory is that the differences between the two gospels reflect more than a different personal mentality. The vast differences indicate that the writers lived in separate Christian communities which were radically different from each other. Parker rightly notes, however, a shortcoming of general oral tradition theories: some material in John is so similar to Luke that it is improbable that it came from general tradition.

Rudolf Schnackenburg (1965), professor of New Testament exegesis at Würzburg, concludes there is probably no direct literary dependence of John on the synoptic gospels. He believes that common use of oral tradition may be the explanation of the similarities between John and the other canonical gospels. The evangelist probably used written sources, but used them freely, the way he used the Old Testament books.

Raymond E. Brown (1967), professor of New Testament at St. Mary's Seminary, Maryland (now at Union Theological Seminary, New York), presents a compound theory of the origin of the gospel: two stages of oral tradition, two editions of the book by the evangelist, and a final editing by a redactor.[23] In Stage 1 there was a body of oral tradition which was independent of synoptic tradition. In Stage 2 that body of tradition was molded into Johannine form and style, probably "through oral preaching and teaching." The premise that there were two stages of Johannine oral tradition apparently is an effort to explain how John could be so different from the other three if all the canonical gospels are based on oral tradition. An unusual feature of this theory is the suggestion that one of the main contributions of the redactor was to add more material from Stage 2 of the oral tradition. This notion will appeal to conservatives, for it defends the early origin and authority of material which was added later. The idea is conjectural, for there is no evidence of the existence and use of stages of oral tradition.

The "theme-history method" of Siegfried Schulz (1957, 1960) should be mentioned because it bears some resemblance to the oral tradition aspect of form criticism. He describes his method in works published while he was *Privatdozent* in New Testament at Erlangen. Whereas form critics assume that pericopes circulated orally as units, Schulz contends that certain themes were transmitted as units. His theory is not *necessarily* an oral tradition theory, for he states that the theme-units could be passed on either orally or in writing.

He states that Christianity very early had a multiplicity of traditions, some of which were later woven together and transmitted as units because of their related themes. Therefore any search for sources in John must be preceded by the discovery of the theme-units, which are to be found by breaking the text into small units of tradition and by grouping them according to their theme, thereby revealing the historical-cultural background and source of each group. He finds six "theme-traditions" in John which he thinks originated in Jewish sectarianism and were gnosticized in early Christianity before they were incorporated in John: Son of Man, the Son, the Paraclete, the Second Advent, the basic theme of the Prologue, and the *egō eimi* sayings with their theme of self-predication and soteriological invitation and promise or threat. He declares that each of the six themes underwent the same process: the original Jewish concept was reinterpreted in the Christian community. Schulz has been affected both by oral tradition views and by the history of religions. The latter influence is especially apparent in his interest in Gnosticism and the Hellenistic *egō eimi* speech form.

There are many valid objections to Schulz's theme-history method. James M. Robinson and D. Moody Smith, Jr., object to the fact that it begins with the relatively unknown (the tradition) instead of with the known (the text), an approach which increases the element of uncertainty and is contrary to normal historical methodology.[24] Both biblical scholars question his manner of determining the background of his themes. For example, the term Paraclete does not occur in Jewish apocalyptic, but this fact does not stop Schulz from forcing the Paraclete theme into that background. He ignores the possibility of non-Jewish backgrounds of his themes.

Another serious objection to Schulz's theory is the fallacy of his central thesis that units with the same theme were transmitted together. In actual practice the material was constantly being reinterpreted and regrouped; within material which originally had the same theme, some traditions were interpreted in one direction and some in another, causing new groupings. Schulz recognizes that reinterpretation occurred, but fails to see its variety and the consequent regrouping of traditions.

Theories of common oral sources behind John and the other canonical gospels continued to be popular through the 1940s and 1950s. The trend was expressed succinctly by Haenchen in 1956: "Today more and more are drawn to the conjecture that John was created out of oral tradition."[25] The theories, indeed, were founded on conjecture. The current trend is away from them, for historians are becoming increasingly aware of the weaknesses of form criticism and the oral tradition hypothesis.[26] The present writer has outlined the case against the theory of an authentic oral tradition of Jesus deeds and teaching.[27] Although it was neither uniform nor universal, there was an oral tradition in early Christianity which originated in the life of the church, but a prevalent authentic oral tradition which reported details of Jesus' actual life and teaching simply did not exist.

Even if we assume--contrary to the evidence--that there was an authentic oral tradition, we are still confronted with problems which oral tradition theories cannot solve. Where is the evidence that oral tradition is the source of the synoptic-like material in John? Or of any material in John? What evidence is there that synoptic tradition is more likely to change in oral tradition than in the hands of writers? Since the use of written sources was prevalent in Hellenistic and Latin literature, why should we conclude that the Gospel of John was an exception to that practice?

Written Synoptic-like Tradition

Oral tradition theories have been superseded in popularity by theories of a written source or sources behind John which contained synoptic-like tradition. These theories began to appear about the same time as the oral tradition theories but did not achieve early popularity because they lacked the support of the fascinating new German form criticism and did not have such persuasive advocates as Gardner-Smith and Dodd. Not typical but nevertheless related to this kind of source theory is Bernard's suggestion (1929) that possibly the author of John used Q, the written source(s) other than Mark used in Matthew and Luke.[28]

In his Introduction au Nouveau Testament (1923) Goguel notes the parallelism between John and Mark in respect to the stories of the purification of the temple, the multiplication of bread, the walking on the sea, and Peter's confession. He observes features which he believes go back to very early tradition. These consist chiefly of certain details in 2:13-22 and two items in chapter 6: the enthusiasm of the crowd for Jesus, and his retreat from it to a mountain. Therefore, concludes Goguel, the evangelist who wrote John used a written source which contained material similar to that in the synoptics but reproduced primitive tradition more faithfully than the synoptics. The evangelist omitted parts of the source , however, and made some alterations in the portions he used. In some passages the source had already been altered by the redactor.[29]

Wilbert Francis Howard (1931), professor of New Testament at Handsworth College, Birmingham, mentions the possibility that John and the synoptists may have used an earlier common source.[30] Joachim Jeremias (1941), professor of New Testament at Göttingen University, has suggested that John was dependent on an unknown written source for his synoptic material, since there are both nonsynoptic and non-Johannine elements present which must come from a third body of material. He believes that the source can be identified even though it cannot be recovered.[31]

Bultmann in the 1941 edition of his commentary on John maintains that the evangelist did not use directly the synoptic gospels. The synoptic-like material comes from three written sources. The Signs Source contains, like Mark, the feeding and Jesus' walking on water and, like Matthew and Luke, the healing of the ruler's son. In the story of the man born blind (9:1-3, 6-7) the same source contains a form of the tradition later than that in the synoptic gospels. Secondly, the aspects of Jesus' death and resurrection in John that parallel those in the synoptic gospels come from the Passion Source. Finally, the evangelist drew from special sources of synoptic tradition his stories of the cleansing of the temple, anointing, entrance into Jerusalem, prediction of the betrayal, and the pericope 12:24-26. In the English translation of the latest edition, however, Bultmann maintains that the evangelist had either a "direct or indirect acquaintance" with the Gospel of Mark.[32]

In the Jordan Lectures in Comparative Religion delivered at the University of London in 1952 and published in 1956, David Daube, professor of civil law at Oxford proposes that John's source of the story of the anointing at Bethany was not the Gospel of Mark, but a"' proto-Markan' account."[33] In Mark the anointing is a burial rite: the whole jar of ointment is poured over Jesus' head, and the act is described explicitly as the anointing of Jesus' body in advance "for burying." In John, however, only Jesus' feet are anointed and Mary is to keep the ointment for "the day of my burial." In Mark the anointing of Jesus' body occurs before his death, whereas in John the anointing is performed by Joseph and Nicodemus when they remove the body from the cross. The author of John must have used a source in which it was Jesus' feet which were anointed and there was an allusion to the future performance by Mary of the actual burial rite of anointing. The evangelist reinterpreted the story as a foreshadowing of the burial rite as performed by Joseph and Nicodemus.

Ivor Buse (1958) in Bangor, North Wales, compares the Passion narrative in John with the strata of the Marcan Passion narrative that Vincent Taylor reconstructed. According to Taylor the Passion story in Mark consists of two layers: A, the basic, non-Semitic narrative, and B, Semitic material containing reminiscences of Peter which Mark inserted into A.[34] In his investigation Buse observes that the Johannine account "has striking similarities to the Marcan material classified as B and no significant likeness to material classified as A"; the resemblances to B are "often word-for-word identity of expression."[35] Therefore Buse concludes that in the Passion story the evangelist must have been acquainted not with Mark itself but with one or more of its sources.

Siegfried Mendner (1958) maintains that the stories of Jesus' feeding the five thousand and walking on the sea in John 6:1-21 are founded on "current" tradition which was not the synoptic gospels but tradition older and better than they (he goes back to Bernard and Bauer for this idea). The original form of that primitive tradition has been lost, but it has been developed and remodeled in two different directions. One of these later forms is in the present text of John, and the other is the synoptic form of these stories in Mark and Matthew. These two later forms contain secondary features that enhance the stories or display legendary traits. Someone added some of these features to the primitive stories and inserted his revised form of the stories into the Gospel of John. Someone else used that gospel to revise Mark and Matthew and at the same time worked his own revised form of the feeding and sea stories into these gospels. In the process he deliberately made the sea miracle a doublet of the stilling of the storm (Mark 4:35-41).

As evidence that John is the source of the Marcan form of the sea miracle Mendner points out the one place in Mark (6:50) where the Johannine expression "speak with" (laleō meta) occurs. Since the story is not in Luke, Mendner reasons that it was not in Mark when the author of Luke used Mark, but it was inserted later.

Mendner's theory is full of unjustified assumptions. There is no sound evidence that the Johannine form of the stories is based on a primitive tradition earlier than the synoptic gospels, and Mendner does not even attempt to examine the evidence that Mark is the source behind the feeding and sea miracle stories in John. Mendner's distinctive error is his theory that John was used to revise Mark! Nearly all New Testament scholars reject that view. Although "speak with" occurs elsewhere in John, it does not occur in the sea miracle story in John. This indicates that the same expression in Mark is a coincidence rather than borrowed from John. If John was used to revise Mark, why does Mark not have any characteristic Johannine ideas or expressions other than "speak with"? The case for this theory is frail indeed!

Peder Borgen (1959), a Norwegian biblical scholar, later reader in biblical studies at the University of Bergen, lists in two categories the parallels between John and the synoptics: these in Johannine passages dependent on synoptic tradition, and those in mutually independent tradition. The first group is in the accounts of the burial of Jesus, Peter's use of the sword, and the mocking of Jesus. Although nonsynoptic Johannine tradition is the basis of these accounts, some synoptic pericopes or parts of pericopes have been assimilated into them. Since John is dependent on synoptic tradition in certain passages only, it is probable that oral tradition had already fused the synoptic material before it came to the evangelist, and he used that tradition. If he had used the other gospels, the synoptic material would be more evenly spread in John, contends Borgen, and it would not deviate so much from the gospels.

The second category of parallels consists of agreements between John and the synoptics in traditions that are completely independent of each other. Borgen believes that the situation is merely that two independent traditions about the same subject have, as one might expect, agreements both in fixed expressions and in features which necessarily belong to the narrative. Unlike the agreements in the passages dependent on synoptic tradition, these agreements are spread through the material rather than grouped close to each other. These accidental agreements occur in the accounts of Jesus before Pilate, Jesus' trial before Annas and Caiaphas, the crucifixion, and the resurrection.

Borgen objects to Buse's study because it considers only the parallels with Mark. Borgen emphasizes that the parallels in his first category contain agreements with all three synoptics. He regards this as evidence that the synoptic material in John comes from oral tradition; he evidently thinks it improbable that the evangelist would use more than one synoptic gospel as a source. The argument disregards the probability that more then one author is involved in writing John. As for his second category of agreements, Borgen does not demonstrate that accidental agreement is more probable than selective use of written synoptic material; in fact, he does not even consider the latter.

In 1960 Buse replied to Borgen's criticism by comparing the forms of the Passion narrative in John, Matthew. and Luke. He found few authentic parallels between John and Matthew, but many between John and Luke. He excludes Luke as John's direct source on the familiar grounds that the author of John would have included more of Luke if he had known that gospel. On the other hand, "the similarities are on such a scale as to make sheer coincidence a most improbable supposition."[36]

His explanation is that Luke and John used the B-stratum document underlying Mark's Passion story. What about the elements which are common to John and Luke but are not in Mark? Buse's answer is that they come from the B source, too, but the author of Mark omitted them because they coincided with material he obtained from his basic source A. The author of Luke used the B Passion source before he handled Mark.

Buse's theory is an interesting one, but some of its presuppositions are difficult to demonstrate. Assuming that the author of Mark employed two written sources, A and B, how can we be sure that he has omitted A whenever it coincided with B? How can we be sure that Luke and John agree against Mark because the authors of Luke and John followed B? What about the agreements of Luke and John against Mark outside the Passion narrative?

Haenchen made a study (1959) of certain narratives in John which convinces him that the evangelist obtained his synoptic-like material from a written source ("Vorlage," or "Grundlage") which was in contact with the tradition taken up by the evangelists who wrote the synoptic gospels. Although Christian tradition was partly fixed, it still was in the process of development, and John's Vorlage exhibits a later, often split-up, form of it. Haenchen claims that we possess six separate compositions of the story of the centurion or official at Capernaum: from Matthew's Vorlage, from Matthew, from Luke's Vorlage, from Luke, from John's Vorlage, and from John. In John's Vorlage the miraculous element is growing, demonstrated in the stories of the royal official at Capernaum, the feeding of the multitude, and the quieting of the sea; the significance of miracle has shifted from that of saving man from calamity to that of demonstrating the divine power of Jesus as the Son of God. Proof that John's Vorlage was written rather than oral is found in the insertions by the evangelist; his insertions often exhibit his hostility to Judaism.

Haenchen admits that he draws apologetic conclusions. He tries to show that the "foremost" (erster) evangelist, who produced John, is as early as Mark and of the highest historical worth in the sense that he displays clear traces of progressive development.

S. Temple (1960), stimulated by Buse's 1958 article, examines Vincent Taylor's theory of two strata in Mark's Passion story, then reconstructs the strata A and B somewhat differently. Taylor's reconstruction runs from Mark 14:1 to the end of the gospel, but Temple includes only the first fifty verses of chapter 14. Temple regards the doublets in the material as proof that there are two main sources.

Whereas Buse finds the parallels with John only in stratum B,

Temple finds the parallels only in stratum A! The contradictory opinions result partly from Temple's transfer of some passages between A and B and partly from disagreement over whether a Marcan passage has a parallel in John. An example of carrying parallelism too far is Temple's claim that Mark 14: 10-11 has an equivalent in John 13:2b; the only common element in the passages is the general idea that Judas betrayed Jesus, a fact too widely known to indicate literary relationship. Temple concludes that John did not use A but a source parallel to it.

Pierre Benoit (1960), professor of Greek language and New Testament in the École Biblique, contends that each of two blocks of material, John 19:31-42 and 20:1-18, contains three corresponding layers: A, 19:31-37 and 20:1-10; B, 19:38 and 20:11b-14a; C, 19:39-42 and 20:11a, 14b-18. The A accounts are primitive, without any connection with synoptic tradition. The C accounts are Johannine material too, but they do reveal some contacts with synoptic tradition. The terms "garden" (19:41) and "gardener" (20:15) show that there is a connecting line between the two C accounts. The B material consists of two insertions derived from the synoptic tradition and used here to introduce the stories of the burial by Nicodemus and Jesus' appearance to Mary Magdalene.

Barnabas Lindars, lecturer in Old Testament at Cambridge University, in his study (1961) of John 20, divides the chapter into two sections, with three episodes in the first and two in the second. He compares the form and vocabulary of the two sections with each other and with the synoptic gospels. Lindars concludes that with the exception of the second episode (20:3-10) in the first section, the two sections probably are based on the tradition behind the synoptic gospels. Further, matter omitted from the synoptic tradition is used as the nucleus of the supplementary incidents (the final episode in each of the sections), and each supplementary incident is concerned with only one person, Mary Magdalene or Thomas. The two sections therefore are alike in form. The second incident of the first section does not conform so well, but it does exhibit some Johannine features.

In his analysis of the vocabulary Lindars finds many parallels with the synoptic accounts. John's sources cannot be confined to any one of the synoptic gospels, so his sources are probably not the gospels themselves but the traditions behind them. In Lindars' opinion the possibility of other sources is unlikely because nearly all of the remainder of the vocabulary is Johannine and Johannine repetitions abound.

Although comparison of chapter 20 with the synoptic tradition is not new, Lindars' brief study is a penetrating anlysis that deserves careful examination. It deserves credit for its apparent honesty. Nevertheless, we must question the validity of the presupposition that the synoptic gospels were not direct sources simply because there are parallels with more than one of them. It is logically possible that several gospels could have been used by one writer, or one writer could have used one gospel and another writer also involved in the composition of John could have used another gospel.

Bailey's work (1963) has been mentioned in connection with his acceptance of the theory that the Gospels of Mark and of Luke are the chief sources of the traditions in John that parallel those in Luke. A feature of the study is its complexity; in addition to the two synoptic gospels, virtually all the kinds of sources that have been suggested for this category of tradition are accepted for one Johannine passage or another. Oral sources were employed in some narratives, and written sources other than Mark and Luke were used for some accounts. Contrary to Martin Dibelius and Bultmann, Bailey concludes that John did not have a continuous written account of Jesus' Passion other than the Gospels of Mark and Luke; instead, the evangelist's nonsynoptic written sources were "isolated pieces." Occasionally Luke's account seems secondary compared to John's; that is, Luke seems to presuppose knowledge of a tradition or its source as reported in John. Finally, the evangelist himself created some of the material in John.

Parker has criticized Bailey's study for its unnecessary complexity and overconfident assertions.[37] Although the Gospel of John is complex in its composition and therefore the correct explanation, if we find it, probably will be complex too, we may ask whether oral tradition, written synoptic-like sources, and the canonical gospels are all involved in the synoptic-type material in John.

Fortna, whose source theory we sketched in chapter 4, finds the synoptic-like material mainly in the Gospel of Signs. The evangelist probably did not know the synoptic gospels, at least in their canonical form, in Fortna's opinion. He adds: "Whether the source had literary contact with any of the synoptic sources it would be impossible to say; there is some evidence of close contact with the material peculiar to Lk, but not necessarily in a literary form."[38]

Ferdinand Hahn (1970), professor of New Testament at the Johannes Gutenberg University in Mainz, compares the numerous parallels between the Passion story in Mark and Luke on the one hand and the Passion story in John on the other. He adopts the view that John is too independent of the synoptics to have used them. He observes that in John the Passion story begins with chapter 11. Hahn's conclusion is that John used a Vorlage, or source, which was similar to Mark, expecially in the order of events, and he revised this material and inserted his own overall conception. One result was that he created an artificial break between chapters 17 and 18. The parallelism between Luke and John in the Passion story is not to be explained as the result of the common use of a special source by those two evangelists. Hahn believes that it is improbable that we can reconstruct the pre-Johannine tradition in John 11:47ff. because the evangelist dealt very freely with his material. Hahn overlooks the fact that his statement that John dealt freely with his material refutes his argument that the evangelist could not have used the other canonical gospels because John varies so much from them.

Redaction

Another kind of explanation of the presence of synoptic tradition in John is that some or all of it was inserted later by a redactor, probably directly from the synoptic gospels. This view has not been so popular as some of the others, partly because it makes the form of the synoptic tradition in John later than the synoptic gospels. Redaction theories which are not limited to synoptic tradition will be discussed in the next chapter; some of them ascribe to a redactor the insertion of synoptic tradition.

Emile Osty (1951), professor of biblical Greek in l'Institut catholique in Paris, accepts assimilation from the Gospel of Luke at the hands of a redactor as the explanation of the Lucan tradition in John. In his article he describes the similarities between Luke and John in the accounts of Jesus' Passion. Although some of the parallels may be caused by the use of the same sources, and others may be accidental, the rest form two groups that require a different explanation. The "lucanismes" came into John from Luke, for Luke was written earlier than John, and these parallels are superficial in nature and scattered throughout John. They are not the result of systematic imitation of Luke but are like spontaneous reminiscences. In the Passion story, at least, they must come from the pen of a redactor who was a disciple of Luke (following Boismard's suggestion) or a reader attentive to the Gospel of Luke.

The second significant group of parallels, the "johannismes" in Luke, are Johannine in origin because they express Johannine theology. Osty maintains that they belong to the original text of the Gospel of Luke, for the evangelist Luke probably had heard the evangelist John preach and had collected some of his remarks, which inspired Luke in his own writing!

A few theories do not fall into any of the categories we have established. One such theory is that of Curtis. K. Peter G. Curtis (1971) compares Luke 24:12 with John 20:3-10 and observes six significant linguistic agreements between them. Two other verbal agreements, "alone" and "lying," are not in some manuscripts of the Lucan verse, and these variant readings indicate that the two terms were added later as a result of efforts to harmonize the verse with the Johannine passage. Curtis judges the linguistic agreements to be more characteristic of John than of Luke [with the exception of historic present tense, however, the features are not much more characteristic of John]. The presence of these "Johannisms" and the extent of the parallelisms argue strongly against dependence on a common source. Did Luke use John, or is the Lucan verse a later insertion into Luke? Curtis chooses the latter solution, because two of its features are especially unlike Luke and because the verse is absent in Codex D, Old Latin manuscripts, and Marcion. His solution is open to question, however, for the verse is in the earliest Greek manuscripts and could be merely a Marcionite omission.

Fundamental Questions

The variety of opinion on the relation of John to the synoptic gospels indicates that this problem is not yet solved. Clearly two important questions are involved.

What is the source(s) of the synoptic-like material in John? Pe haps it has come directly from the synoptic gospels or from written sources, or from late oral church tradition, or from several of these. If several writers are involved in John, we would like to know which one(s) is responsible for this material.

Secondly, what is the source(s) of the Johannine variations when the accounts in John differ from the corresponding traditions in the synoptic gospel? Perhaps the differences were in sources used by the evangelist, or they were created by the evangelist, or they were inserted by a redactor. We may ask whether the differences are the result of revision of tradition behind the synoptic gospels or the result of revision of material drawn from the synoptic gospels.

Blinzler has some comments which are pertinent to these questions. Gardner-Smith argued against synoptic influence on John on the grounds that the latter contains more divergences from them than agreements. Blinzler rightly rejects this argument and remarks that this merely shows that the Fourth Evangelist did not use the canonical gospels the way Matthew and Luke used Mark, but that he used them with "sovereign freedom." He also observes that the fact that John did not follow Mark more closely should cause little wonder, for John used Old Testament quotations freely and in new combinations, as shown by Bultmann, Goodwin, Lindars, and Noack.[39]

CHAPTER 7

REDACTION THEORIES

A redaction theory explains the aporias by attributing them to later revision of the original gospel. In this type of theory the original gospel was not a source but was similar enough to our present gospel to justify our calling it the Gospel of John. Some theories combine the source and redaction explanations in that they present both the use of sources by the evangelist and later revision by another writer as major factors in the development of the book. A different kind of combination theory is one in which the redactor has not only revised the gospel but has added material from a written source(s).

The German biblical scholar Karl Frommann in 1839 concluded that a few passages are later additions in John: certainly 5:3b–4 (healing resulting from an angel's stirring the pool), 7:53–8:11 (woman caught in adultery), and 21:24–25 (final verses of the present gospel), and probably 21:1–23 (the body of the final chapter.[1] Frommann was theologically conservative and wrote his book to oppose Strauss's interpretation of the gospel. Frommann charged that Strauss's rejection of apostolic authorship removed the fundamental basis for accepting the historicity of the gospel. Frommann sought to omit the obvious insertions and thereby restore confidence in the Johannine authorship of the rest of the book.

Frommann got his lead from textual criticism, for the first two passages do not appear in Greek manuscripts of the New Testament until after the sixth century. Changes in the text made later than the second century are not in the category of redaction but of textual criticism; they are changes made by the scribes in the monasteries as they copied the text.

On the other hand, all codices, other than the fragmentary ones, contain chapter 21, although the last verse is a later addition in Codex Sinaiticus (fourth century). Thus the evidence from textual criticism so far dates the origin of 21:1–24 early enough to be the result of redaction. Although Frommann's motive was not legitimate, the view that chapter 21 is a later addition helped to open the way for the development of one type of redaction theory, according to which the redactor revised the gospel and added the final chapter.

Interpretations of chapter 21 as supplementary are important background for the development of the theory that a redactor added the chapter. Alexander Schweizer reported that Wilhelm De Wette (1826), professor of theology at Basle, had pointed out briefly that the style in chapter 21 is different from that of the rest of the gospel. Schweizer added that Gustav Seyffarth had proved this completely by observing that the narratives in the chapter are so legendary in nature and so un-Johannine in style that they are foreign to the gospel.[2] Schweizer (1841) decided that chapter 21 must be an appendix, for the gospel comes to a close in 20:30. He made two more important observations. He noted that the same person who added chapter 21 has made some changes and insertions in the rest of the book, and he concluded that chapter 21 is itself composed of layers (verses 1-14, 15-19, 20-23).[3] In Schweizer's theory the redactor's insertions consist more of material from sources than of matter he composed himself.

Heinrich Ewald (1861), professor of Old Testament in Göttingen, and Jan H. Scholten (1864), professor of theology at Leiden, concluded that there are in John interpolations based on misunderstanding of the text. Ewald proposed that after the gospel was "published" another hand wrote the insertions.[4] In his source theory Renan (1863) held that after the disciples of John the Presbyter in Asia Minor had finished the gospel, a redactor made scattered corrections and added chapter 21.

Spitta (1893), according to Bousset, was the first to recognize that 6:51b-59 are interpolated verses.[5] Their emphasis on the Eucharist sets them apart.

Although Adolf Harnack (1897), professor of church history at Berlin, regarded John 21:1-23 as a part of the original gospel, and Adolf Jülicher (1894), professor of theology at Marburg, accepted the whole chapter as authentic, many German New Testament scholars around the turn of the century viewed chapter 21 as an appendix added later. Even Harnack acknowledged a little redaction when he suggested that those who added verse 24 made also four insertions to identify John the son of Zebedee as "the disciple whom Jesus loved."

Friedrich W. Blass (1902), professor of classical philology at Halle, believed that the original gospel was written by the apostle John and therefore must have been a unity. Blass recognized some bad connections and other disunity in the book as we now have it, so he concluded that the original text had been corrupted. He tried to restore the original by deleting, altering, and transposing the text. As a guide he adopted the presupposition that the original gospel contained no heresies, and he made many improvements in style on the assumption that the style of the original could not have been bad! Wellhausen severely (and rightly) criticized him for this.[6]

In 1906 Wilhelm Heitmüller, Privatdozent for New Testament exegesis at Göttingen, adopted the suggestion that a redactor has inserted small glosses in John and added the final chapter. In 1907 Roland Schütz (in Wilmersdorf, Berlin), without knowing the work of Schwartz and Wellhausen, asserted that the trips of Jesus to the feasts in Jerusalem and the resulting festival chronology in the first part of the gospel are later additions; when these journeys are removed, the plan of John approaches that of Mark.

Eduard Schwartz, a classical philologist and patristic scholar at Göttingen, in a series of articles published in 1907 and 1908 set forth a detailed redaction theory. In his hypothesis the original gospel, "proto-John," is a poem about the divine Jesus who performs miracles, a poem which did not claim to be the report of an eyewitness. In it Jesus speaks of himself in the first person and not as "the Son." Later "the redactor," who was the author of the Johannine epistles, inserted material based on the synoptic gospels, the homilies (e.g., 12:44-50), and the four passages in the Passion story which mention the Beloved Disciple. The redactor inserted also the matter which represents Jesus as deliberately delaying his visit to Lazarus, so that Lazarus definitely will be dead and Jesus can perform the unquestioned miracle of bringing him to life again. "The interpolator," who in effect was a second redactor, added chapter 21, the feast chronology which represents Jesus as making frequent trips to Jerusalem to attend Jewish feasts, Peter's second and third denials of Jesus, and the term "Caiaphas." Schwartz claims that in chapter 21 the interpolator tries to identify the Beloved Disciple with John the son of Zebedee; Bousset disagrees.[7]

Julius Wellhausen, orientalist and biblical scholar, while professor of Semitics in Göttingen wrote two books (1907, 1908) in an attempt to solve the literary problem of John. The first is a brief study of the "expansions and alterations" in John concentrating on certain passages. Wellhausen investigates chapters

15-17 and decides that they are supplemental insertions written by a different author; he calls attention to internal linguistic evidence and asserts that the end of chapter 14 fits the beginning of chapter 18 instead of the beginning of chapter 15. He accepts Adolf Jülicher's suggestion (1894) that originally chapter 5 followed chapter 6. A later hand has made changes in the account of Jesus before the high priest in chapter 18, added the story in chapter 20 about Thomas's doubts, and put in various small interpolations. Often features and motifs which are in the original gospel are repeated, altered, and expanded by the later hand, the redactor who made all these changes. The expanded repetitions are often closely related to 1 John, but Wellhausen gives no weight to the conjecture that the redactor of the gospel was the author of the first Johannine epistle.

Wellhausen's second book dealing with the literary problem was a short commentary on the Gospel of John into which he blended his by then more developed theory. He states that his earlier book caused a lively exchange of ideas "between me and Eduard Schwartz, in which he was more the giver than the receiver. Some of his suggestions are in this present work of mine, especially in the footnotes."[8]

In this commentary Wellhausen presents the hypothesis that the gospel's Grundschrift, A, consists of individual pieces which form a running but not unbroken line. To these pieces has been attached the B material, layers of expansions of A which far surpass it in range. The expansions are not sources;[9] they are the work of more than one redactor and originated gradually. In addition an interpolator inserted a few small statements. Although Wellhausen regards A as a string of pieces (and thus sources) and not "the real (eigentliche) Johannine gospel," his view is described here with redaction theories because he regards redaction as the chief factor in the gospel's development and because the hypothesis is closely related to Schwartz's redaction theory.

Influenced by the plan of Mark, A consists of three parts: the Galilean period of Jesus' career, his first stay in Jerusalem until the flight, and the return to Jerusalem motivated by the Lazarus story. In A Jesus is the Messiah with some human characteristics, and utters a few of the gospel's speeches. The redactors omitted portions of A and probably worked over most of the remaining A material.

The speeches in B are in two sections: the speeches of Jesus to the Jews are inserted between the first two parts of A, and his esoteric speeches to the disciples before his Passion are inserted between the second and third parts of A. The connecting links, transitions, summary statements, and the insertion of festival trips are also from B. The redactors deliberately transposed certain sections of A;[10] this idea differs from the theories of accidental displacement in chapter 8. Although B came from the same Christian circle as A, it was written to eliminate A's tolerant attitude toward Jews and its messianic and eschatological ideas.

Some of their contemporaries recognized that the works of Schwartz and Wellhausen are landmarks in the history of the interpretation of the gospel. Spitta hailed their writings as "epoch-making."[11] Bousset regarded their works as "distinctly important" and made them the basis of his own study of the subject. Although he disagreed with some details of their theories, he commended them for offering so much that was "new, stimulating, and challenging."[12] The studies of Schwartz and Wellhausen are outstanding for their detailed linguistic analysis, their literary approach, and their opinion that redaction might be a major factor in the formation of the gospel and not merely responsible for chapter 21 and a few minor insertions. Above all, their work seems to have been more objective than that of many others, both before and since.

Wilhelm Bousset (1909), professor of New Testament exegesis at Göttingen, made some important modifications in the theories of Schwartz and Wellhausen. According to his hypothesis there are two main strata in John: the original material, the Grundschrift, for which Mark and especially Luke and Acts were used as sources; and the writing of the "interpolator" who inserted material based on Matthew. In addition, there is the work of a glossarist whose often senseless and unhistorical glosses are scattered throughout the gospel. In contrast, the insertions of the redactor are often historical. Perhaps there was more than one redactor, for 12:36-43 and 12:44-50 are from different hands and chapter 21 is composite. Contrary to the opinion of Schwartz and Wellhausen, the Grundschrift was not a uniform work but a conglomeration of rubble from tradition (in this respect Bousset's theory is a source theory). The Grundschrift exalted Andrew and Philip, but the redactor exalted Peter and the Beloved Disciple. The Grundschrift in 7:3-4 tells of a permanent migration of Jesus to Jerusalem, but the redactor changed it into one of Jesus' journeys to a feast.

Bousset ascribes to the work of the redactor many characteristics which he believes are late. These features include Jesus' self-designation as "the Son" and "the Son of God," the "signs" of Jesus, the homilies, the passages containing the term "Pharisees," and one member of each pair of doublets. The redactor introduces his quotations from the Old Testament with "in order that it may be fulfilled," and he added 13:36-38 because that passage has the same emphasis on Peter's martyrdom as chapter 21, which also comes from the redactor.

Friedrich Spitta (1910), while professor of New Testament and pastoral theology at Strassburg, used as a springboard the redaction hypotheses of Wellhausen and Schwartz for his theory. He commended them for their philological approach and complemented Wellhausen as one of the first to base a partition theory of the gospel on detailed exegesis. Spitta, too, examined the text closely. From Wellhausen he borrowed the symbol A for the Grundschrift, and B for the revision, the Bearbeitung.

Nevertheless, Spitta's theory departs from the work of Wellhausen and Schwartz at significant points. He dislikes their Grundschrift because it does not seem to be a good source for the life of Jesus. His most significant divergence from them, however, is his inclusion in the Grundschrift of both narrative and speech material on an equal basis. His hypothesis is a combined source and redaction theory in that the redactor added source material.

According to Spitta, A is earlier and superior to the synoptic gospels. It contains no Galilean narratives. In it Jesus is the prophet, teacher, and Messiah, loyal to Jewish law and festivals. His second advent will occur in the lifetime of his disciples. Although Jesus' death is necessary so that he can return to the Father, it is not necessary for salvation. The author, the apostle John, must have been the unnamed disciple in John 1:35-40 who originally belonged to the circle of disciples of John the Baptist.

B consists of the redactor's own reflections and of source material from older gospel literature including the synoptics. It reflects second-century theology. In it Jesus is the preexistent and incarnate god, his death is necessary for salvation, and his second advent is off in the distance. B is hostile to the Jews and to the Mosaic law. The insertion of B material into A made the latter disjointed and ambiguous and changed its point of view. The reviser added the Beloved Disciple in chapter 21 and changed the unnamed disciple in A into the Beloved Disciple by means of interpolations. The doublets indicate the use of a source, for no one writes that way unless he has separate written reports of the same event, states Spitta.[13] The doublets in their dogmatics and legendary elements display later developments in the church.

Spitta recognizes that the view of the apostolic authorship of the whole gospel as a literary unity rests on apologetic interest and could not be defended after the publication of the works of Wellhausen and Schwartz.[14] But Spitta has his own bias. He is determined to find a Grundschrift which would be superior to the synoptic gospels for constructing the life of Jesus. He claims that he approaches his study without a definite view about the origin of the synoptics, but actually he assumes throughout his book that they are inferior to his Grundschrift. Spitta criticizes his predecessors for not allowing the text to speak for itself, yet he himself fails to listen to the text. He claims that not A but B is hostile to Jews, yet he includes in A the later Christian charge that the Jews seek to kill Jesus (5:18). He claims that A reports Jesus' Jewish teaching and practices better than the synoptics, yet he includes in A the hostile attitude toward the Jewish law reflected in the phrase "your law" (8:17). Above all, he closes his eyes to the fact that far more and closer parallels to Jewish thought occur in the synoptic gospels than in his A.

F. Warburton Lewis, an English clergyman, in a series of three articles (1910, 1911), lists fourteen passages in John which in his opinion are "interpolations by a hand other than the Evangelist's." His main basis for regarding them as later insertions is that they misunderstand and misinterpret the saying or incident which immediately precedes them. Interruption of the narrative or sequence of ideas is another basis for suspecting that a passage was not in the original gospel. Other criteria which Lewis employs include the failure of a passage to fit the context, inconsistency with the rest of the gospel or the teaching of Jesus or of John the Baptist, and the fact that some passages bear the same marks as 12:33, which is widely acknowledged as a misinterpretation. Two of the interpolations, however, are not really misinterpretations according to Lewis: John 18:32 is the result of the reviser's obsession with the manner of Jesus' death, repeated from 12:33; and John 21:24 (and 25 ?) is a note composed by the reviser.

There is a very unreliable presupposition in Lewis's study. He assumes that the gospel and the Johannine epistles were written by John the apostle and that the gospel therefore accurately reflects the views of Jesus and John. His assumption leads to his refusal to accept as part of the original gospel any passage which disagrees with 1 John, or a motive or action which is a discredit to Jesus, or an insight foreign to John.[15]

Johannes Weiss, professor of New Testament at Heidelberg, concluded in 1912 that the original gospel was written by the Beloved Disciple. He maintains that a redactor added chapter 21, inserted passages to make clear to the reader that the author was the Beloved Disciple, and interpolated many comments, explanations, and expansions of the text.

Paul Wendland, professor of classical philology at Göttingen, in his examination of early Christian literary forms (1912) maintains that the redactor of the gospel was the author of 1 John and inserted the miracle stories and his interpretation of them. The same literary technique is present in the writings of Phlegon, a Greek author in the second century A.D. The redactor composed also the longer speeches, in which he combined words of Jesus with beliefs originating in the church. Wendland went farther than Schwartz and Wellhausen in the degree of deliberate change he ascribed to the redactor.

In an article published in 1917 James S. Thompson discusses "some editorial elements" in John. In his day the typical discussion of the subject started from chapter 21 and linked together the "we" passages in verse 24, in 19:35, the Prologue, and 1 John. Thompson discounts that method as unsatisfactory, for he thinks that the evangelist's "we" cannot be distinguished from the later editor's "we." Instead, the "editorial footnotes" provide the key for distinguishing the redactor's work. These are "not notes upon his sources by the author of the Gospel, but comments upon the author's work by an editor who misunderstands his meaning."[16] There are analogies in the synoptics (e.g., Mark 7:3-4, 19b) where the "footnotes," or comments, reduce "a spiritual principle into an ecclesiastical rule."[17] Examples in John are 7:39; 12:33; 18:9, 32; 21:19, 24.

Thompson then proceeds to reconstruct briefly the literary origin of the gospel. The author of the gospel incorporated some fragments of sources which contained relics of primitive Christology and apocalypticism.

tology and apocalypticism. The author did not eliminate entirely the literalistic elements in his sources, but his own point of view was closer to that in the discourses than to the narratives. Later some of the pages were accidentally disarranged, and the gospel was re-edited by persons who were not in sympathy with its mystical point of view. The "footnotes" which misinterpret passages in the gospel are examples of the editorial work.

H. J. Flowers (1921), at Union Theological Seminary in New York, in his study concludes that a redactor added chapter 21 and interpolated these passages: 2:21-22; 4:2; 5:28-29; 6:39, 40, 44, 54; 7:39; 12:33; 18:9. Later a group of men added 19:35 and 21: 24-25 to authenticate the whole Gospel of John, as the "we" and eyewitness claim for the author indicate.

G. H. C. Macgregor (1928) produced a combined source and redaction theory. According to his hypothesis the evangelist probably incorporated the written memoirs of an eyewitness and used the Gospel of Mark too, but left his own imprint on the material. Afterwards a redactor changed the order of some of the passages, inserted comments which show that he misunderstood the text, and added chapter 21 as an appendix. Macgregor believes that some of the text is disarranged, so he attempts to reconstruct the original order. He follows Moffatt's rearrangement in general, for he is commentating on John in Moffatt's translation, but he makes independent relocations at a few points. The dislocations are not accidental, but as in Wellhausen's theory they are made deliberately by the redactor. However, in 1961 Macgregor abandoned redaction as an explanation and adopted Morton's source theory.

J. H. Bernard, Provost of Trinity College, Dublin, in his classic commentary on John published in 1929, relies on accidental dislocation as the main cause of the aporias, and ascribes to the evangelist nearly all the brief comments. Nevertheless, he lists six glosses by a later hand [textual criticism has shown that two of these are not in the earlier manuscripts]. He accepted chapter 21 as part of the original gospel.

During the first three decades of the twentieth century the view that chapter 21 was added later by another hand gained widespread acceptance. Biblical scholars in that period who adopted this interpretation include, in addition to those we have observed, Bacon (1910, 1933), Friedrich von Hügel (1911), Moffatt (1911), Soltau (1916), Strachan (1917), V. H. Stanton (1920), A. E. Garvie

(1922), Carpenter (1927), and Dibelius (1927). This view now predominates over any other theory of the authorship of "the appendix." This interpretation was combined frequently with the conviction that the same redactor inserted a few glosses, especially the parenthetic explanations and short misinterpretations of the text; Moffatt, Soltau, Garvie, Carpenter, and Dibelius reached this conclusion.

Emanuel Hirsch (1936), professor of church history at Göttingen, presents the hypothesis that the evangelist wrote in Syria around 100 and a redactor extensively revised and expanded it in Asia Minor about 130-140. Hirsch separates and rearranges the two strata, using thought-content more than style as a guide because he believes that the redactor tried to imitate the evangelist's style. This last point is a major development of the view held by Bacon as early as 1910, the view that the redactor who added the final chapter adjusted his own style to that of the gospel. With Hirsch this idea has far more effect on interpretation, for in his theory the quantity of material written by the redactor is far greater. The redactor's purpose was to produce a "church edition" which would be accepted generally by Christians; he tried to accomplish this by making five groups of additions and alterations. These groups are (1) matter assimilated with some mate rial in the synoptic gospels; (2) insertions to identify the Beloved Disciple with the author, John; (3) proof texts from the Old Testament interpolated chiefly into the Passion story; (4) matter to combat pagan-Christian Gnosticism; (5) the chronological framework. The original author portrays Jesus as going to Jerusalem only once, to attend an unidentified "feast" of the Jews; the reviser changed the account so that Jesus attends several feasts, which are identified by name.

In 1950 Hirsch defended his theory against the criticism of E. Schweizer. He charges that Schweizer's assertion of the gospel's unity on the basis of a stylistic approach proves nothing, for the redactor imitated the evangelist's style, and the strata are to be found more on the basis of substance. Hirsch concludes that the evangelist's writing, E, consistently has the term "life" and the redactor's work, R, has "eternal life" and never vice versa except that R has "resurrection of life" (5:29) and "bread of life" (6:48). R tends to make abstract generalizations (e.g., 6:40; 14:21; 15:12; 17:3). R breaks some of the rules of style in E when R is inserted into the midst of statements in E; this situation places limitations on style analysis. R's additions to the speeches in E caused the speeches to lose their conciseness, because these insertions run to copious repetition and formlessness. The additions tend to end with an expression corresponding, often verbally, to the one at which they interrupted the original text, for example, 6:36, repeating "believe" from 6:35. Hirsch calls this technique, used in the Hellenistic period, the "technique of similar insertion."

Hirsch's detailed analyses are worthy of study, and Wilkens used them extensively. Yet Hirsch fails to recognize sources in the gospel, and many of the characteristics of his redactor are really those of the editor.

The theories of Loisy (1921, 1936), Bacon (1933), and Bultmann (1941) have been described with source theories in chapter 4. They are really combination theories. The redaction aspects of Bacon's and Bultmann's theories call for special comment.

In Bacon's hypothesis the amount of redaction is moderate, standing between the minimal amount in the early theories and the almost maximum amount in such theories as that of Hirsch. Bacon maintains that the redactor transposed some passages including chapters 5 and 6, and thus intentional displacement is a feature of his theory. His notion that the redactor inserted some more material written by the author of the original gospel is very questionable. In his book The Gospel of the Hellenists Bacon tries to reconstruct the growth of the gospel by separating the evangelist's gospel, the redactor's writing, and the evangelist's writing inserted by the redactor. He attempts to restore to their original position the passages allegedly displaced by the redactor.

Bultmann combines accidental displacement with the idea that the redactor relocated some of the passages. Bultmann believes that the ecclesiastical redactor found the gospel with the pages broken into fragments and he unintentionally disarranged the material when he attempted to restore the gospel. Although the redactor used the synoptic gospels when he revised John, he added only a small portion of the synoptic material.

Joachim Jeremias (1941), professor of New Testament at Göttingen, adopts a very conservative redaction theory. In his opinion the gospel may have been edited and published later by the evangelist's disciples with a few of their own interpolations but without major change in its theological view. He rejects Bultmann's source theory and rearrangement of the text of John. In 1953 he repudiated his own earlier acceptance of the view that 6:51c-58 is a redactional insertion.

Siegfried Mendner in a series of articles (1952-1958) concludes that the gospel was extensively revised. The story of the temple cleansing in John seems to be closest to that in Matthew, for in it Jesus casts out "all," whereas in Mark and Luke he only "began" to throw them out. There are signs that the Johannine account is composite; for example, a different Greek word is employed for "money changer" in 2:15 than in 2:14, and in verse 15 the "all" that Jesus casts out is defined as "both sheep and oxen" when one would expect the sellers and moneychangers to be included. Mendner remarks concerning the temple cleansing: "The Johannine composition in its whole compass appears as a literary remodeling of the synoptic tradition."[18] The writer of this passage was not the evangelist who composed the original Gospel of John, but a later redactor. Not all synoptic elements in John are necessarily redactional, contrary to the claim of Wellhausen, Schwartz, Loisy, Goguel, and Windisch, states Mendner.

He points out incongruities in the story of the conversation between Jesus and Nicodemus, 3:1-21. He concludes that the original story consisted of only certain verses and portions of verses, and that after 125 it was transposed to its present position from its original location in chapter 7. Relocating it in its original position eliminates all evidence of textual disturbance in chapters 7 and 8. Not later than 175 a redactor expanded the story to its present form.

Günther Bornkamm (1956), professor of New Testament at Heidelberg, accepts the widely-held view that the eucharistic speech (6:51c-58) was inserted by an ecclesiastical redactor. The redactor used the speech on the Bread of Life to aid him in composing his eucharistic speech. He wrote to support the traditional view of the Eucharist, represented by Ignatius, in opposition to docetic Gnosticism.

Pierson Parker (1956), in an article describing his theory of redaction by the original author, maintains that there were two distinct editions of John, the first devoted to tradition with a Judean setting and the second enlarged with narratives set in Samaria and Galilee. The expansions in the second edition consist of 2:1-12 and chapters 4, 6, and 21.

Parker's line of reasoning runs as follows: The aporias show that additions were made to the gospel. The additions were made after the original gospel was written, for internal evidence indicates that the passages assigned to the second edition are later in composition. One writer made all these additions, because the striking parallels between chapters 6 and 21 indicate that the same writer composed both. Further, the similarity in vocabulary and style throughout reveals that the same author wrote both the added passages and the original gospel.

The contacts with some passages in Luke suggest that Lucan tradition was known to the author, perhaps by oral transmission. This fact indicates a late date for the second edition, as does its allusion to the death of Peter. But in his 1963 article on the similarities between Luke and John, Parker tries to explain them by claiming that the Fourth Evangelist must have been associated with Luke in the latter's missionary work.

Why would the same author want to produce a second edition? Parker's answer is that he had a new point of view, a concern to reach Diaspora Judaism, prompted by his own activity in the church's mission, his growing dismay at the Jewish failure to accept Christian faith, and perhaps his contact with Alexandrian modes of thought.

Parker's theory does not explain the differences in vocabulary and point of view among some of the sections in the gospel, and it does not account for the variation within chapters 4 and 6. Also, the sections he selects as later additions are not so close to "Alexandrian modes of thought" as other portions of John.

Wilhelm Wilkens in his book published in 1958, proposes a very elaborate theory of redaction by the author. His thesis that John is a Passion gospel is derived from an unpublished study made by his father, Johannes Wilkens.[19] The book is essentially Wilkens' doctoral dissertation at Basel (1957) and shows the influence of his adviser, Oscar Cullmann.

According to Wilkens, the evangelist first wrote the <u>Grundschrift</u>, which Wilkens refers to more frequently as the <u>Grundevangelium</u> (basic gospel). In harmony with 20:30-31, the verses with which the <u>Grundevangelium</u> closed, the book should be characterized as a "Gospel of Signs." It contained narratives and conversations, but not speeches. It cannot be recovered by separating the narratives from the rest of the present gospel, for the evangelist later added other narratives. Wilkens denies that the theology of the Gospel of Signs is that Jesus' miracles are proof he is the Christ. Instead, he claims, the theology is that the signs are the acts of the crucified and resurrected One (and therefore proof that Jesus is the resurrected One).

The Grundevangelium consists of three main parts. The first section, the Signs of Jesus, is within the first twelve chapters of the present gospel. Wilkens states that the first three signs in Galilee relate symbolically to the Eucharist, and the three in Jerusalem relate to baptism. Even in this first composition of the gospel the evangelist is influenced by the arrangement in Mark and Matthew; the feeding of the 5,000 is followed by the story of Jesus' walking on the sea.

The second section of the Grundevangelium contains the stories of the cleansing of the temple, the anointing, the Last Supper, and much of chapter 13. It formed the bridge to the third section, the Passion and Easter story. The motivation behind the third section was to present Jesus as the true king of Israel. Jesus' crucifixion is the high point of the Grundevangelium, and his death is described as a kingly deed. Jesus is the paschal lamb, for he is called the "Lamb of God" (1:36) and he dies on the day that the lamb was slaughtered and prepared for Passover (19:31). A major purpose of the Gospel of Signs is to counteract Docetism, although Wilkens is uncertain whether the gospel ever circulated in this early form.

According to Wilkens the evangelist later revised the gospel by inserting large speech complexes, thereby joining the words of Christ to the acts of Christ. The speeches have an anti-docetic tendency, for they oppose the Christology of Docetism (1:14) and the eschatology of Docetism (5:28-29). Wilkens claims that the speeches were composed earlier and afterwards inserted by the evangelist himself throughout the gospel. He denies that there is any difference in theological point of view between the Grundevangelium and the speech complexes.

He postulates that still later the evangelist produced a third stage of his book, a stage that is a deeper reconstruction than the second. Not only is new material inserted, but the earlier arrangement of the composition is dissolved and some of the material is transposed to other locations in the book. The new arrangement (Neugliederung) is dominated by the Passover point of view; that is, the doctrine that Jesus is the true paschal lamb. To convert the book into a Passion gospel, the evangelist moved the story of the temple cleansing to the front of the book and connected it with the first sign, located the Lord's Supper in chapter 6, advanced the story of the anointing to chapter 12, and in chapter 1 changed the original two days into four days of events. The third stage of the gospel, too, is anti-docetic. Finally, a redactor added the two last verses and a few other passages.

Wilkens has investigated his subject deeply, building upon the work of Wellhausen (whose theory he concludes is vindicated), Bultmann, Hirsch, and others. Much can be learned from his study, but there are valid objections to his hypothesis. He does not use vocabulary and syntax sufficiently as objective criteria. He has overworked his theory of a Passion gospel, for some of the phenomena are better explained as the result of other causes. He overestimates the extent of the sacramental aspect, for the effort to connect six miracles with either the Eucharist or baptism gives most of them a connotation they never had. His denial of the fact that the purpose of the signs is to prove that Jesus is the Christ is a contradiction of the plain statement in 20:30-31. Another error is his failure to recognize that the theological point of view in the speeches differs from that in the narratives of his _Grundevangelium_, which lack the gnostic flavor of the speeches. James M. Robinson asks a legitimate question: "Why did this Passover theology assert itself through radical rearrangement and never state itself theologically?"[20] The lack of express statements of the view and the vagueness of any evidence that the present arrangement of the gospel makes John a "Passover gospel" are sufficient grounds for raising doubts about Wilkens' theory.

Both Haenchen and Fortna recognize that Wilkens' purpose is to show as much of John as possible to be apostolic in authorship and that consequently he glosses over the contradictions in the gospel and insists that all three strata were written by the same man.[21] Wilkens' adoption of the old belief that the evangelist was an eyewitness should make us suspicious of Wilkens' work.

Eduard Lohse, professor of New Testament at Göttingen, in a brief study (1960) concludes that the sacramental passages 3:5, 6:51c-58, and 19:34 have been interpolated by a redactor. Many exegetes before him reached the same conclusion concerning the last two passages.

Octave Merlier, in his 1945 doctoral dissertation published in 1961 with tables and index added, contends that first there was an anonymous source containing _logia_, or sayings, some of which appear in papyri such as the fragments of "the unknown gospel" that Bell and Skeat made famous by editing and publishing. The author of John, whom Merlier calls "A," composed a life of Jesus, then enlarged it with materials from the logia source. Next the first redactor, R2, added the discourses in chapters 14-17. Another redactor, R3, added a few pieces, including the pericope of the adulterous woman; perhaps R2 and R3 were the same person. Finally, R4 added chapter 21 to represent R3 as the disciple whom the Lord loved.

M.-E. Boismard (1961-1963), professor of New Testament at the École Biblique, explains the similarities between John and Luke-Acts as the result of the redaction of John by the evangelist Luke himself! Boismard observes that the present Johannine account of the healing of the official's son presents difficulties showing that it is not homogeneous: internal repetition, inconsistency, and variation in vocabulary. His explanation is that there are two strata, a primitive account in which miracles are the accepted basis for faith in Jesus, and the additions made by the redactor in which miracles are unnecessary for faith. In retouching the text the redactor tried to imitate the Johannine literary style. Certain Lucan features indicate that the redactor was Luke.

Boismard contends that the Prologue has been revised and expanded by Luke. Verses 1-5 come from the primitive Johannine hymn; 6-8 are Johannine but originally immediately preceded 19; the rest of the Prologue is essentially Lucan. Boismard separates the remainder of chapter 1 into two categories: X, the original text, and Y, the revisions made by Luke. Redaction is found too in sections of the last three chapters.

Boismard notes the discrepancy between chapters 1 and 3 concerning John the Baptist. In chapter 1 the Baptist testifies that not he but Jesus is the Messiah, while in chapter 3 the Baptist's own disciples are astonished that all men are going to Jesus to be baptized. If John had told his disciples that Jesus was the Christ, why should they be surprised when many people went to Jesus? Wellhausen and Goguel interpreted 1:19-36 and 3:22-30 as two different accounts of the same incident, but Boismard decides that they are two distinct scenes, the first corresponding to Mark 1:9-11 and the second to Mark 1:7. Both are Johannine, so the evangelist must have written one account, then replaced it with the other account; later the redactor inserted the first one and added 3:24, 26, and 28. Boismard sees the redactor's hand at work in sections of the last three chapters also.

Although Boismard's evidence for redaction deserves careful study, his theory that Luke revised the Gospel of John is rightly rejected by nearly all Johannine scholars. Boismard assumes that parallels with Luke-Acts in material he assigns to the redactor necessarily indicate that Luke is the redactor, and he ignores other explanations of the parallelism. He fails to show why he thinks it more probable that the author of another gospel revised John than that the editor or a redactor of John has used the Gospel of Luke or Lucan tradition. Boismard rejects the use of sources as an explanation of the literary phenomena.

In an article published in 1963 John A. T. Robinson, Bishop of Woolwich, accepts the view that the gospel is a stylistic unity, but he also recognizes the "seaminess" of the "seamless robe." He is convinced that there were two recensions of the gospel, written by the same hand. He regards the evidence for this in the body of the gospel as "somewhat subjective," so he approaches the question from the ends, the Prologue and the Epilogue (chapter 21).

Robinson points to some similarities of theme between the Epilogue and Prologue on the one hand and the body of the gospel on the other. Following B. T. D. Smith's suggestion in 1912, he believes there is parallelism in structure between the Prologue and the rest of the book (excluding the Epilogue): 1:3 and 1:35-4:42; 1:4 and 4:43-6:71; 1:4-5 and 7:1-9:41; 1:10-11 and 13:1-20:29. The unity of style, theme, and structure convinces him that one author wrote all. On the other hand, the beginning and ending do differ somewhat from the body of the gospel. The Epilogue is separated from it by a clear line as a definite appendix, and the Prologue has unique vocabulary. The parallels with the Johannine epistles indicate to Robinson that the Prologue and Epilogue were added by the same author soon after he wrote the epistles. Robinson argues against the presence of a poetic source in the Prologue.

Evidence Robinson cites for his theory actually is evidence against it; the differences between the ends and the body of the gospel are so great that they indicate different authors, not merely different editions by the same author. His assumption of literary unity ignores the aporias in the body of the book. Some of his alleged parallels in theme are not equivalents, and the "parallelism" in structure is quite farfetched.

Redaction by the original author is a very weak explanation of the literary phenomena. First of all, it is highly improbable that an author would revise his own work without smoothing out the rough connections and other aporias. A later editor or a redactor often created aporias by inserting blocks of material from a source or from his own mind into a writing, but the original author usually felt free to rewrite his earlier material, producing a smoother, more uniform document. Brown makes a valid comment concerning Wilkens' interpretation which applies to this kind of theory in general: "Also, in Wilkens' theory the process of editing consisted in adding material and rearranging it but never in rewriting what was originally written; that does seem to be a curious way of editing one's own work."[22] Wilkens tries to account for this by claiming that the evangelist did not want to transpose even his own material because he was a witness through whose mouth the Paraclete, the Holy Spirit, had spoken to the Christian community and when this testimony was written down it was too sacred to change. This claim overlooks the fact that if the evangelist believed his earlier work was inspired, he probably believed that his later work was also, and as such the later could supersede the earlier. It was typical of Christian prophets to believe that the latest revelation replaced the earlier, even if the earlier had been ascribed to Jesus.

In the second place, it is improbable that the same author would express the conflicting views which occur in John. Several writers tend to have more variety of outlook and belief than a single writer, even over a period of time. Wilkens minimizes the variation in view by ignoring some of the contradictions and by assigning to both the first and third editions a concern for the Passion theology and by finding in all three editions an opposition to Docetism. Parker tries to meet the problem by postulating that the evangelist must have changed his ideas between his editions. But it is improbable that an author would change his point of view that much; and if he did, why did he not simply omit the material which conflicted with his later views? Fortna raises a valid objection along this line: ". . . it is unlikely that a writer would alter his earlier work so radically that elements which are really the creation of a single mind will appear foreign to each other."[23]

In the third place, it is implausible that one author would alter his vocabulary so much. This objection is especially valid when different terms are used for the same person or the same concept.

Haenchen includes redaction as a factor in his study of the growth of the Prologue (1963). Sometime after he finished the gospel, the redactor, whom Haenchen calls the Supplementer (Ergänzer), inserted verses 6-8, 12-13, and 15. Haenchen gives three arguments against assigning verses 6-8 to the evangelist: (1) The verses describe John the Baptist as "sent from God," but the gospel as a whole restricts this phrase to descriptions of Jesus. If the evangelist applied the expression to John, we would expect to find it used in this way elsewhere in the gospel. (2) The verses describe John as a "witness" to Jesus, but in 5:34 Jesus says he does not accept the witness of any man. (3) In verse 7 the purpose of the Baptist's witness is that all might believe through him. The reason for his witness is not expressed in those terms elsewhere in the gospel, and the inclusive "all" does not fit the historical situation of the Baptist's preaching. Haenchen believes that the "all" was suggested by the synoptic tradition (Mark 1:5) which states that "all the Judean countryside and all those in Jerusalem" went out to John to be baptized. The redactor made the insertions because he misunderstood the text and because he wished to depreciate John's role as the baptizer of Jesus.

Haenchen's first and third arguments rest on the mistaken premise that the evangelist would not insert in the Prologue any ideas which he does not repeat in the rest of the gospel. As for the second argument, it is not valid, because the evangelist was not always consistent, and John is a witness to Jesus elsewhere in the gospel.

Rudolf Schnackenburg (1965) maintains that the gospel went through three stages of composition. First, John, "the disciple whom Jesus loved," is at the source of the primary tradition; then the evangelist, who was not John, shaped the book; finally a redactor produced the final form of it. The work of the various writers can be distinguished by their views on eschatology, faith, and the sacraments. In an article published in 1958 Schnackenburg interprets the Nicodemus story in John 3 along similar lines. He concludes that in the original gospel, the Evangelium-Bericht, the account ran 3:1-12, 22-30; 4:1 ff. Later the evangelist composed a homily, 3:31-36, 13-21 (in that order), which is a meditation on 3:1-12. Finally, the redactor, a disciple who gave to the unfinished work of the evangelist its last form, inserted the homily in two parts, reversing their order.

C. Dekker (1966) maintains that there was a basic gospel, which another writer has revised later. In Dekker's opinion the original gospel applied the term "the Jews" to the inhabitants of Judea, but the redactor in 6:41, 52, applied it to Galileans. The evangelist used the word "crowd" to designate Galileans in the sense that Pharisees used "people of the land" to refer to Palestinians who were ignorant of the Torah; the redactor in 6:22, 24 applied it to Jews. The original gospel reflects a Palestinian background, whereas the redactor was a non-Jewish Christian. The whole of chapter 6 was inserted by the redactor. Without chapter 6 Jesus' public career in John lasts one year as in the synoptic gospels, and runs from one Passover (2:13) to the next (when he was crucified).

Although there is strong evidence that at least part of chapter 6 is a later addition, Dekker's thesis has serious weaknesses. Some of chapter 6 has definite affinities with other parts of the gospel, and therefore if a redactor wrote it, he probably inserted other material too. Dekker tries and fails to find reliable evidence of a Palestinian environment for the basic gospel. He collects examples of the use of the term "Jews" in the ancient world, but overlooks the fact that both Greeks and Hellenistic Jews applied the term to Jews anywhere, not just in Judea. Therefore "Jews" in John could refer to any Jews, and it is only a coincidence whether the term occurs in a Judean or in a Galilean setting. Similarly, "crowd" in John is not necessarily used in the sense of "people of the land." Dekker overlooks the non-Palestinian flavor of passages outside chapter 6.

Raymond E. Brown (1966), like Parker and Wilkens, believes that the evangelist revised his own writing. According to Brown's theory, there was first a stage of oral traditional material; second, traditional material was shaped into Johannine patterns in the oral preaching and teaching, and some of this was put in writing; the third stage was the first edition of the Gospel of John, written by the evangelist; the fourth stage was the second edition, written by the evangelist to adapt the gospel to a later situation in the church; finally, the second edition was revised by a redactor who was of the same school of thought as those who produced the second stage, and he inserted more material from that stage--he probably was a close friend or disciple of the evangelist.[24] The conservative attitude behind the theory shows through in the statement, "while preserving the substantial unity of the Gospel, this theory explains the various factors that militate against unity of authorship."[25]

Wilkens' book published in 1969 continues his earlier (1958) hypothesis that one author wrote the whole gospel in three stages. Consequently Wilkens minimizes the variations and ascribes the tensions within the gospel to the differences between narrative and discourse. He presents a detailed exegesis of the whole book in opposition to the interpretations of other Johannine scholars, especially Bultmann and Käsemann.

Wilkens' exposition of the terms sēmeia, "signs," and erga, "works," in John is intended to demonstrate that there was not a pre-Johannine signs source, and that the author of the gospel used each term to fit his purpose. John, states Wilkens, regarded Jesus' miracles, or "signs," (including his passion and resurrection) as actual revelations of Jesus' divine glory, while "works" is a broader term which includes theology and Jesus' words as well as miraculous deeds. In his review of the book Fortna criticizes Wilkens for excluding a pre-Johannine signs source, and he rightly remarks that Wilkens seems to be too anxious to defend the gospel as representative of normative Christianity.[26]

J. Becker (1970) has examined John 13-17 and concludes that this section displays the theological development within the Johannine community. The passage 13:31-14:31 reduces future eschatology to anthropology. Contrary to prevailing opinion, chapters 15-17 are not a unity. In 15:1-17 the interest is in Christology, which is a trait of the evangelist. In 15:18-16:15 the concern has shifted to ecclesiology, and Jesus' departure is treated accordingly. John 16:16-17:26 contains some of the evangelist's theology, but it emphasizes ecclesiology. This last section must have been written by a pupil of the evangelist who adapted the latter's words to the situation in the church at a later time.

When there is evidence that another hand has been at work on the gospel, a difficult question is whether the second writer was the editor modifying his written source material or whether he was a redactor revising the gospel. The answer can be found only by thorough, detailed examination of the whole gospel. Guidelines can be found by determining the characteristics of the work of the editor and the work of the redactor, if there was one. As we have seen, in some theories the redaction is extensive, but others limit it to the insertion of a few glosses and the addition of chapter 21.

If the Gospel of John was revised later, was chapter 21 added by the redactor? Thompson argued in 1915 that, although John has been revised, most of chapter 21 is part of the original gospel. On the other hand, even some prominent biblical scholars who argue for the unity of the gospel (e.g., Dodd, Barrett, Lightfoot)[27] concede that the last chapter is an appendix. If the last two verses of chapter 20 were originally the end of the gospel, then chapter 21 is indeed an appendix. But if one or both of those verses were the conclusion in a source the evangelist used, did he allow them to serve as or be part of the closing of the gospel, or did he continue by writing chapter 21?

CHAPTER 8

THEORIES OF ACCIDENTAL DISPLACEMENT

Displacement theories form another type of solution to the problem of the literary structure of John. The fundamental idea in these theories is that the incongruities and poor connections are largely the result of later incorrect arrangement of the writing, so it is necessary to restore the original order before the gospel can be properly understood. The view that the author himself combined into a single speech words which Jesus uttered on different occasions[1] is not strictly a displacement theory, because the writing of the author has not been disarranged.

The Sinaitic Syriac manuscript of the canonical gospels has the central section of John 18 in this order: verses 12-13, 24, 14-15, 19-23, 16-18, 25. The manuscript was written in the fourth century, but the translation it preserves was made in the late second or early third century. As Macgregor has observed, this order probably does not indicate that the scribe knew a manuscript that preserved that order, but rather that "the confusion of the present text was early recognized and that there were skilled textual critics before Spitta!"[2] In short, someone noticed that certain elements in the story of Jesus' trial before the high priest do not fit each other very well, so he changed the order of some verses. He may have believed that he was restoring the original order.

In the fourteenth century Ludolphus de Saxonia assumed that the sixth chapter of John ought to precede the fifth.[3] In 1880 Karl Bertling proposed that John 7:15-24 originally was connected to the end of chapter 5.

Advocates of displacement vary in their opinions of the cause and manner of the disarrangement of the text. Modern theories may be classified into two categories: intentional and accidental displacement.

Intentional displacement can occur when an editor combines the author's work with other source material; this is a form of source theory. Intentional displacement happens also if the editor composes material himself and inserts it in the author's writing; the material following the insertion is displaced from its connection with the passage which originally preceded it. The displacement is more pronounced if the editor (or a later redactor) transposes some of the original writing.

In 1871 J. P. Norris concluded that chapters 6 and 21 are supplemental sections written later, presumably by the apostle John, who wrote the rest of the book too; early copyists attached chapter 21 to the end and spoiled the connection between chapters 5 and 7 by inserting chapter 6 between them. This kind of notion still survives, for in 1963 M. Làconi contended that the author of the gospel was the apostle John, who died before finishing it; after his death his disciples found more of his writing and inserted it wherever it seemed to fit.[4]

Ernest De Witt Burton, professor of New Testament interpretation at the University of Chicago, in 1904 set forth an editorial displacement theory. His explanation of the literary structure is that a company (probably disciples of the apostle John) of writers of the same school wrote thirteen "booklets" while John was living and a fourteenth (John 21) after his death. Originally these existed "as separate books, not as a connected series." An editor produced the literary roughness when he assembled the booklets and added a few phrases to link them together. He inserted "after these things" and "the disciple whom Jesus loved" and verses 3:28, 4:26, and 4:44.[5] This hypothesis does not explain the displacements Burton postulated within six of the booklets, but these dislocations could come under his further suggestion that possibly a careless copyist or binder may have contributed to the disarrangement.

Our concern in this chapter, however, is with accidental displacement. This type of theory rests on the hypothesis that the leaves of the manuscript accidentally fell out of place, someone reassembled them in incorrect order, and all our copies of the gospel have descended from the disarranged document.

Spitta in 1893 argued that there is a group of transpositions caused by an accidental exchange of leaves. He placed chapters 15-16 after 13:31a and located 7:15-24 behind 5:17. In his opinion editorial expansion disturbed the arrangement of the text elsewhere, for example, the account of the trial of Jesus in chapter 18. The following year Bacon made the same transposition of 7:15-24 and concluded that originally chapter 15 connected directly to 13:20. At the same time Jülicher proposed that chapters 5 and 6 were both written by the original author and were transposed by a redactor. Wellhausen adopted this suggestion in 1907. He explains that the redactor transposed the two chapters so that the feast in 5:1 would no longer refer to a Passover, for by removing the second of the three Passovers in the original gospel, and by regarding the remaining two as the terminal points of Jesus' work, the duration of Jesus' career becomes one year. In this way the redactor accomplished his purpose of making John agree with the synoptic gospels.

F. W. Lewis developed transposition further in his Disarrangements in the Fourth Gospel, a small book published in 1910. He transfers 3:22-30 because it separates the two parts of the speech on the only-begotten Son. Following Norris's proposal, he reverses the order of chapter 5 and 6 because of the geographical confusion. He notes that chapter 4 ends with the anticipation of Jesus' ministry in Galilee, but chapter 5 brings him to Jerusalem and leaves him there; chapter 6 begins with the presupposition that he is in Galilee; chapter 7 opens "with a statement that Jesus would not walk any longer in Judea, and therefore resorted to Galilee, where, according to the preceding chapter, He already was."[6] Lewis agrees with Bertling, Spitta, Wendt, and Burton in placing 7:15-24 immediately after chapter 5. He advances chapters 15-16 to a location behind 13:32 because the end of chapter 14 is the closing of the discourse and requires a change of scene, which, as the gospel now stands, does not occur until 18:1. He observes that the statement in 16:5, "None of you asks me 'Where are you going?'" could hardly have occurred after 13:26, where Peter asks, "Lord, where are you going?" Although he states that the reason for the disorder cannot be proved, he accepts as a tentative hypothesis the notion that the cause was accidental disruption of the order of an early copy of the gospel.

James Moffatt, while professor of New Testament at Mansfield College, Oxford, rearranged the text in his famous translation of the New Testament (1913), which was the first English translation to arrange the text of John in accordance with a displacement theory. His reconstruction of the original order is similar to that of Lewis, except that Moffatt makes some transpositions within chapters 11, 12, and 18. Howard credits him with extending the knowledge of displacement theories from the realm of the scholars to the world of laymen.[7] Although Moffatt concludes that a little editorial revision of the gospel took place, he attributes the dislocations mainly to the work of copyists.

Bernard, in his commentary on John (1929), rearranges the text and favors accidental transposition of the pages of the original manuscript as the cause of the dislocation. The similarity of the literary style of the passages in the gospel is responsible for his conclusion. He adopts as an objective test of his rearrangement the method which had been adopted by certain other scholars.[8] This method may be called the "unit-length test." Theoretically, the dislocated passages and the sections between them should all be approximately the same length or else multiples of a unit length. This is because usually each page of a manuscript has the same number of lines and the lines are filled. Within each early Greek New Testament manuscript the number of letters in each line, although not identical, tend to average about the same. Therefore, if a leaf has been moved ahead of the next leaf, the number of letters in the two transposed passages should be approximately the same. Consequently, every disarranged passage should be the equivalent of a leaf or a multiple of a leaf. Bernard was convinced that the six passages that he transposed passed the test, although he admitted that three did not conform as well as the others. According to his hypothesis there were about 750 letters to the leaf. The average number of letters to the leaf in each of his transpositions is 726 (chap. 5), 763 (7:15-24), 780 (13:31-14:31), 730 (3:22-30), 747.5 (10:1-18), and 598 (12:36b-43). The first five are close enough to be plausible, but the last with only 598 letters is not very persuasive evidence.

In 1944 there appeared the rearrangement of the text made by the Roman Catholic scholar, F. R. Hoare. He alters the order of the material in chapters 2 to 16 only. He recognizes that if a displacement theory is valid, it must meet both the test of sense and the physical test (i.e., the unit-length test). He describes the physical test as follows:

> Every passage we propose to remove from its present position in the Gospel to some other position must be equal in length to the matter contained in one or more physical units of the original document. Nor is this all. At every point from which we have removed a passage we shall have made a break in the text; and at every point at which we insert a transferred passage we make another break in the text; and every interval between these breaks in the text throughout the book must be the equivalent of one or more physical units. At the same time, the breaks must not mutilate a continuous narrative or discourse,

> and every transferred passage when set between its new neighbours must make better sense at least at one end, and at least as good sense at the other end as it does in its present position.[9]

To meet the unit-length test Hoare employs the arithmetical approach. He counts the letters of the whole gospel in Merk's Greek text and again in "the more easily identifiable passages requiring to be transferred." Then he concludes that the original manuscript contained 185 columns (omitting the story of the woman taken in adultery), each containing twenty-one lines averaging 18.9 letters per line--an average total of 397 letters per column, or unit. Counting both the transpositions and the sections between them (in 1:1-16:23), he arrives at a total of twenty blocks of material, which he terms "segments," ranging in length from two to seventeen units. He notes that precision is difficult to attain, however, because of uncertainty as to the reading of the original text and the extent of the use of abbreviations in it.

Although Hoare works out his arithmetical approach in great detail and with considerable ingenuity, there remain major shortcomings in his theory. One weakness is that a standard number of letters for each column or page does not agree with the evidence so he varies the length of the columns to make them fit his theory. In an effort to explain this variation in the length of the columns, Hoare theorizes that the original gospel was divided into chapters, "capita," and the scribe left between them a space equivalent to four lines (a partial line would count as a space). Some columns would contain a chapter ending and some would not; those which did would contain a correspondingly smaller number of letters. In strong opposition to this conjecture is the fact that no early manuscript of the gospel (or any other New Testament book) is divided into chapters. Hoare's chapters are shorter than our present divisions, which, of course, were not in the original text. If chapters stood originally in the Gospel of John, why did the copyists omit them?

Equally serious is the fact that his arithmetical basis, instead of the aporias in the text, determines his relocation of many of the passages. He admits that the "necessity of making the transpositions conform to some consistent arithmetical scheme was, as has been said, a governing condition in my mind."[10] Consequently his theory, not the evidence, determines the length of some of his "dislocated" passages. Nevertheless, he is certain that he has discovered realities in the gospel that neither he nor arithmetic put there. Some of the rest of us are not so confident of the results.

Bultmann (1941) accepts displacement as one cause of the literary phenomena. As we have seen, his total theory combines source and redaction. He maintains that the ecclesiastical redactor who added chapter 21 found the leaves unbound and in fragments. After rearranging the leaves in an effort to restore the text, the redactor "published" the gospel. Bultmann points as evidence to the nearly equal size of some of the "dislocated" passages. He rearranges the text more than any other advocate of displacement. In his effort to restore the text to its original order he breaks it into sixty-eight units. The disorder of so many bits of text cannot be explained entirely by the theory of displacement of pages, as D. M. Smith has noted.[11] The small size of some of the units which are claimed to be out of place necessitates the implausible conclusion that leaves not only were loose, but were broken into fragments which invariably were syntactically complete!

Thomas Cottam (1952), in his theory of accidental dislocation, made a "general rearrangement," but did not attempt to correct the possible "minor rearrangements of the text within the sections."[12] Even if his rearrangement is only "general," it is quite extensive: forty-one sections, second only to Bultmann's number of transpositions. It is surprising that he includes the <u>pericope adulterae</u> (7:53-8:11), a passage not in the earliest manuscripts; his explanation is that the story has been suppressed because it presents Jesus as defending an adulteress. This suggestion is not plausible, for in the story Jesus does not defend adultery ("sin no more"), and no extant manuscript has suppressed the story of the sinful woman who kissed Jesus' feet and his words in her defense (Luke 7:37-50) or the mention of Jesus' association with sinners (Mark 2:15-17). Further, in the history of the transmission of the text, the tendency was to add stories rather than delete them.

Cottam's approach apparently is biased, for he claims the result of his rearrangement is that the Gospel of John "is now seen to be historically correct in its general presentation of the ministry of Jesus," written by an eyewitness who chose to present the inner meaning of the facts.[13] Why the removal of the rough connections and inconsistencies proves that the gospel is historically correct is not clear!

Hubert Edwards (1953), Canon of Blackburn, maintains that all twenty-one chapters of John were written by the same author. The evangelist, who was the Beloved Disciple, dictated to a stenographer his memoirs of what Jesus had said and done more than thirty years earlier. The literary unevenness is the result of an editor's placing side by side in the gospel documents of the evangelist that originally were separate, and the editor may have omitted some passages, especially miracle stories. The originally independent sections include the Prologue, chapter 5, 8:31-59, and chapter 21. The allusions to Mary, Martha, and the anointing of Jesus in chapter 11 show that the author is familiar with tradition about which he has not yet told us; Edwards claims the reference is not to the synoptic gospels but to documents which the evangelist previously wrote but were omitted from the gospel. Chapters 14 and 17 have been interchanged, and the lack of an introduction to chapters 14-16 suggests that the editor omitted a document there.

How should we evaluate the displacement theories ? At first glance, the transposition of the leaves of the exemplar (the manuscript being copied) seems to be a possibility, especially in the light of what happened to the exemplar of Codex C. Harold H. Oliver, while a graduate student at Emory University (now professor of theology at Boston University, School of Theology), solved the mystery of the strange order of two passages in the Book of Revelation in Codex C. He determined that the exemplar was a multiple-quire codex in which one folded sheet (four pages) was accidentally bound in the reversed position, that is, the leaf was turned over so that the side of the sheet which should have faced up, faced downward instead.[14] An accident of this kind could occur, but it is surprising that the scribe who wrote Codex C did not correct the error when he copied the text of the exemplar. The scribe evidently copied in a routine manner, without examining the material.

The situation in the exemplar of Codex C, however, is quite different from that of the hypothetical displacement in the exemplar of the present text of John. In the case of the gospel all surviving manuscripts have the same order, whereas with Revelation, Codex C is the only one out of order. A further difference--an important one--is that in this known case of displacement in the exemplar of Codex C, the result is four unintelligible sentences where the transferred passages join the context. This is not the pattern in the Go pel of John, for there all the sentences are understandable.

As an explanation of the literary phenomena in the Gospel of John, displacement theories have major weaknesses. First, it is improbable that such an accident occurred. The lack of any manuscript evidence or any tradition attesting to another order of the text has led the proponents of the more recent theories to conclude that the accident must have happened soon after the manuscript was written. But if the manuscript was a codex, the leaves probably would not come loose until the manuscript was old and worn; if the leaves did get out of order soon after "publication," the author and his amanuensis, the scribe who took down his dictation, would be available to advise on the proper order of the leaves. If the original manuscript was a scroll, there would be no separate leaves to get out of order. Frederic Kenyon observes that in the production of ancient scrolls the sheets were glued together before the scribe wrote on them; this is proved by the fact that "the writing frequently runs over the junction of the sheets."[15]

A second weakness of displacement theories is the fact that if the leaves had accidentally fallen out of order, they probably would have been restored properly. Whoever rearranged them would have realized that they were in disorder and would have made a conscious effort to assemble them correctly. If a better order of the leaves were possible, it is hard to believe that any copyist would make such an unintelligent effort at restoration that he chose rough connections instead of smooth ones and split speeches when he could have left them whole. The exemplar of Codex C may seem to be evidence against this argument, but in it only one leaf was out of order (installed wrong side up), and only one known manuscript follows its arrangement.

If the leaves in John had become loosened as the result of wear from much use of the manuscript, there would be many readers who could correct a faulty assembly. Probably by that time copies of the original would have been made, and they, too, could serve to correct a disarrangement.

The manner in which manuscripts in Greek were written renders implausible the theory that very many leaves could have been rearranged incorrectly. The lines of a page were filled with letters, even if the line ended in the middle of a word. In most cases the bottom line ends in the midst of a clause, phrase, or a word which is completed at the top of the next page. This evidence of the original arrangement would have enabled the copyist to assemble the leaves in the right order. If he had ignored the evidence and arranged the sheets improperly, forming the model for our present text, it would contain broken words, broken phrases, and broken sentences, as Codex C does. Although the gospel contains poor connections,they are not that rough. Instead, the alleged transposed sections are usually nearly complete units.

Cottam tries to meet this objection by suggesting that the original must not have been "a properly written fair copy, but . . . a first draft written at least partly on odd sheets which were afterwards deranged." In a rough draft the writer would not be concerned with the appearance of the page and, reasons Cottam, would finish a word and even a sentence before beginning on the next page.[16] This is sheer conjecture, for there is no evidence that there was a first draft of the gospel or that ancient writers wrote first drafts in that manner.

Another answer offered to the objection is the suggestion that the copyist inserted connecting links wherever the pages did not fit each other. This does not seem probable either, for writing the connections would require more effort than correctly arranging the text.

Paragraph length is another argument, ably presented by A. Q. Morton,[17] against displacement of leaves. Employing the analogy of tearing a page out of a book, he calls attention to the fact that relocation of sheets tends to produce some short paragraphs. Since a sheet rarely starts at the beginning of a paragraph and rarely ends at the conclusion of another, the removal of the sheet divides both its first and last paragraphs into two shorter ones. When the sheet is inserted into a new location, it splits another paragraph. Therefore, if the Gospel of John had suffered a number of accidental dislocations, it would contain a relatively high percentage of paragraphs shorter than the average length in that book. In a table Morton points out that this is not the case: the number of paragraphs of less than half average length in John is 25.8%; the percentages in the synoptic gospels are 23.2% in Matthew, 27.5% in Mark, and 26.8% in Luke (these three together average the same as John: 25.8%).

The irregular length of the transferred sections and of the spaces between them is further evidence against displacement. If the leaves had been disarranged, the length of the misplaced passages would have been determined by the size of a page, making the dislocations approximately the same length or a multiple of a unit length. This is the basis of the unit-length test. Some proponents of displacement have estimated the number of letters on an average leaf of two pages in the disarranged manuscript. Lewis estimates the equivalent of 9.3 lines in the Westcott-Hort Greek text. Bernard estimates 750 letters and Cottam estimates 736.

Most advocates of displacement claim that their theories meet the unit-length test. We have noted that Bernard and Bultmann regard the nearly equal length of some of their transpositions as evidence of displacement. On the other hand, W. G. Wilson in his study of the subject in 1949 sharply disagrees. He observes that if the leaves of a codex had been disarranged, the length of each dislocation and of the space between its original position and its present position would be a multiple of the length of the text on a leaf, that is, two pages. With the exception of Hoare, advocates of displacement usually overlook the test of the length of the space between the old and new locations of a passage. Wilson proceeded to examine seven frequently alleged dislocations and found that none of the spaces met his test.

Actually, the value of the unit-length test is limited to the extreme discrepancies, for the number of letters on a leaf of a manuscript varies greatly. In a spot check of three of the earliest New Testament papyri (ca. 200) I found much variation. In Papyrus Bodmer II (P^{66}) the number of lines per page range from sixteen to twenty-two and the number of letters per line from twenty-two to twenty-seven. In Papyrus Bodmer XIV (P^{75}) the number of lines ranges from thirty-nine to forty-five and the letters per line from twenty-four to thirty. In Papyrus Bodmer XV (part of P^{75}) the lines run from forty to forty-four in number, though most pages have forty-four; the number of letters runs from twenty-seven to thirty per line. If the exemplar manuscript was as regular as Bodmer XV, the unit-length test would have some value, but if it was as irregular as the other two, such a test would prove little. Dislocation theories usually rest on the presupposition that the number of lines was constant on all pages, but this is not the case in our earliest New Testament manuscripts. This is a serious blow to the unit-length test.

Schnackenberg rightly rejects displacement theories because the pieces, or blocks of material, do not occur meaninglessly here and there in the present text, as one would expect if the blocks were the result of an accidental exchange of leaves. Instead as he observes, the blocks are inserted into certain textual connections.[18] Barrett observes an additional shortcoming of displacement theories: "While the proposed alterations generally improve some connections, they often worsen others."[19]

The arguments against the displacement theories are so strong that most New Testament scholars today rightly reject them. We must look in other directions if we are to find the solution to the puzzle of the literary origin of John. Yet displacement theories do have a certain value: they point out places (aporias) in the text where some biblical interpreters have felt that the connections are so irregular that the original must have been different from the present text.

CHAPTER 9

HOW CAN THE PUZZLE BE SOLVED?

The enormous variety among the "solutions" to the puzzle of the literary origin of the Gospel of John is quite confusing! The extent of the disagreement arouses the suspicion that no one is on the right track. The fact that no theory has gained general acceptance by scholars in the field also raises some doubts, although we must admit that in religion human bias has often prevented widespread acceptance--even by "scholars"--of sound scholarship. Also, no hypothesis satisfactorily explains all the evidence, and at least portions of each fail to stand up under intensive and extensive scrutiny. Evidence against the theories remains, evidence that the author has overlooked or misunderstood. The Gospel of Signs hypothesis of Fortna and Nicol, however, is close to solving the problem of one source in John, and their theory is gaining support.

The apparent failure of the "solutions" has led to two negative reactions formulated as conclusions: the gospel must have been written by a single author after all, or the work of the various writers has been harmonized to such an extent that solution is impossible. But if source, redaction, and displacement theories have failed, so have the theories of single authorship. No one has yet given a satisfactory explanation of why a single author would have different points of view, different vocabulary, and--least probable of all--different syntax in different portions of his book, even when presenting the same subject matter. The theory that John is an unfinished gospel, and the view that one author wrote it in several stages, fail to explain the phenomena, as we remarked in Chapter 3. I once accepted the creative ability of the author as a possible cause of the literary structure of the gospel,[1] as a result of the present study I now reject completely that facile explanation. The persistence of efforts for more than a century and a half to find the solution on the basis of multiple authorship strongly suggests that there must be considerable evidence that the book was written by more than one hand. The gospel is not a "seamless robe," but a mass of tangled threads.

The other negative reaction, the view that the work of the writers has been harmonized beyond detection, fails to recognize that the gospel is far from uniform and that many distinctive features remain. These features are sufficient in number that they should enable us to discover at least the main strands in the literary fabric. The biblical interpreters who have adopted this negative view have been too easily discouraged and have not made a sufficiently thorough examination of the text.

Our survey of the theories discloses a wide range of method. We soon suspect that a major cause of failure is a lack of reliable methodology. If we are to solve this puzzle, we must avoid the mistaken presuppositions and erroneous procedures of the past. As we have observed, accidental displacement of the leaves cannot be the answer. Neither can sources be determined on the simple basis of speeches vs. narratives. It is a mistake to assume that oral tradition is the source of much of the editor's material; the persistence of certain stylistic traits points to written tradition in which the style was fixed. We should not assume that the evangelist would necessarily include all of a source he used; the evidence indicates that he selected only portions of his source documents. We should not conclude, as Goodenough and Dodd did,[2] that the evangelist would not conflate written sources, piece by piece; the conflation of Mark and the Q material in Matthew and Luke demonstrates that early Christian writers could combine material in that manner.

Many mistakes have been made in respect to the synoptic tradition. We should not attempt to settle the question of the relationship of John to the synoptic gospels before making a source analysis of John. This gospel is late enough in origin that theoretically the other canonical gospels could have been used by the author of a written source as well as by the editor or by the redactor. Thus more than one Johannine writer could have used the synoptic gospels, but we must determine what material comes from each writer before we can decide who used what synoptic material.

Stylistic characteristics are valid criteria, and my respect for this type of evidence has increased greatly. It was the misuse of stylistic evidence that led to false conclusions and brought linguistics into disrepute. Style should not be employed exclusively, but in conjunction with other significant aspects such as literary structure (aporia, catchwords, etc.) vocabulary, and thought content. Improper selection of the stylistic characteristics is the chief source of error in the use of this type of evidence. If we assign to one writer all occurrences of a term or a syntactical feature, when actually that stylistic trait was used by two or three writers in the gospel, we consequently assign too much to one writer. The proper selection of stylistic features as criteria and the accurate recognition of precisely which writers used which features , is absolutely crucial in this investigation. The worst error of this kind is the E. Schweizer-Ruckstuhl approach which selected as criteria the stylistic characteristics that occur the most frequently in John. It is astonishing that such a method was ever accepted seriously! The traits that occur the most frequently naturally tend to be those used by several writers, and hence are least valuable in detecting the work of an individual writer.

I confess that I stumbled around quite a bit while searching for the valid methods. At first I assumed that a redactor was responsible for most of the aporias, and tentatively I assigned passages to him. Then I surveyed the theories of others who have attempted to solve the puzzle. Although some of these studies contain valuable insights, none of the solutions seemed adequate.

Next, I began in earnest my own investigation by repeatedly reading through the Greek text, testing hypotheses of others as well as my own, and making vocabulary, syntax, and thought-content tests in an effort to find consistent patterns that reflect the work of different writers. Moulton and Geden's A Concordance to the Greek New Testament was used for the vocabulary tests. Textual variants in the Greek manuscripts made it necessary to establish the text; no reading was accepted which is not in at least one of the earliest four major manuscripts of John: Codices P^{66}, P^{75}, B, and Sinaiticus.

Later I recognized that most of the aporia are the result of the work of an editor, not of the redactor who added chapter 21 and made some insertions in the text. The evidence that convinced me was the difference between the redactor's writing in chapter 21 and the writing at the aporia in the other chapters.

Then I wondered if the same writer who added chapter 21 made the obvious insertions about John the Baptist in the Prologue (1: 6-8. 15). If he did, was this writer the editor or a later redactor? Some interpreters have concluded that the editor added chapter 21, while some others have decided that a redactor contributed this addition. If there were both an editor and a redactor, which one wrote the Prologue insertions? Or are these insertions later glosses? Chapter 21 clearly contains material from sources, and therefore this material must be determined and screened out before we can discover the characteristics of the author who added this final chapter. To my surprise, I found that this writer, unlike his sources, always uses the article "the" with personal names, while in the insertions in the Prologue the article is always omitted with personal names. These constructions are known as arthrous and anarthrous, respectively. In Greek, unlike English, the article can be used with names without affecting the meaning of the sentence, and the use or non-use of the article with personal names was a matter of personal style with some writers. The anarthrous personal names in the Prologue insertions indicate that the author of the final chapter did not make the insertions; further evidence is the fact that anarthrous personal names are characteristic of the other material apparently written by the editor. Also, John the Baptist is a special interest of the editor elsewhere as well as in the Prologue insertions, but the Baptist is not an interest of the redactor. Comparison of the insertions with the work of the editor in the body of the gospel reveals other traits of his in the insertions. On the other hand, the interests, point of view, and to some extent the style in chapter 21 differ from those in the editor's work. Finally, traits of the editor occur in the last verse of chapter 20, where he drew the original Gospel of John to a close. Thus it became evident that the editor made these insertions in the Prologue and that a later redactor added the last chapter.

The investigation of the Prologue insertions proved to be more profitable than anticipated! The discovery that anarthrous personal names are characteristic of the editor provides an essential tool for detecting his writing. To the best of my knowledge, no one has previously noticed this trait of the editor. In contrast, with the exception of Old Testament and definite names, personal names are arthrous in the sources and the redactor's work (even the Old Testament names are arthrous in the redactor's writing). The influence of the Septuagint and the Jewish background accounts for the anarthrous Old Testament names. Other books in the New Testament demonstrate that some writers used the article with personal names and some did not. In a recent report on the occurrence and non-occurrence of the article with personal names in the synoptic gospels, I point out that in the Q material in Matthew and Luke, personal names in the narrative portions are arthrous, while in the sayings portions the personal names are all anarthrous, with one exception.[3] This indicates that the narrative Q material and the sayings Q material come from separate written sources. Furthermore, a preliminary examination of Paul's letters indicates that he, like the editor of John, wrote personal names in the anarthrous style and that some of the later insertions (though not all) contain arthrous personal names.[4]

Next, I observed one way in which the editor operated in using source material. Sometimes he inserted material from another source because it contained a term which was in the source he was copying; sometimes a term in a source induced him to insert a passage of his own composition either just before it or just after it. In other words, at times he combined source materials, or else wrote material to insert, on the basis of catchwords. When I observed this I thought that I had discovered something new, but later I found that Hirsch had already called attention to it.[5] The same literary technique occurs in Mark 9. The author of Mark placed two distinct sayings next to each other in spite of the fact that the idea in each has no relation to the other; his reason for combining them is that both contain terms from the same root, "salt."[6] Occasionally the editor's insertions are based on an idea in a source instead of a catchword.

A characteristic of the editor's writing, observed by others as well as myself, is his tendency to restate some passages or scattered sentences that are in his sources; knowledge of this trait aids us in recognizing restatements as his work. Analysis of his restatements, especially his changes from the source material, discloses some of his stylistic traits and points of view which are useful in detecting his writing outside of his restatements. Another characteristic of the editor's own composition is its "shotgun shot" nature; that is, often it is a scattered miscellany without close logical consistency, in contrast to the source material, in which the thought usually develops logically. An insertion that makes little or no sense, however, invariably is either from the redactor or a later gloss.

Assigning on a tentative basis the material in John to various writers was a continuing process almost from the start. Looking back at it, I would recommend postponing that process until most of the evidence has been collected. At first I listed the features which I assigned to each author; later this material was reorganized in charts, some of which are in the appendix of this book.

After many of the literary features had been noted and tentative assignment of authors made, I translated John into rather literal

English, reassigning the material to the various writers as I went. It is impossible to convey in English all the variations in style that occur in Greek, including some word order that would be confusing in English. The assignment of authorship was still premature. A further problem was that at the time the translation was made I was not yet sure which terms and which elements of syntax are significant for source-redaction criticism of the gospel; after the research was finished the translation was revised to show the final selection of the features of the Greek text that serve as criteria of authorship. The translation was used as a working tool for recording certain criteria.

General Principles

If an investigation of the literary origin of John is to be valid, it must observe certain principles of scholarship. These principles apply to this kind of study of any ancient composite document.

The most fundamental of all is the necessity of objectivity. It is disillusioning to see that prejudice has been such a dominating influence in so-called "biblical scholarship." In our survey of theories of the literary origin of John, we found bias to prove apostolic authorship, bias to preserve unity of the book, bias to preserve the earliness (and hence the authority) of at least a portion of the gospel, and bias for certain other types of theory. Theological prejudices have been excused on the grounds that even a scientist has presuppositions. That excuse overlooks the fact that a genuine scientist is willing to change his presuppositions in accordance with new knowledge, whereas a biased person will not change them regardless of the evidence.

A second principle is that the establishment of sound scientific methodology is a vital prerequisite. The discovery of valid methods is a major concern of this book. Next to bias, lack of sound methodology is the greatest cause of failure to solve the literary puzzle of John.

Thirdly, the evidence should be collected and investigated as fully as possible. Many biblical scholars have erred by examining only a portion of the available picture. The internal evidence in the gospel is primary and should be examined first, comprehensively and intensively. The environmental evidence is essential too. We need to know the Jewish, pagan, and above all the

Christian backgrounds in order to understand the vocabulary and the point of view of each writer of the gospel.

Another principle is that we must try to think of all the possible ways in which the present form of the gospel may have been produced, and test these possibilities against the evidence. At the start we do not know how many writers are involved, the characteristics of each, or, in the case of an editor or a later redactor, just how he operated. Therefore we must test all possibilities. Both inductive conclusions drawn from the evidence and deductive suggestions drawn from possible theories must be invoked and examined. When someone has made an insertion in source material, it must come from the editor, or redactor, or be a later gloss. When there is a comment on something the editor has written, the comment obviously does not come from the source material.

A fifth principle is that if a theory is valid, it must be consistent with all the evidence. It is dishonest to ignore or misinterpret that portion of the evidence which disagrees with one's interpretation of the gospel.

Another principle is that variation, inconsistencies, and abrupt shifts in linguistic or ideological content must be accounted for. The numerous claims that the book is a unity simply are not supported by the text. Disunity is there, and must be satisfactorily explained.

Specific Techniques

Certain specific techniques are recommended as essential procedures for the task of detecting the literary origin of John. Many of these would apply as well to the study of the origin of any ancient work of multiple authorship. Additional techniques appear in the following chapters.

1. Use a Greek text of the gospel, a text with a good critical apparatus which records accurately the readings of the recently discovered early manuscripts P^{66} and P^{75}. Until two decades ago the earliest known manuscripts of the text of John, with the exception of a few small fragments, were Codex B, or Vaticanus, and Codex Sinaiticus, both written in the middle or latter half of the fourth century. Now we have the papyri P^{66} and P^{75}, written about A. D. 200. P^{75}, unfortunately, consists of only the first fifteen chapters of John; the remaining portion of the manuscript is lost. As for the best printed Greek text to use, the Nestle-

Aland text is preferred.[7] A good working knowledge of Hellenistic Greek is, of course, a prerequisite for the researcher.

2. Establish the text. The text in even the earliest manuscripts varies. Therefore we must know well the principles of textual criticism so that we can determine which variant reading is the original or at least the closest to the original.

3. Make a literal translation of the Greek text leaving ample space for later insertion of evidence.

4. Mark the location of aporias or breaks in thought or style.

5. Using a Greek concordance to the New Testament, record in the translation the location of Greek terms which appear to be characteristic of a particular writer or type of passage. At the beginning this will be tentative, and as the investigation proceeds you will need to make deletions and additions.

6. Search the Greek text for distinctive features of syntax. Then comb through the text systematically to locate and record every instance of each of these features.

7. Search for and record any other features which may be distinctive of a writer in John.

8. Examine the evidence you have recorded to see what patterns emerge. On the basis of the patterns assign the material to the various writers. Do the passages assigned to a certain writer form a consistent group? Are the characteristics ascribed to a writer consistent with the passages assigned to him? If not, either some characteristics are not valid criteria of his work, or some material has been erroneously assigned to him. Do your conclusions form a consistent theory?

9. Recognize that there is no <u>one necessary</u> starting point for this investigation, contrary to Faure. No matter where you start, you will have to employ all possible approaches before you finish, for solution depends upon your comprehension of the whole picture. Start with any passage which seems distinctive, analyze its traits, and then look for other passages with the same traits. After determining that 1:6-8 was written by an editor and 21:18-24 by a redactor, I used those passages as my starting point.

10. Working out the solution is a continuing process. There are two basic operations in solving the literary puzzle: the assignment of characteristics to each writer, and the separation of the work of each writer from the rest of the gospel. Neither operation can be performed alone. You cannot make a <u>final</u> list of each writer's characteristics until you know what each one

wrote, because the writing of each is the source of knowledge of the characteristics of each. On the other hand, you cannot make a final separation of the work of each writer until you know definitely the characteristics of each writer, for knowledge of those traits is a fundamental guide in detecting the composition of each writer. Therefore you must make tentative assignments of characteristics and tentative separation of authorship, constantly checking each operation against the other.

11. Finally, after authorship has been assigned tentatively on the basis of vocabulary, syntax, and thought content, check each assignment against the context and your overall hypothesis. For example, expansion of the editor's work cannot be from a source he used, nor can material written by the redactor be commented on by the editor; the editor wrote later than the authors of his sources, and the redactor wrote later than the editor. Incidentally, there is no valid evidence that any of the writers later revised his own material (in spite of the recurrent popularity of this type of theory).

CHAPTER 10

THE PROLOGUE

The first eighteen verses stand apart from the rest of the gospel. This Prologue is distinctive in its vocabulary, for its following terms never occur in the body of the book: "Word" (logos) as a title for Jesus, "grace," "fullness," and the verb in verse 18 translated as "declare." Only here is Jesus called "god" (the correct reading in 18 is "god," not "Son," because "Son" is the result of later harmonization by scribes who copied the manuscripts). The uniqueness of these terms is significant because wnen essentially the same topic is mentioned elsewhere in John, a different term is used. For example, when alluding to Jesus' preexistence and descent to earth in the rest of the gospel, he is called "the Son of Man" or "Son," not "the Word."

The Prologue also contains distinctive ideas not found elsewhere in John. Only here are Christians "children of God" (the expression refers to Jews in 11:52) and "born of God" ("born of the Spirit" in chapter 3 is not identical). Only in the Prologue are "all things" and "the world" created through Jesus, who gave to all who received him "the authority" to become children of God. Only here is the Incarnation doctrine expressly stated (in verse 14), and only here is Jesus the "only-begotten god"--in 3:16, 18 he is the "only-begotten Son." Only in the Prologue does the gospel contain the notion that Christians have received "grace" from Jesus' fullness.

The unique vocabulary, distinctive ideas, Semitic-style poetry in certain verses, and abrupt change between the Prologue and the body of the gospel all indicate that one author did not write both the Prologue and the rest of the book. Advocates of the unity of the Prologue have failed to explain why, if the evangelist wrote it all, he did not use in the rest of the book the distinctive terms, ideas, and style in the first eighteen verses.

Landmarks in Prologue Reconstruction

The church fathers, followed by Friedrich Lücke (1820), regarded 1:1-5 as a distinctive section of John. In 1840 Edward Reuss observed the different nature of the first five verses and viewed them as a sort of preface. By 1873 Daniel Schenkel had concluded that verses 1-5 form a prologue in a narrow sense and verses 6-14 a beginning in a broader sense. In the latter half of the nineteenth century B. Weiss, Albert Réville, and Otto Pfleiderer divided the Prologue into three parts: verses 1-5, 6-13, 14-18; some other biblical scholars divided it slightly differently.[1]

The difference in subject content among the sections of the Prologue led Albrecht Ritschl in 1875 to transpose the verses into this order: 1-5, 10-13, 6-9, 14, 16-18, 15.[2] In the same year Julius Wagenmann placed together the statements about John the Baptist by transposing 6-8 with 9-14.[3] In 1892 Harnack recognized enough difference in point of view between the Prologue and the remainder of John to cause him to reject the theory (upheld by Baldensperger in 1898 and Réville in 1901) that the Prologue is the key to the gospel. He interpreted the Prologue as an introduction intended to prepare Hellenistic readers for the book.[4] Although all of these views recognized either differences within the Prologue or differences between it and the body of the gospel, none went so far as to claim that a different author wrote the Prologue or that a source is incorporated in it.

Around the turn of the century a few biblical scholars began to recognize that more than one hand wrote the Prologue, but these interpreters were confused over what was original and what was written later. Wendt (1886-1911) rightly recognized that verses 6-8 and 15 are secondary. He concluded that the rest of the Prologue comes from a source, but he seriously erred by believing that the author of the source was the apostle John.[5] Delff (1890) decided that verses 6-8 belong to the original and that the remainder of the Prologue was interpolated later. Baldensperger in 1898 recognized that verses 6-8 were inserted for apologetic reasons.[6] As Brown has noted, it is generally agreed today that 6-7, 9, 11-12, and 14b, d belong to the original gospel, the Grundschrift, and that the editor added the rest from sources or from his own imagination.

James Rendel Harris (1917) pointed out that Wisdom in Jewish sapiential literature (in Proverbs 8, Wisdom of Solomon 6-9, and Sirach 24) has some of the same attributes as the Word in the Prologue, and that Wisdom is identified with God's Word in the Wisdom of Solomon. He concluded that there originally was a "Sophia-Hymn" (i.e., a hymn to Wisdom) incorporating Jewish developments of the Old Testament idea of divine Wisdom. Harris held that Jesus was early identified with Wisdom, for he is called "the Wisdom of God" in 1 Corinthians 1:24. The author of the Gospel of John recast the hymn by substituting logos for sophia and attaching this "Logos-Hymn" to the gospel as its preface. C. F. Burney (1922) adopted and expanded this theory, claiming that the primitive hymn consisted of eleven couplets in Aramaic.

Harris makes two major mistakes in his argument. First, he overlooks Philo and the fact that there was enough identification of Wisdom with the Word in Hellenistic Judaism to make it quite probable that the term in the original Prologue was Word, not Wisdom. A second mistake is that Harris devotes much space to discussing the interpretations of the church fathers. Their views are too late to throw any light on the origins of the Prologue.

Cecil Cryer (1921) set forth the hypothesis that the evangelist himself had written earlier a hymn on the Logos, consisting of a series of tristiches and disticheses. Later he used it as a preface to his gospel and added verses 6-8 and 12c (he labels the last "12d") in prose. After the gospel was finished someone added 13c and 15 as marginal glosses, and verses 17 and 18 were retouched. Although Cryer erred in thinking that the evangelist wrote the original poem, he correctly recognized verses 6-8, 12c, and 15 as insertions. He was mistaken, however, in believing that 15 was written by a different hand than 6-8 and 12c.

Bernard (1928) decided that the Prologue was written by the same hand that wrote the body of the gospel "to express the writer's conviction that Jesus the Christ was Himself the Divine Logos,"[8] but the evangelist composed it after he had written the gospel. The author wrote first a Logos Hymn consisting of verses 1-5, 10-11, 14, and 18, then added other verses as his commentary on it. Bernard regarded the Logos Hymn as similar to the Odes of Solomon in its mysticism.

Bacon in 1933 maintained that verses 6-8, 12b-13, 14b, and 15 were added by the redactor, who added also many other passages in the gospel, including chapter 21.[9] Thus Bacon looked to a later redactor as the author of the later insertions, and he opened the question of whether the evangelist or the redactor added this material.

Paul Gächter (1936), like Cryer and Bernard, decided that the evangelist wrote a shorter form of the Prologue and later made insertions in it himself. A. Wikenhauser in his commentary on the gospel (1948) also followed this interpretation.

Bultmann (1923, 1941), as we have seen, conjectures that the Prologue and the rest of the Revelation-Speeches source was originally written in Aramaic. This is a serious error,[10] for it overlooks the possibility that the Prologue may be from a different source than the Revelation Speeches and written in a different style. He fails to recognize the significance of the fact that the Semitic-style poetry is in only a portion of the original Prologue. There is no valid evidence supporting Bultmann's opinion that the Prologue and the Revelation Speeches emanated from the followers of John the Baptist. His basis for the conjecture, in addition to the Mandaean literature, is the evangelist's anti-Baptist polemic in verses 6-8, 15, which suggests to Bultmann that the source was a hymn of the Baptist community which regarded John as the Revealer, and the evangelist, a Christian convert from the Baptist community, made the insertions to counteract the beliefs of that community.[11] Bultmann overlooks the existence of anti-Baptist polemic in early Christian literature that definitely was not written by former members of John's sect. Bultmann's reconstruction of the hymn source is: verses 1, (2 ?), 3-5, 9a-b, (10a ?), 10b-c, 11-12b, 14, 16; he excises "man" in 9 and "authority" in 12 for the sake of rhythm. He strongly suspects that verses 2 and 10a were added by the evangelist.[12]

Ernst Käsemann (1957), professor of New Testament at Göttingen, has evaluated Bultmann's analysis of the Prologue. He rejects Bultmann's theory that the basic elements of the Prologue came from a pre-Christian writing, and he concludes that the evangelist used a Christian hymn (verses 1, (2 ?), 3-5, 9-13) as a source. Käsemann divides it into two strophes, the first ending with verse 4, and the second beginning with verse 5. The remainder of the Prologue was composed by the evangelist. Käsemann observes that the "chain-like interweaving" ends with verse 12, and consequently concludes that the source must not extend beyond it.[13] He believes that verse 5 is already a reference to the Incarnation, so he rejects Bultmann's view that the incarnated Logos is first mentioned in verse 14.[14]

Schnackenburg (1957) observes that the Prologue is a unity neither in thought nor in literary structure, and he concludes that there was an original Christian hymn to the Word in which the latter was not incarnated. The hymn has a Jewish background but is wrapped in Hellenistic ideas; it was written in a church located in a syncretistic milieu where Judaism and paganism were borrowing from each other. For the purpose of refuting docetic Gnosticism, the evangelist made additions to transform the Word into Jesus, the incarnate god. According to Schnackenburg the source consists of verses 1, 3-4, 9a-b, 10a, c, 11, 14a-b, e, 16. He divides it into four strophes, ending with verses 3, 9b, 11, and 16, respectively. The remaining material and the rearrangement come from the evangelist.

Schulz (1960), influenced by Bultmann, concludes that verses 1-5, (9), 10-12b, 14, (16), and (18), are from a pre-Christian hymn produced by followers of the Baptist; the verses in parentheses have been retouched by the evangelist. On the basis of rhythm criticism, he regards 6-8, 12-13, 15, and 17-18 as prose supplements to the hymn. Using statistics of the literary style, he finds the most linguistic characteristics of the evangelist in 7, 8, and 12c, and he decides that 5, 13, and 18 have been revised or perhaps composed by the evangelist. Verses 6-8 and 15 are definitely secondary additions.

Haenchen's article published in 1963 analyzes the Prologue in respect to the Christian hymn underlying it and its subsequent revision. Haenchen maintains that the hymn contained a variety as in free rhythm, and therefore a longer verse need not be interpreted as an addition by a different writer. He disagrees with Käsemann's opinion that verse 5 originally referred to the Incarnation. The original hymn consisted of verses 1-5, 9-11, 14, and 16-17. The evangelist added verse 18, and afterwards the redactor who added chapter 21 inserted 6-8, 12-13, and 15. Haenchen rejects flatly Bultmann's claim that the hymn was a gnostic work dedicated to John the Baptist.

Boismard (1963) concludes that in the primitive stage the Prologue of the gospel consisted only of verses 1-5. He does not, however, regard it as a source within a source.

J. A. T. Robinson (1963) presents anew the thesis that the whole Prologue is a unity. He argues that this is shown by the themes and by the structure that are common to it and to the body of the gospel. He believes that the Prologue was added later, however. The same author wrote all the Johannine writings, but in three stages: the body of the gospel, the epistles, and the Prologue and the Epilogue (chapter 21) of the gospel.

Walther Eltester (1964) also defends the unity of the whole Prologue. He contends that the evangelist shifted from poetic to prose forms for the sake of variety to avoid the monotony of the couplet form, and therefore the rhythmic portions are not from a hymn source but merely reflect the manner in which the evangelist wrote.

Josef Blank's reconstruction (1966) is similar to that of Boismard. The source is a Christian hymn in four strophes: verses 1, 3, the divinity of the Logos and his participation in creation; 4, 9, the Logos asarkos ("Word without flesh"; i.e., the preexistent Logos before the Incarnation) as light and life of men; 10-11, the Logos asarkos repelled by men; 14, 16, the Incarnation and the distribution of graces. The evangelist added the remainder, forming the present Prologue in three strophes: 1-5, 6-13, 14-18.

Brown (1966) separates the original hymn into these four strophes: 1-2; 3-5; 10-12b; 14, 16. He concludes there are two sets of additions: one consists of 12c-13 and 17-18, "explanatory expansions of the two lines of the hymn"; the second set consists of 6-9 and 15, "material pertaining to John the Baptist."[15] We observe that verse 9 should not be classified in the second group, however, for it does not pertain to the Baptist. Brown is not certain whether the two sets of additions are the work of one man.

Christoph Demke (1967) believes that the Prologue incorporates a source, which he divides into two parts. The Logos Hymn consists of verses 1, 3-5, and 10-12b, a song used in the Christian community's worship service, and verses 14 and 16, a confession of faith that the community made in response. The evangelist inserted the other verses, except 13, which is a marginal gloss. Käsemann's doubts about verse 2, and the definite exclusion of it from the hymn source by Bultmann, Blank, and Demke constitute an important advance, for it reveals one of the editor's practices; restatement.

Jeremias (1967) observes that the Prologue is constructed with all three basic types of poetic parallelism (synonymous, antithetic, and synthetic), but in addition it contains "step parallelism," a literary device in which the second part of a parallelism repeats and elevates the material or term in the first part. He distinguishes between the "Urprolog" (the hymn source), in which "step parallelism" is characteristic, and the prose commentary added by the evangelist. The verses in his Urprolog are 1-5. 9-12b, 14, 16, 18. He observes that the hymn source is distinguished by certain vocabulary which occurs nowhere else in John, while the prose verses demonstrate the linguistic characteristics of the evangelist. A weakness of Jeremias's position is that much of his Urprolog does not exhibit step parallelism.

A. Feuillet (1968) bases his interpretation on the views of predecessors such as Cryer, Gächter, and J. A. T. Robinson.[16] He agrees with them that the Prologue is an independent hymn that the evangelist composed first, then retouched (only "lightly") when he incorporated it in his gospel. In this conservative view we recognize a return to the effort to maintain the authority of the Prologue by claiming unity of authorship of the Prologue and the rest of the book. He argues that there are numerous lines connecting the doctrine of the Prologue with that of the body of the gospel, especially "its fundamental theme, the revelation of the divine world by the Logos." But, we ask, how can this be when in the Gospel Jesus is never the "Logos," except in the Prologue?

J. C. O'Neill (1969) separates the Prologue into a source, the evangelist's additions, and later glosses. The source consists of three strophes of ten cola each emanating from a Hellenistic Jewish community. The evangelist added verses 6-9, 14a, and 15a. Later glosses occur in verses 4, 12c, 13c, 15b-d, and 18. O'Neill's determination of later glosses on the basis of textual variation is not a reliable approach; textual variants can arise also in material from a source or from the evangelist's pen.

Is the Prologue a unity? Is it from a single source, or from several sources? Has either the editor or the redactor made insertions in it? Johannine scholars today are generally agreed that at least verses 6-8 and 15 are later insertions. Ruckstuhl (1951), Barrett (1955), Dodd (1955), and Eltester (1964) are among the few who have held out for the old view that the Prologue is a unity. We suspect that the influence of traditional interpretation and doctrine and the reaction against Bultmann's conjectural reconstruction are largely responsible.

Knowledge of whether it was the editor or the redactor who abruptly inserted verses 6-8 and 15 is of vital importance, If the insertions were made by the redactor who added the final chapter, they are not evidence that the evangelist used sources. Further, insertions made by a redactor are of no value in determining the literary characteristics of the editor, knowledge which is essential for separating his writing from possible sources. On the other hand, if the editor inserted the four verses, they are definite evidence that written source matter confronts us.

To determine if the Prologue insertions were made by the author of chapter 21, we must compare them with the matter that its author wrote, excluding his source material. Portions which he definitely composed are verses 7a and 18-24. A striking feature of these verses is that personal names are arthrous, that is, accompanied by the Greek article, whereas in the source material utilized in that chapter, personal names usually lack the article. This indicates that the use of the article with personal names is a trait of the writer of the last chapter.

When we turn to the insertions in the Prologue, we find just the opposite. A personal name, John, occurs twice, and in both instances lacks the article. The anarthrous construction here, contrasting with the arthrous syntax of the writer of chapter 21, indicates two different writers and shows that the insertions in the Prologue were not made by the author of the appendix.

As we observed in chapter 9, intensive examination of the rest of the gospel reveals that an editor has produced the book by using written sources and by composing some matter himself. A characteristic of the editor's writing is the absence of the Greek article with personal names, the same trait observed in the Prologue insertions. This fact indicates that it was the editor who made the insertions, and that a later redactor has added chapter 21.

The possibility that the Prologue insertions were composed by a copyist or anyone other than the editor is unlikely because both the subject matter of the insertions (John the Baptist as a witness to Jesus) and the syntax of the insertions[17] are characteristic of the editor's work. The combination of so many traits of the editor in only four verses is very strong cumulative evidence.

A few other passages in the Prologue were inserted by the editor and display some of his characteristics. Verse 2 breaks the chain-linkage style of the adjoining source material, uses introductory houtos as a substantive, and is a restatement of verse 1. At the end of verse 9 the editor added his participial phrase, "coming into the world" (cf. 6:14 and 11:27); he probably was influenced too by the fact that he found in a gnostic speech in 12:46 the idea of Jesus coming as light into the world. His awkward insertion caused confusion through the ages as to whether it is "the light" or "every man" that is coming into the world! In the passages from which the editor derived it the expression refers to Jesus, and it does here too.

Considerable evidence indicates that verse 10 was composed by the editor. (1) Although the style is somewhat similar to the source in verse 1, verse 10 lacks the latter's chain linkage. (2) The source in the next verse uses *idia*, "own things" (i.e., the things the Logos created) as the term for the world, but the editor's term is *kosmos*, used here and in his insertion in 9c. (3) Verse 10 is a continuation of the editor's thought in 9c. (4) Verse 10 exhibits the editor's trait of restatement of source matter: the world was made through the Logos, from verse 3, and the world rejected him, from verse 11. (5) The editor's remark here that the world did not know him is an idea suggested by his gnostic source in which the world does not know the Father, 17:25 (cf. E in 14:7). (6) Verse 10 causes a chronological error: Jesus comes into the world (verse 11) *after* he is already there (verse 10); such confusion often results from insertions and conflations. (7) In verse 9b the relative pronoun is neuter to agree with its antecedent "light," but in verse 10 the pronoun is masculine even though the antecedent is still "light." This indicates that the writer of 10 is not the writer of 9ab.

Turning to verse 12, we find that the editor added at its close the participial phrase, "to those believing on his name." Schnackenburg lists the participle in apposition as a characteristic of the evangelist's style.[18] The expression "believe on his name" occurs three times in John, each written by the editor,[19] as was the related statement in 20:31, "that believing, you may have life in his name."

Verse 17 is a later gloss, as Bultmann recognizes. It is an insertion, for it breaks the line of thought. It was not inserted by either the editor or the redactor, for only here in John occurs the Pauline antithesis "law" vs. "grace," and only here and in 17:3 is found the compound "Jesus Christ" (anarthrous). The editor and redactor use the historical name "Jesus," but not "Jesus Christ." The editor combines the two nouns only in 20:31, and there he preserves the early distinction that "Christ" is a title ("Jesus the Christ"), not a proper name. Further evidence that 17:3 is by neither the editor nor the redactor (nor a source) is that only here in John the word order is "eternal life" instead of "life eternal." In verse 18 of the Prologue *ekeinos*, "that one," is an insertion by the editor for clarity.

After the later insertions are stripped off, the remainder is not a unity but contains two types of material: poetry characterized by chain-linkage construction (word, word: God, God; etc.) and hymn-like material which lacks chain linkage. The single-source theories which have been offered fail to explain this phenomenon satisfactorily. If all but the editorial insertions come from a single hymn source, why is only part of the source written in chain-linkage style? On the other hand, if the source consisted only of the chain-linkage poem, and the rest was written by the evangelist, why did the evangelist write in his part of the Prologue terms and ideas which he never uses elsewhere in the gospel? The solution is that neither situation occurred, but rather the editor used a source, a Christian gnostic hymn, which in turn had incorporated a source, a Hellenistic Jewish poem.

The Jewish Poem

The material from the poem consists of verses 1, 3-5 (except 3c), and 11, and reads as follows:

> 1 In the beginning was the Word, and the Word was with God, and the Word was God. 3 All things came to be through it, and without it nothing came to be. 4 In it was life, and the life was the light of men. 5 And the light shines in the darkness, and the darkness did not overcome it. 11 It came to its own, and its own did not receive it.

Observe the pattern of chain linkage: Word, Word; God, God; came to be, came to be; life, life; light, light; darkness, darkness; its own (*idia*, own things), its own (*idioi*, own people). Although single units of chain linkage occur in John 6:37 and 8:32, this poem is the only passage in the gospel containing a continuous string of this type (seven units). The passage is also the only block of material in John consisting of Semitic parallelism, both synonymous (verse 3) and synthetic (verses 1, 4, 5, 11).[20] The final clause ("which came to be") in verse 3 is a relative clause inserted later by the author of the hymn, for all the clauses in the poem are connected by "and" (*kai*), not by subordination. The reason for assigning 3c to the hymnist instead of the editor of the gospel is that the hymnist uses relative clauses in 9b and 13, whereas when the editor inserted modifying clauses in 9c and 12c, he used participial construction. In fact, the editor prefers--though not exclusively--participles to relative clauses throughout the gospel. *Auton* (masc.) in the present text of verse 11 probably originally read *auto* (neut.), and the hymnist changed it to *auton* to agree with *auton* in the preceding verse and make it refer to Jesus; for this reason *auton* here is translated as "it" instead of "him."

The poem is Jewish; nothing in it is specifically Christian. It springs from the Hebrew Creation story, in which God created by oral commandment. "In the beginning" (en archē) and "came to be" (egeneto) are verbatim from Genesis 1:1, 3 (LXX). In Psalm 32:6 (LXX) logos is the Greek term for the means by which God created: "By the word of the Lord the heavens were made." This kind of thought must have been prevalent in Alexandrian Judaism, for it appears not only in the Septuagint which was translated there, but also in Philo and Wisdom of Solomon.[21] Philo associates the Logos with Light.[22] The warfare between darkness and light is mentioned in the Qumran War scroll.[23] Wisdom of Solomon 7:29-30 states that Wisdom is superior to light because night overcomes light, but "evil cannot overpower Wisdom."[24] Wisdom in Proverbs 8:30 and Wisdom of Solomon 9:9 was with God when he created the world. In Wisdom of Solomon and 1 Enoch Wisdom comes to earth and is rejected;[25] verse 11 presents this kind of thought, not a reference to the Incarnation.[26] Verse 11 is not gnostic, for as Robert Grant has noted, in Gnosticism the divine power which comes from above is received by its own.[27] The Logos in this poem is not gnostic, for it did not originate as an emanation from the Father, either directly or indirectly.

The fusion of life, light, and the creative word occurred also in Graeco-Egyptian syncretism, as Bréhier observed.[28] In the Hermetic cult God the Father created by Logos the existing things,[29] and the Logos is associated with the terms "life" and "light" (CH 1:6).

The poem is simply a statement of an idea prevalent in Judaism at the time. The notion of the rejection of the Word , the idea of the Word as God's creative agent at the beginning, the verbal parallelism with Genesis, and the similarity to Alexandrian Jewish thought all indicate Hellenistic Judaism as the background.

The Christian Gnostic Hymn

Later a Christian Gnostic, probably in Alexandria, added to the Jewish poem verses 3c, 9ab, 12ab, 13, 14, 16, and 18, thereby producing a Christian gnostic hymn. These are the additions he composed:

> 3c which came to be. 9ab He was the true Light, who enlightens every man. 12ab But as many as received him, he gave to them the authority to become children of God, 13 who were begotten, not from bloods nor from the will of the

> flesh nor from the will of man, but from (the will of) God. 14 And the Word became flesh and tented among us, and we have beheld his glory, glory as the only-begotten from the Father, full of grace and truth. 16 So that from his fullness we all received, even grace on grace. 18 No one has ever seen God; the only-begotten god who is in the bosom of the Father has declared (him).

The hymnist added 3c, as the relative clause construction suggests. Verse 9ab does not belong to the Jewish poem, for it contains a relative clause instead of parataxis, and it lacks the chain-linkage style. Verse 12ab is separate from the poem source, for it has a different term for "receive" than in verse 11 (*lambanō* instead of *paralambanō*) and a different word for "and" (*de* instead of *kai*). In verse 13 the term for "man" is *aner*, whereas in the poem and in the editor's composition the term is *anthrōpos*. This writer's work stands apart from the rest of the gospel by virtue of its distinctive expressions ("grace," "fullness," "declare," and "only-begotten god").

The background of the hymn is complex. Its author is a Christian, as the Incarnation in verse 14 shows. There are only a few Jewish aspects. The notion that the Logos "tented among us" has a partial parallel in Sirach 24:8 with its reference to Wisdom pitching its tent in Israel. Somewhat similar to "grace on grace" is Philo's statement that God gives men "ever new graces in exchange for the old."[30] God is invisible, according to Philo and Sirach,[31] but the idea was very prevalent in pagan philosophy too. Perhaps Psalm 84:10-12 (LXX; 85:8-9 Heb.) influenced verse 14 of the hymn, for it too contains the terms "glory," "truth," and a similar verb for "to tent." The passage could seem suggestive to a Christian who was looking for scriptural support for his Incarnation doctrine:

> 10 His [God's] salvation is near to those who fear him, so that glory may tent in our land. 11 Mercy and truth have met together, . . . 12 . . . And righteousness has stooped down from heaven.

The Prologue hymn has more affinity with paganism, however. The author has converted the Logos from the abstract Word of God in the poem to a definite being, a god. In the Hermetic cult literature, too, the Logos is a definite being, the Son of God, and is associated with light. God is "the Father."[32] In the *Corpus*

Hermeticum Pomandres, a god, is "the Logos of Absolute Authority" (CH 1:30). "Grace" has religious significance, for the devotee prays, "With this grace I will enlighten the races that are in ignorance" (CH 1:32). Here, too, the will of God is associated with rebirth: the child of God, by the will of God, is the "creator of rebirth" (CH 13:4). One aspect of the Hermetic Logos is similar to the Logos as creative agent in the Jewish poem: God, the Father of all, "by Logos has constituted the existing things" (CH 1:31).

The universalism of verse 9ab of the hymn suggests the Stoic-Platonic background, especially the Stoic belief in the illumination of all men by the divine Logos, Reason. To express the idea of "true light" our hymn does not use the noun "truth" (alētheia) in the style of the Semitic genitive construct, "light of truth";[33] instead it displays traditional Greek style with its adjective "true" (alēthinos). "Authority" (exousia) in verse 12 is a term used in some pagan mystery cults to express the right bestowed upon the reborn initiate to become immortal by becoming the god himself.[34] Bultmann[35] and Haenchen[36] rightly see Greek influence in verse 13 in the plural "bloods"; compare the hymn's "born from bloods" with Euripides' "bred from other bloods."[37] Although in Wisdom of Solomon Wisdom has an "only-begotten" spirit (7:22), the term "only-begotten" (monogenēs) was more prevalent in paganism. Plato applies the term to the cosmos,[38] and the Stoics adapted the notion to their philosophy by saying that the cosmos, or the Logos which animates it, is "the only-begotten Son of God."[39] In the Orphic hymns the goddesses Demeter, Persephone, and Pallas Athene are each called "only-begotten."[40] "Declare" or "interpret" (exēgeomai) in verse 18 was used in paganism to refer to priests' diclosures of divine prophecies and to describe the direct statements of Apollo at Delphi and the proclamation of the miracles of Serapis.[41]

The Prologue hymn has a strong affinity with Gnosticism, too, especially with the Gospel of Truth. The suggestion[42] that the author of the Gospel of Truth may have used the Gospel of John is not a valid explanation of the parallelism. The parallels are not close enough to indicate necessary literary dependence, and they consist only of features which are not limited to John but were in the general gnostic milieu. In the Gospel of Truth, as well as in John, God is "the Father," he is invisible (20:30), his bosom is mentioned (the Father opens his bosom and reveals his hidden self,

24:9-12), and his "will" is very important ("nothing happens without the will of the Father," 37:24; each of his words is the product of his will alone, a revelation of his Word, 37:4-7). The will of God, however, is vital in Judaism, too (e.g., 1 QH 10:2, 9). In the Gospel of Truth, as in John, Christian Gnostics are God's children ("his children are perfect," 43:20; they who have knowledge of the Father are "little children," 19:28-29). "Truth" has vital religious significance (God is the Father of truth," 16:33; the gnostic doctrine is "the gospel of truth," 16:31). The revealer makes the Father known ("the beloved Son" taught Gnostics about the Father, 30:31-33; Jesus "proclaims what is in the heart of the Father," 20:39-21:1). The plērōma, "fullness," is the source of "grace" (the plērōma fills with grace the deficiency, which has no grace, 35:37-36:8). Jesus serves to enlighten men (the Father [or perhaps "the gospel of truth"] has "enlightened" through Jesus those who were in darkness because of forgetfulness [i.e., they had forgotten that their souls came "from above"], 18:17-21; cf. 24:35-37). Divine glory is cherished, though in the Gospel of Truth it is "the glory of the Father" (which is shared by Gnostics, 42:3-4) and "the glory of the Father's name" (38:5-6) instead of the glory of the Logos.

Admittedly, there are differences between the hymn and the Gospel of Truth; for example, the Logos is not identified with Jesus, the Son, but is quite distinct from him. The differences are not sufficient to indicate lack of gnostic background, however, for there is much variation among other gnostic writings too.

Judging from Irenaeus' report, several early Christian Gnostics exhibited parallels to the thought and terminology of the hymn, though in less concentration than the Gospel of Truth. Saturninus, Basilides, Carpocrates, and Marcion called the Supreme God "the Father." All four Gnostics had a low opinion of physical man and the material world, an attitude implied in the hymn's statement that the children of God are not born of the will of the flesh. Christ is the Light (but not the Logos) in the Christology of the Barbelo-Gnostics. Concern with birth and begetting is characteristic of Gnosticism. Typically the Father is "unbegotten." Irenaeus (i. 1. 1) regards as characteristic of the Gnostics the view that Mind is the Father's "only-begotten." Basilides maintained that Mind (Jesus) is the Father's "first-born," and the Barbelo-Gnostics held that the first angel is "only-begotten." "Truth" and

"Logos" as separate emanations from the Father appear frequently in Gnosticism.

Clearly the author of the Prologue hymn was a Christian Gnostic who lived in a syncretistic environment, and probably was a Gentile. He had some familiarity with Jewish thought and the Septuagint, but had a fuller knowledge of pagan and gnostic beliefs. He was anti-docetic, judging from verse 14, but nevertheless a Gnostic, for not all Christian Gnosticism was docetic (contrary to a prevalent opinion).[43]

Why did he use the Jewish poem? Probably he was attracted to it by its ideas of the preexistence and nonacceptance of the Logos. The latter notion was useful in Christian apologetics to explain the nonacceptance of Jesus as the Christ by the large majority of Jews. In Colossians 1:16 Jesus is the preexistent Son through whom all things were created, although he is not the Logos. If the author of the Prologue hymn knew of this idea, he may have used the Jewish poem because of the similarity. Some pagans believed that the Logos would descend to earth; for example, the Roman Stoic Cornutus (ca. A. D. 65) stated that the divine Hermes "is the Logos that the gods have sent from the sky to us."[44] If the author of the hymn knew of this kind of thinking, it might suggest to him that the Logos of the Jewish poem could be interpreted as a divine figure who descended from heaven and became incarnated. Other connotations of the term *logos* in the Hellenistic world may also have been factors.

What is the origin of the Logos Christology in Christianity? Jesus is not the preexistent Logos elsewhere in the New Testament, not even in the Gospel of John. He is the "Logos of God" in Revelation 19:13, but he is not preexistent. In the earliest Christian gnostic books Jesus is not the Logos. Basilides and the Barbelo-Gnostics included the Logos in their emanations from the Father, but the Logos is not Jesus or the Christ. Ignatius states that "God was manifest as man" (Eph. 19) and once refers to Jesus in gnostic terms as the Logos that has come forth from *Sigē*, "Silence" (Magn. 8), yet in anti-docetic fashion he stresses Jesus' birth from Mary and descent from David. Are we witnessing in the Prologue the birth of the identification of Jesus with the preexistent Logos? If so, the notion originated not from systematic theological thought, but from the chance incorporation of a Hellenistic Jewish poem into a gnostic Christian hymn!

The editor of the gospel, too, lived in a syncretistic milieu, but had a broader knowledge of Judaism and of the issues in the church than the author of the hymn had. The hymn must have appealed to him because its preexistent Logos seemed to fit the notion of a preexistent Son of Man. He, too, was probably attracted to the notion that the Logos was not received by its own. Nevertheless, he did not absorb the content of the hymn into his own thinking, for he did not use in his own composition any features of the hymn, including "Logos" as a title for Jesus.[45]

ERRATA

When there is a difference between the listing of linguistic criteria in chapter 11 and in the Appendix, the Appendix represents the later view of the author.

The Gospel of John consists of four main literary strands, in addition to the Christian Gnostic Hymn used by the editor in the Prologue, a possible post-resurrection stories source or sources in chapter 20, the post-resurrection stories source or sources used by the redactor in chapter 21, and occasional scribal glosses made later by copyists. The main strands are two written sources, the work of the editor who interwove and expanded the sources, and the writing of the redactor who made insertions and added more material at the end. The "unity" of style and thought which has been claimed for the gospel results from two factors: first, the work of all four writers is scattered throughout the book, and second, both the editor and the redactor made modest attempts to unify the diverse material. Faure rightly recognized that the work of the editor, or evangelist as Faure called him, gave some unity to the gospel and obscured the fact that other writers are involved.

One of the editor's sources was a narrative document which I label "S" because of the author's interest in Jesus as a worker of miracles, or "signs." The editor's other major source was a collection of documents expounding a Christian theology of Hellenistic mysticism; I designate it "G" because of its semi-gnostic nature. The source S corresponds only roughly to Bultmann's "Signs Source," "SQ," and Fortna's "Gospel of Signs," while G corresponds only roughly to Bultmann's "Revelation Speeches," "RQ." My assignment of authorship differs considerably from theirs because I selected some other criteria. Bultmann's Signs Source does not go beyond 12:38, whereas Fortna and I agree that the narrative source extends into the Passion story. Unlike my G, Bultmann's RQ includes the source in the Prologue and excludes all narrative material. The editor used only portions of S and G, so we cannot reconstruct the original source documents. "E" designates the work of the editor, and "R" indicates the work of the redactor. All four symbols are employed also to refer to the respective writers themselves.

The ideal type of evidence consists of terms, syntactic constructions, and ideas which only one of the writers uses, and uses repeatedly. Such evidence provides criteria which enable us to detect passages by that particular writer. Many tests of the evidence must be made however, before we can be sure that a feature is a trait of one writer only. Most of us have made the mistake, at least temporarily, of wrongly assuming that only one writer exhibits a certain trait, and on the basis of that assumption we have assigned to one man some work of another. Nevertheless, each writer in John does have traits peculiar to himself, and failure to recognize this fact has led to the erroneous conclusion that the work of the different writers cannot be separated. After these criteria are determined with certainty, they are necessary tools.

Even if a feature is used by three of the writers, recognition of its absence in the writing of the fourth writer can be valuable. For example, if S, G, and E have a trait which R does not have, and we encounter an insertion into source material, the presence of the trait in the insertion tells us that the insertion was made by the editor, not the redactor.

In general, syntax and vocabulary preference among synonymous terms are more reliable guides than vocabulary with different meaning. Two terms which mean "go" illustrate preference among synonymous terms: S and E prefer hupagō, but G prefers poreuomai. Sometimes the editor borrows ideas and synonymous terms from G, especially if at the moment he is using a G passage containing them. Therefore great care must be exercised in using vocabulary and ideas as guides in separating the sources from the editor's writing.

S

The S source was not written very early. In 11:48 it alludes to the destruction of the temple in Jerusalem, which occurred in A.D. 70. In various passages S displays the influence of the Gospel of Mark and possible the Gospel of Matthew. Since Mark was written after A.D. 75, S is later that that date.

The author was familiar with Jewish Christianity, for he incorporates some of its terms and ideas. In S Jesus is the messianic Prophet (4:19; 6:14; 7:40), while the Baptist is not (1:21). Jesus, like Hebrew and Hellenistic pagan prophets, has extraordinary knowledge, and this is a cause of belief that he is the Messiah (4:29, 42). Jesus is human, "the son of Joseph" (1:45). Peter's name is his original, Hebrew name, "Simon." Jesus is addressed as a Jewish teacher, "Rabbi." The author knows the Gospel of Matthew, which was written in a Jewish-Christian community. S knows the Septuagint, for in 2:4 he quotes verbatim 3 Kings 17:18 (1 Kings 17:18 in Hebrew and English Bibles): "What (is that) to me and to you?" This feature does not necessarily indicate a Jewish background, however, for gentile as well as Jewish Christians used the Septuagint.

S knows the Semitic world, for he uses the Aramaic term "Cephas," the Aramaic form of the word "Messiah," and "Rabbi" (which is either Hebrew or Aramaic), then explains them to his Greek-speaking readers with an expression such as "which is interpreted." He writes in Semitized Greek, introducing sentences with kai more frequently than any of the other writers in John. His usage of poieō, "make," in 6:10 ("make the men recline") reflects the Semitic causative construction.

Although S reflects the Semitic background, he is not a Jewish-Christian. This fact is shown by his usage of the expression "the Jews," placing them in a separate category from Christians, and by his hostile attitude toward them in the Passion story. He employs the expression in 11:19; and eight times in chapter 19. His attitude toward Jews (but not Pharisees) is neutral or even friendly (11:19) until he reaches the Passion story, then like the other gospel writers, he blames them for Jesus' death (19:14-16).

The author is acquainted with Jewish criticism of early Christianity, and tries to meet some of the objections. In response to the claim of the Baptist's followers that John, not Jesus, was the Christ, S represents John as emphatically denying that he is the Christ or the messianic Prophet. To combat Jewish denials that Jesus was the Christ, S (in common with the other writers in John) stresses the necessity of believing in Jesus as the Christ. S tries to counteract the Jewish charge that Jesus could not possibly be the Christ because he came from Galilee and was not a descendant of David (7:41-49).

It is not an accident that S is so concerned with "signs." The Pharisees maintained that if Jesus were the Christ, he would perform signs (Mark 8:11; Matt. 12:38). Others besides Jesus claimed to be the Christ, and they displayed "signs and wonders" as proof (Mark 13:22). Apparently the historical Jesus did no signs, for in Mark 8:12 we find the answer that no signs will be given. S goes farther than Matthew or Luke in claiming that Jesus performed miracles, for in it Jesus performs seven of them of which the first two are specifically called "signs."[1] To S the signs are of vital importance because they lead to belief on Jesus (2:11; 4:53), they arouse the desire of the chief priests and Pharisees to arrest Jesus (7:32a), and they form the central theme on which the book closes (20:30).

The controversy between the early Christians and the Pharisees apparently reached its peak in the last quarter of the first century, especially after the Pharisees at the "Council of Jamnia" excommunicated the Christians. Consequently S and the Gospel of Matthew, both of which were written shortly after the Council, represent the Pharisees as the main opponents of Christianity. Only one passage in S (3:1-2) presents a Pharisee in a favorable light: he calls Jesus "a teacher from God." According to S, many Jews believe on Jesus as a result of his miracles, and therefore S's attitude towards them is friendly. But in chapter 11 the author's attitude changes to hostility as he shifts from the Jews who believed in Jesus to the mass of Jews who did not (11:46-50, 54).

S suggests that many Jews believed on Jesus and that this caused the Romans to destroy the Jewish temple (11:48). This claim is not true, of course, for the Romans destroyed Jerusalem with its temple because the Jews revolted against Roman rule. The claim is only Christian apologetics.

The doctrine that belief on Jesus is the basis of salvation is sufficient evidence alone to disprove any theory that S represents primitive Christian tradition, either oral or written. Jesus (Mark 1:15) and his disciples (Acts 2:38; 3:19) preached that repentance --not belief on Jesus--is basic, but neither the verb "to repent" nor the noun "repentance" even occur in S or in any other part of the Gospel of John. All the writers in John reflect the later stage in which deification of Jesus by gentile Christians and the Jewish disbelief that Jesus was the Christ had caused Christians to shift the basis of salvation from repentance to belief on Jesus.

S's syntax and vocabulary provide criteria for detecting the S material. In John only S uses *te* for "and" or "both," "after this" at the beginning of a sentence, and *hōs* in the sense of "about" with numbers. Except in P, only S has *tote oun* for "then." Only S (and a source used by the redactor in chapter 21) uses the term *ploion*, "boat," instead of *ploiarion*, "little boat." "Crowd" as the subject of a plural verb occurs only in S, except that E borrowed it in 11:42. With the exception of E in 8:44 and 52, only S has a compound subject with a singular verb. There are some syntactic traits which are not exclusive in S, but are quite characteristic of it. The author tends to use indefinite subjects of verbs, such as "one of [prep. ek] his disciples" (6:8) and the indefinite "they" (1:21; RSV supplies "people"). E and R often feel compelled to correct this trait by supplying some name or other (e.g., 1:40). Nevertheless, S likes to give his account the appearance of historical accuracy by stating a specific passage of time (2:1; 4:43; 11:6); he gives a precise measurement of quantity in 2:6. Although personal names are arthrous in S, Old Testament personal names are anarthrous; this presumably is the result of Septuagint influence. Unlike E, S uses apo for "from" in the expression "from a city." The non-exclusive features are not so reliable as criteria as are the exclusive ones, but still are valuable because evidence is cumulative.

On the other hand, certain terms and elements of syntax never occur in S but are present in two or more of the other writers: "the Son," "the Son of Man," "it is necessary," "truly, truly, I say to you," the verb "be about to," pempō for "send," and reference to Jesus' "word" (logōs). This knowledge helps us to recognize non-S material.

Contrary to Bultmann and Schnackenburg,[2] the narrative source in John extends into the Passion story. This is demonstrated by the presence of many of S's characteristics in the Passion, including the repeated article in narrative material (18:10), a compound subject with a singular verb (18:1), and tote oun for "then" (19:1, 16). The opinion that the narrative source does not extend into the Passion story is partly the result of too much influence from Faure's mistaken theory that the first half of John is completely different from the second half.

An interesting theory is that S was a story of miracles Jesus performed after his resurrection. One bit of evidence for the theory is that S labels Jesus' first miracle as the beginning of the manifestation of his glory, and in early Christianity the risen Jesus was described as glorified. Post-resurrection stories about Jesus must have originated early, for the Transfiguration in Mark is such a story which the evangelist incorporated in his gospel. Further evidence is the fact that S is very concerned with the disciples' disbelief in Jesus, and his first sign causes the disciples to believe on him (2:11). According to early Christian tradition the disciples at first had difficulty in believing that Jesus had risen from the dead; as I have explained elsewhere,[3] belief in Jesus' resurrection soon became crucial for belief that he was the Christ.

Historically, the disciples' disbelief in Jesus' messiahship was a problem after Jesus' death, not before, because it arose from their disbelief in his resurrection. Consequently, there was need for miracle stories in the post-resurrection setting, and some stories must have been created to meet that need.

In spite of the evidence, S itself could not have been a post-resurrection narrative, for it concludes with the story of Jesus' death (and resurrection ?). What the total evidence does suggest is the probability that S has been influenced by an account of miracles performed by the risen Jesus. This explains the presence of post-resurrection features in a narrative which is in a pre-crucifixion framework. All the canonical gospels push back into Jesus' lifetime issues which first arose after his death. In S, as in the Transfiguration in Mark, it is probable that miracle stories which originally were in a post-resurrection setting have been transferred into Jesus' earthly career.

G

The use by the editor of a written source, "RQ," which consisted of a collection of revelation discourses, or speeches, is a major feature in Bultmann's hypothesis. Schnackenburg, however, flatly rejects the existence of any "logia or discourse source" and ascribes to the redactor the "clearly defined complexes of discourse which interrrupt the flow of the presentation . . . "[4] Although Bultmann erred in his views on the nature and content of the speech source, he, not Schnackenburg, is right on the issue of the existence of such a source.

It is easily demonstrated that most blocks of speech material were not composed or inserted by the redactor: the editor, who preceded the redactor, has made many insertions in them. Also, some units of the speech material were composed by the editor himself, for they exhibit his traits, including anarthrous personal names (e.g., 14:4-6a, 8-9) and restatement of source material (e.g., 17:7-12a, which restates several of G's ideas).

Some of the speech material definitely comes from a written source. It contains linguistic features not found in the writing of either the editor or the redactor. One feature in particular is prevalent enough and distinctive enough to prove the existence of the source G: the possessive adjective, with the article repeated with both the adjective and the noun, occurs in John 29 times, and every occurrence is in G.[5] The fact that this construction never occurs in S, E, or R demonstrates that it is in a source and the source is not S. Also, the editor has treated this source in the same ways he treated S: he has expanded it by using catchwords as a connecting link (e.g., 6:29, 36), he has restated it (e.g., 6:33, 40), and made block insertions into it to expound his favorite themes (e.g., 8:44-47a). The fact that distinctive ideas, distinctive syntax, and distinctive vocabulary coincide in the same material, apart from S, E, and R, demonstrates amply that we are dealing with a separate source.

A mistake frequently made in the past has been to regard chapters 14-17 (or 15-17) as quite distinct from the rest of the gospel because they are much longer than any other blocks of speech material. Actually, the same kinds of material are in the rest of the book. This section differs from the rest of the gospel in that the editor has inserted more of his own composition and he has not incorporated any of S in it. This lack of narrative material from S makes this section appear unique.

There are certain syntactic features and vocabulary which distinguish G. Only in this source do we find in John the expressions "fill joy" and "fill sorrow," the verb "walk" in a figurative sense, "even as . . . thus" (kathōs . . . houtōs), "the Father's word" (logos), eipon (2nd aorist tense ending) for "they said" (except 6:25), the repeated article with the possessive adjective, "everything" instead of "everyone," the verb "complete" (teleioō), "never" (pōpote plus a negative), "pass" (metabainō), idou instead of ide for "behold," and ek for "from" in the phrase "from God." Only in G does this word order occur: "answered" plus indirect object plus subject plus "and said."

Some linguistic features occur in the work of one or more of the other writers too, but G uses them consistently and thus they are among G's characteristics. These include pempō for "send," the preposition ek used instead of the partitive genitive, aiteō instead of erōtaō for "ask" in the sense of "request" or "pray," skotia instead of skotos for "darkness" (except in 3:19), and the expression "from (apo) self."

G has a strong tendency to use a third group of linguistic characteristics, although not necessarily consistently. These include "the Son," "commandment," "it is necessary," "truly, truly, I say to you," "Jesus' word" (logos), poreuomai for "go," phileō for the verb "to love," Jesus' "name," the article repeated with both noun and adjective, "Son of Man," the possessive adjective instead of the genitive of the personal pronoun, the dative of time instead of a preposition in the expression "on the last day," and the cognate accusative ("work the works" in 3:21, 6:28, and 9:4; "rejoice with joy" in 3:29; "will to do his will" in 7:17).

Was G written by more than one writer? The possibility is suggested by some variety within the G material. We must be careful not to assign to G any matter written by another writer, thereby making G appear to contain more diversity than it does. Nevertheless, in a few source passages which are similar to other G material we find a distinctive trait or two which suggest either that they are from a different source or sources, or that G was composite. The passage in 3:16, 19-21 stands out as different from the rest of G. In it agapaō is the verb for "love," epi is the preposition instead of eis in the expression "believe on," and skotos instead of skotia is the noun for "Darkness." Possibly it was composed by the editor, but the repeated article in verse 16 makes this doubtful.

In the conflation of two stories of a Samaritan woman, one at a spring (from S) and one at a well (from G), we find a G passage (4:20-23) that differs from the rest of the gospel. Only here is Jesus addressed with "you" in the plural, and only here is the name "Jerusalem" both anarthrous and plural. Is this passage from a different source entirely, or does it reveal that G was composite?

A surprising result of this investigation is the discovery that there was more narrative in the "speech source" than previously recognized. Only part of the narrative has been transmitted to us, for the editor used only portions of his sources. The big surprise is that G apparently contained a Passion story account. The fragments of it are in 18:15-18, 25b-29, 31, 33-40. Here "another disciple" is superior to Peter because he can enter the high priest's court, but Peter needs the disciple's help in order to do so; Peter denies three times that he knows Jesus; Pilate tries Jesus on the charge of being king of the Jews; Jesus, in semi-gnostic fashion, assures Pilate that his kingdom is not of this world.

The redactor did not compose this material, for it lacks his characteristics, and his writing lacks the distinctive features in these passages. He did not insert it, because the editor has made insertions in it, and it contains two of G's most distinctive traits: the repeated article with the possessive adjective (18:36, three times), and "from (apo) self" (18:34).

No definite indication of date is given in G. Its use by the editor shows that it was written before he produced the gospel, but its semi-gnostic ideas and its blaming all the Jews for Jesus' death indicate lateness. Plainly it was written after the relations between gentile Christianity and Judaism had reached the breaking point. G can hardly be earlier than A.D. 90-100.

The author of G is a gentile Christian, for he separates himself and Christianity completely from Jews and Judaism. In 8:17 he refers to the Old Testament as "your (i.e., Jews') law," not as "the law" or "our law." Rejection of the Mosaic law was typical among Christian Gnostics.[6] Jews as descendants of Abraham are apart from Jesus, since his word has no place in them (8:37). G refers to Jews as "the Jews" and puts the responsibility for Jesus' death on Jews as a whole, not on the Sadducees or any other group, and above all, not on the gentile Pilate!

The background of G is gnostic or at least semi-gnostic. The following notions indicate this: God is "the Father," who transfers his own authority to the Son and has sent him into the world to give it life eternal; "the world" is inherently bad ("its works are evil," 7:7) and (consequently) the disciples are not of the world (15:19; 17:14); being "born from above" is fundamental for salvation (3:3, 7; cf. Gospel of Truth 22:3-4 where the Gnostic is "from above");[7] Jesus came from the Father and to the Father he is returning. The idea that God's Son seeks to do the will of God (5:30) is similar to the statement in pagan Gnosticism that God's Powers accomplish his will (Poimandres 31).

Although there are some Semitic linguistic expressions in G, there is little Jewish thought. G's background is pagan, not Jewish. He illustrates the validity of Colwell's conclusion that Hellenistic Greek in pagan society had absorbed some Semitisms. The Semitisms in G include "do the truth" (3:21), "sons of Light" (12:36), "Spirit of Truth" (16:13), and "walk" in a figurative sense (8:12; 11:9-10; 12:35).

Unlike E, G displays only a little knowledge of the issues between Jews and Christians. He does, however, know that some Jews have believed in Jesus and have lost that faith (8:31, 37). G stresses the idea that Jesus is the "Son of Man" who has come down from heaven and that it was absolutely necessary for him to return to it so that everyone who believes in him may have life eternal (3:13-15). This view is intended to solve a problem in the early church. Christians claimed that Jesus was the Messiah who fulfilled prophecy, but Jews must have pointed to the obvious fact that Scripture does not predict a Messiah who would ascend to heaven and return to earth. Apparently Hellenistic Jewish Christians (cf. Acts 7:56) were the first to identify Jesus with the Son of Man type of Messiah (the type in the Parables of 1 Enoch) in an effort to meet the Jewish objection. The Son of Man in the Parables is preexistent in heaven and will descend to earth to conduct the judgment, but he does not return to heaven. Thus the identification of Jesus with the Son of Man was only a partial solution to the problem; it provides apocalyptic support for the notion that the Messiah is presently in heaven and will come down to earth in the future, but gives no support to the Christian invention that the Messiah has been on earth first, then ascended to heaven, and will come to earth a second time. Our deduction that the Christian problem caused the identification is supported by the fact that G usually associates the title "Son of Man" with Jesus in heaven or with his descent and ascent. The identification is carried a step farther in 5:27 by associating the Son of Man with the resurrection, as in the Parables. R (and G ?) states that one must eat the flesh and drink the blood of the Son of Man (6:53-58); R thus loses touch with the earlier concepts of the Son of Man.

In primitive Christian faith the belief that Jesus has ascended to heaven is combined with the necessary belief that he will return to earth and establish the kingdom of God. In Gnosticism, however, eternal life is in heaven, not on earth; Jesus' ascension is fundamental for believers' salvation because Jesus as the savior god must first pave the way by his example for the ascension of Christian souls to heaven. G is less unorthodox; in it the Son of Man will return to conduct the resurrection and judgment. G's position on eschatology is not clear, probably because in this encounter the tenets of eschatology and of Gnosticism are not reconciled. Immortality is in heaven (14:2-3) and Jesus' kingdom is not of this world (18:36); these ideas are compatible with Gnosticism. Jesus judges, but not necessarily at the last judgment (5:30; 8:16). On the other hand, on the last day Jesus will raise all that the Father has given to him (6:39); this idea is compatible with Hellenistic Jewish Christianity and "orthodox" gentile Christianity.

P ?

Is there a separate written source in the Passion story, as Bultmann claims? If there is, it is only in 20:1-8, for S and G apparently are the only sources in the rest of the Passion narrative.

A source has been used in this section, for the editor has made insertions into the basic material. Some of the editor's traits which appear are anarthrous personal names, "Simon Peter" without the article, and restatement.

A few traits of the redactor are present in this source material: arthrous "Peter," the preposition eis for "to" in the expression "come to," and the title "the Lord." Nevertheless, this must not be R's writing, because the editor has made insertions in it and he wrote earlier than R.

Two of S's characteristics occur: a singular verb with a compound subject (v. 3) and tote oun for "then" (v. 8). But verse 3 contains a feature which is contrary to S's practice: "come" is followed by eis instead of pros.

Although verses 3-5a and 8 have essentially the same theme as G's story in 18:15-18, 25b-27 (the superiority of "the other disciple" to Peter), they probably are from a different source because they lack the repeated article which occurs twice in G's story. In G "the other disciple" has the repeated article except when he is introduced (where the expression means "another disciple"); in the P source "the other disciple" occurs three times and never has the repeated article.

I found the passage 20:1-8 extremely difficult. Perhaps the redactor has been active here. My conclusions concerning P are only tentative.

E

In 12:42 the editor alludes to the Pharisees' exclusion of the Christians from the synagogues; this excommunication began about A.D. 90. As we have concluded, one of his sources, S, was written around the year 95. Thus the editor wrote after 95. On the other hand, the redactor wrote before the famous John Rylands Library fragment, P^{52}, was produced, because that papyrus contains R's insertion in 18:32. The date of P^{52} apparently is the second quarter of the second century, and considering the respective points of view of E and R, E probably wrote soon after G was written, but several decades may separate the work of E and R. Therefore E probably wrote around A.D. 100-110, and R probably around 125-

135.

The editor's vocabulary and syntax provide us with many objective criteria for detecting his work. The features which occur only in E include *rēma* (always in the plural) instead of *logos* for "word"; the plural "Scriptures" instead of the singular; "even as . . . also" (*kathōs* . . . *kai*); "Father's name" and "believe on Jesus' name"; "hide"; "say to" with the preposition *pros*, preceding the subject; "Peter" and "Simon Peter" without the article (R has them with it); "is having been written"; "Sabbath" without the article; "ruler of this world"; *theaomai* for "see"; the demonstrative pronouns *houtos*, "this," and *ekeinos*, "that" as *repeated* subjects or objects; *legō*, "say," without a preposition to refer to the person spoken of, as in "whom I said" (1:15) instead of "concerning whom I said" (1:30). Especially useful because it occurs often, is E's characteristic of always omitting the article with personal names; only R's source or sources in chapter 21 share this trait. Although other writers omit the article with Old Testament names, compound names, and in definite constructions, E is the only major writer in John to make *all* personal names anarthrous.

E uses certain other linguistic features consistently, but one or more of the other writers use them too. These include *hupagō* instead of *poreuomai* for "go"; *eipan* (1st aorist tense ending) for "they said"; *agapaō* instead of *phileō* for "to love"; "Judas, (son) of Simon Iscariot," instead of "Judas the Iscariot"; "Devil" instead of "Satan"; a preposition instead of the dative of "day" in the expression "on that day"; *erōtaō* for "ask" instead of *aiteō* in the sense of "request," "pray"; and unlike S, *ek* for "from" in the expression "from" a city.

Less reliable, but nevertheless of some value as criteria, are the features which are neither exclusively nor consistently used by E, but for which he has a strong preference. As we will presently observe, sometimes the inconsistency results from the editor's temporary attraction to the style of the source material he is quoting. These include "the Son of God" in arthrous form; *apostellō* preferred to *pempō* for "send"; *para* for "from" in "from God"; the personal pronoun in the genitive case instead of the possessive adjective to indicate possession; "it is necessary"; the disciples "remember" (only E uses the verb *mimnēskomai* for "remember"); the demonstrative pronoun used as a substantive (demonstrated in E's insertion in the Prologue in 1:7-8); the verb *mellō*, "be about to," substituted for the future tense; "was/were saying" (lego̅ in the imperfect tense); "on account of this"; nun preferred to arti for "now"; meta for "with"; "not . . . but in order that"; "crowd" as the subject of a singular instead of a plural verb; para for "from"; the preposition pros used in the expression "go to"; and the phrase "my Father." The editor has a strong tendency to use the expression "answered and said," and only he has this word order: "answered" plus noun subject plus "and said" plus indirect object, as in "answered John and said to him."

E frequently uses a few expressions which he apparently borrowed from his sources. That E has derived "truly, truly, I say to you" from G is indicated not only by its presence in G (and not in S), but by the fact that it occurs in E only when the editor is reworking G material. In G "you" is always in the plural, for it is always addressed to a group; this is not always the case in E and R.

The term palin, "again," is used occasionally by S and G, and frequently by E and R. The editor may have derived it from his sources, while the gospel as a whole must have suggested it to the redactor. E and R employ it in their own compositions: for example, E in 8:21 and R in 21:1. E and R also insert "again" in material they incorporate in order to tie together pericopes in the same setting or various repetitions.

E's material exhibits the typical characteristics of insertions: abrupt change in subject matter and abrupt change in vocabulary and syntax. The editor's insertion of verses 6-8 in the Prologue illustrates these traits. The topic shifts from the Word (source) to John (E), then back to the Word (source); this is the ABA pattern. The syntax abruptly changes too, for the chain linkage in the source disappears, while participles, dangling construction, omission of the verb "be," hina purpose clauses, and demonstrative pronouns used as substantives suddenly appear.

The editor's method of constructing the gospel is very interesting to observe. A good point at which to start our observation of his technique is his typical treatment of narratives in his source S. Sometimes he copies essentially the whole story in S and merely inserts a few expansions and interpretations. This is the case with John's "confession" that he is inferior to Jesus in chapter one, and the miracle at the wedding in Cana in chapter two. It is more characteristic of the editor to copy only the beginning of a narrative and use it merely as a framework for ideas he wishes to promote, which he presents by writing his own material and by quoting extracts from G. An example is the story of the Pharisee to whom the editor gives the name "Nicodemus." This concrete story in which a Pharisee praises Jesus as a miracle worker is used to introduce abstract, semi-gnostic themes. E's procedure here illustrates another technique: the presentation of his ideas through the medium of "conversations." Another example of that technique is in 14:4, 8, where we encounter "Thomas says to him," "Philip says to him." As many biblical interpreters have observed, the people serve to ask questions or make comments to give Jesus an opportunity to state the author's view (including those in G with which he agrees.). A semi-conversational form is "(some) were saying . . . others were saying" (9:8-9); E apparently borrowed this literary device from S (7:40-41; 9:16).

Occasionally E reports much of a story, but censors a statement he dislikes by substituting something else. In 18:30 E substitutes an exonerating statement for the Jewish accusation against Jesus in G.

At times the editor writes a paragraph or more consisting of abstract ideas, which often are related to the G source. When he does, his thoughts are liable to be quite rambling, loosely connected. This trait supplies us with a test for distinguishing E from G material: the reasoning in a G paragraph is more logical.

In the ancient world some thinking was on the basis of catchwords, and much illogical reasoning and many foolish conclusions were the result. Both Jews and Christians lifted Old Testament passages out of their context and misinterpreted them on the basis of a term they contained. The editor of John uses this method in 2:17 when he quotes Psalm 69:10 LXX (69:9 Heb.). "House" in the Psalm refers to the family, but E applies it to "my Father's house," the temple! Non-biblical statements, too, were associated with each other on the basis of keywords. Luke 16:13 is linked to the Parable of the Dishonest Steward by the term "mammon," yet disagrees with it. The point of the parable is that you should use unrighteous mammon "to make friends for yourselves," but in verse 13 you should have nothing to do with it because "you cannot serve God and mammon." The two sayings in Mark 9:49-50 are grouped together because they contain the catchword "salt," but they do not belong together because in 49 salt is punishment to avoid, while in 50 it is something good you should have.

Our editor, too, uses catchwords as a basis for connecting extracts from source material. Verses 8-16 in chapter 3 furnish a good example. E refers to his semi-gnostic teaching as "heavenly things" which should be believed. This suggests to him that this is a proper place to insert a passage from G which speaks of the necessity of the ascension of the Son of Man into "heaven" so that everyone who believes in him may have "life eternal." The thought in the two passages is unrelated; E has associated them merely because of the terms "believe" and "heaven"/"heavenly things." Next E inserts an extract from a source because it too contains the expression "life eternal"; the type of thought, however, is quite different.

Often E employs a catchword or an idea in a source passage as a springboard for writing an insertion of his own. For example, the statement in G in 14:3 about "going" to prepare a place for the disciples induces E to expand the notion by adding "where I am going, you know the way," a gnostic idea. E here substitutes his favorite term for "go" for the one in the source. Then E continues in verse 5 by means of the catchword "way" (in G in verse 6) to build up his notion that one must know the way. In E "way" is the literal way to heaven, but in G here Jesus is the Way in a more abstract sense.

At times E's connecting link is an idea rather than a term. An illustration of this is 9:4-5; here the specific terms are "day" and "Light," but the linkage rests on the notion of light. E's insertion of 1:6-8 is on the grounds of a negative idea. The interpretation of Jesus as the Light in the Christian Hymn source, and the editor's deep concern to persuade readers that John the Baptist is inferior to Jesus, suggest to E that this is a good place to point out that John was not the Light.

Occasionally the editor's insertions that are less than a sentence in length produce unnecessary double construction, such as two subjects or two objects. When he inserted 1:12c he created a double indirect object. His additions within 17:21, 23, produced a double set of purpose clauses in each of these verses.

He can confuse the thought as well as the syntax when he makes additions. This is the case in chapter 8. The Jews who formerly believed in Jesus are not beyond hope in G: they can still be again his disciples and know the truth (8:31-32). But E's insertions make them sons of their father the Devil, who will never believe (8:44-45); E is really thinking of Jews in general, not just apostates.

Does the editor imitate the style of his source, as Bultmann maintained? He does not systematically do so, for if he did, he would be more consistent in adopting their linguistic characteristics and he would not have used so many of his own traits that differ from those in his sources. Earlier in this chapter we listed 15 traits which occur only in E, and we have observed, too, that some of the traits in S and G are not in E. Clearly the editor did not try very hard to "cover up his tracks."

Occasionally, however, the editor was temporarily influenced by the style of his sources. This applies to vocabulary more than to syntax. When the editor is quoting and expanding source material, he is sometimes attracted, perhaps unconsciously, to terms in the source. When E varies from his customary diction, the uncommon term can usually be found nearby in the source material. We have already noted that "truly, truly, I say to you" occurs in E only when he is using G material. The editor's favorite verb for "send" is *apostellō*, but at times the G source induced him to use its term, *pempō*; apparently E uses *pempō* in 15:26 under the influence of G in 16:7. *Blepō* is not E's usual term for "see," but in chapter 9 he uses it seven times, apparently as a result of the influence of the source story in S (9:7, 15). The influence of the diction in the hymn source in the Prologue is clear in E's use in 1:6-8 of "through him" and *egeneto* for "was." From S the editor borrowed the syntactic expression "believe on" (from 2:11) and the idea that Jesus did "signs" (from 2:11; etc.). Many college students today demonstrate in their term papers the tendency to be inconsistent because they are influenced by the style of source materials which they are using at the time.

The editor's policy in respect to the formulas introducing sayings is important to recognize, because it aids in separating his writing from that of the sources. If the passage he was quoting did not begin with an introductory formula (e.g., "Jesus said"), he wrote one; if it already had such a formula, he quoted it.

A prominent literary trait in E's writing is restatement of source material for the sake of emphasis, modification, or expansion of thought. From the reader's standpoint, the repetition often seems unnecessary. Often the original statement is near the repetition. Examples of the editor's restatement are 1:2, 5:25, 6:33, 6:40, 8:52b, and 14:21a which restate 1:1, 5:24 and 28-29, 6:32 and 51, 6:39, 8:51, and 14:15 respectively.

The editor's restatement of source material provides information that is very valuable for the discovery of his linguistic characteristics, which in turn, supply objective criteria for recognizing his work. In his very first restatement (1:2) his fondness for using the demonstrative pronoun as a substantive appears. E likes the personal pronoun in the genitive case instead of the possessive adjective; a clear example is his restatement in 8:52 of G in the preceding verse. Where G has the possessive adjective, "my word," E changes to the personal pronoun, literally "the word of me." E prefers the articular participle ("the one having," etc.; e.g., 14:21a) and the demonstrative pronoun ("that one") used as a repeated subject. When in 6:40 he restates the preceding verse, he changes pas from neuter gender to masculine, displaying his preference for "everyone" to G's "everything."

The editor's restatements not only provide objective criteria for recognizing his writing, but also furnish valuable insight into his procedure. Although he often changed the text when he restated source material, he allowed the text to stand when he quoted it. Contrary to E Schweizer's conclusion, the editor did not revise his source material stylistically and therefore it is possible to separate the source material from the editorial work.

When E restates source material, he naturally repeats some, but not all, of the vocabulary in the source. For example, in 1:2 he repeats from the source in the preceding verse the expressions "in the beginning" and "with God." This explains why vocabulary alone is not a reliable guide in separating the sources from the editorial writing. Other tests must be applied, and vocabulary criteria must be used intelligently.

The editor's insertions are of many types. In 1:2 he neither changes nor adds to the thought in the source. In 1:6-8 he inserts an idea which is entirely different from that in the source. In 1:9c he inserts a phrase of his own (cf. 12:46) in order to expand the thought in 1:10a. His addition of 1:12c is intended to explain what is meant by "receiving" the Logos: they who receive him are those who believe on his name. E frequently makes explanatory remarks or commentary on his source material, as Bultmann recognizes.

When E cites Old Testament, he quotes from the Septuagint, but he quotes quite loosely. An example occurs in 12:40. Another literary trait of the editor is his tendency to make definite the persons who are mentioned indefinitely in S. Accordingly he assigns the names "Andrew" (1:40; 6:8), "Nicodemus" (3:1), "Lazarus" (11:1, 11, 14, 43), "Mary" (11:1, 19, 20, 28), and "Malchos"

(18:10). He has inserted names also in 11:49, 12:22, and 18:13.

The editor's religious beliefs are much closer to those of G than of S. He generally agrees with the semi-gnostic theology and Christology of G. Although he follows S in claiming that Jesus performed miracles and that one must believe on him to have life eternal, his doctrine of the nature of Jesus, of the world, and of the process of salvation is definitely semi-gnostic, like G. In chapter 3 he repeats for emphasis G's statement that a person must be born again. E's "where I am going, you know the way" in 14:4 rests upon the belief that the Gnostic will be saved because he knows the way his soul can ascend past the planets into heaven. E agrees with G emphatically and repeatedly that Jesus has descended from heaven and that God sent him. Knowing whence Jesus has come is essential in both G (7:28) and E (8:14).

Sometimes, however, E's hostility to the Jews causes him to disagree with statements in G. In 7:28 G has a friendly attitude towards the audience: "you know me." E proceeds to interpret this as being addressed to the Jews, so he reverses the tone: the audience does not know God and it tries to seize Jesus.

Much of the editor's thought deals with issues in early Christianity. He tries to solve the problem of the late origin of some Christian ideas by claiming that later "the disciples remembered" (2:17, 22; 12:16) or "will remember" (16:4). To counteract the charge that Christians have violated monotheism by making Jesus equal to God, E represents Jesus as saying "the Father is greater than I" (14:28). He attempts to defend Christians from the charge of blasphemy resulting from their claim that Jesus is the Son of God (10:36). E often attempts to foster the idea that John the Baptist was inferior to Jesus. This notion is very prominent in chapter 1 and appears again in 3:27-28 and 5:33, 35. This concern about the Baptist arose from the rivalry between the disciples of the two men; after the deaths of John and Jesus each group claimed that its founder was the Christ. The conflict between Judaism and Christianity underlies much of the editor's thinking. He mentions the excommunication of Christians when the Pharisees banned them from the synagogues (9:22; 12:42). The controversy between Jews and gentile Christians over the observance of the Sabbath is on his mind in chapter 5 and in 7:19-24. He attacks not just the Pharisees, but Jews in general whenever he can. According to him the Jews as a whole seek to kill Jesus. He represents Jesus as denouncing Jews as being sons of their father the Devil (chap. 8). In 15:20b-

22, 24, he reacts against the Jewish persecution of Christians. The editor reflects the bitter hatred existing between Jews and gentile Christians at the beginning of the second century.

We are justified in regarding the product of the editor's work as the earliest form of the Gospel of John. S probably deserves to be called a gospel, because it consisted of a story of Jesus' life and death. We cannot call it the Gospel of John, however, because much of it was omitted by the editor and the portion he used is only a fraction of the present gospel. The same is true of G, which had less of the gospel format.

Why did the editor produce the gospel? Judging from its contents, his primary motive was to combine the semi-gnostic Son-Father theology of G with the Hellenistic miracle-worker Christ of S. A second motive was to provide support for Christians in the controversy between them and Jews. The editor produced a syncretistic gospel because he lived in a syncretistic environment --probably Alexandria-- in which different forms of Christianity were in close contact and all were in frequent confrontation with Judaism.

R

Was there a redactor, or reviser, of the gospel in addition to the editor? It is easily demonstrated that there was.

The editor brought the gospel to a close by writing 20:31 as a supplement to the preceding verse, which was the end of the narrative S. He would not have put the conclusion in that location if chapter 21 existed then, so the last chapter obviously was written later. We have observed that while the editor consistently writes personal names without the article, the practice of the writer of chapter 21, except when he is quoting source material, is the opposite; this shows that the editor and the redactor are not the same person. Further, there are insertions in the gospel which bear some of the same characteristics as the redactor's composition in chapter 21. Above all, some of these insertions are into the editor's own writing (e.g., 2:22c-23a; 5:13b, 34, 36), thus proving that there was a redactor who operated later than the editor.

The redactor, as well as the other writers, has linguistic traits which assist us in detecting his work. In John only R has the following: "fulfill" Scripture or Jesus' word; <u>trōgō</u> for "eat"; hour comes "and now is" or "has come"; Scripture "be fulfilled" or "be completed"; "after these things"; "in Hebrew"; "about" (hōs apo) with numbers; "being called"; "Judas the Iscariot"; sun for "with"; "Satan" instead of "Devil"; "little boat"; "Peter" is arthrous; arthrous compound personal names; arthrous Old Testament personal names; "persecute"; "having been written" in the past tense; and eis for "to" in "go to."

Certain other traits are used consistently in R, but occur in the other material too. These include: "Jerusalem" in the plural form (usually arthrous--only R has this trait); apostellō for "send"; partitive genitive instead of the preposition ek in expressions such as "one of," "many of"; eipan (1st aorist ending) for "they said"; agapaō for "to love"; arthrous personal names; arti for "now"; and apo for "from" in "from God." R has a strong tendency to use the following: "Scripture" in the singular; "near"; Jesus' "word" (logos, sing.); "on account of this"; eis for "to"; and the article with "Sabbath."

Whereas S gives the Greek translation of Aramaic terms, R gives the Aramaic translation of Greek terms (5:2; 19:13, 17). R labels his Aramaic as "in Hebrew," which indicates that he really did not know Hebrew. "In Hebrew" is probably R's insertion in 20:16, unless P^2 is R's composition.

R has introduced only a few extracts from written sources. Like E, he quotes a few sentences from the Septuagint version of the Old Testament, but does so more accurately than E. In chapter 21 he has used three short stories from a written source or sources. In 5:17-47 he apparently has rearranged some of the gospel at the same time he inserted some sentences of his own. Perhaps 6:51c-53 is from a written source the redactor used, for its doctrine of the Eucharist distinguishes it from E and G.

R's method of writing differs from that of E in that his work was mainly that of making insertions into a gospel which already existed. Some of his insertions are intended as explanatory notes. He inserts "of Tiberias" in 6:1 to give the current name of the Sea of Galilee. He inserts 3:24 to try to reconcile the gospel to the synoptic account (Mark 1:14) in which John was imprisoned before Jesus began his career. Other insertions are in 4:8, 5:13b, 6:64b, and 12:6. Some insertions add details drawn from R's imagination, as in 12:2bc, 9-10, 17b. Occasionally he inserts geographic details (e.g., 11:18).

R is obsessed with Jewish feasts, for he inserts some mention of them ten times. The Passover is mentioned more than any other feast, but this does not make the book a "Passover gospel" as Wilkens claims. The only evidence of pascal Christology in R is the title "Lamb of God" in 1:29, repeated from S. R calls the Tabernacles, as well as the Passover, "the feast of the Jews" (7:2), so the Passover is not unique in the redactor's sight. When R labels the Passover as a feast "of the Jews," as he does in 2:13, 6:4, and 11:55, he plainly is not associating it with Christian theology. The reason that R mentions the Passover repeatedly is that he is fascinated with Jewish feasts as a device to give the story the appearance of historicity.

R's insertions are often needless and even foolish. The insertions about Jewish feasts do not fit the context, and the remark about Judas and the money box in 13:29 fails to improve the story. The settings R intrudes in 5:2-3 and 6:59 are quite unnecessary. In 21:7 he inserted into his source material the clause, "for he was naked," as the reason that Peter tied an outer garment around himself. The statement in the source implies that this was not the case, but that Peter had merely taken off his outer garment while working. Both E and R ignored chronology when each introduced material he inserted in chapter 1 with a phrase borrowed from S, "on the morrow." In S the first day is the beginning of the story, the second day is "the morrow" in 1:35, and the wedding at Cana is "on the third day." The "morrow" insertions of E and R make the wedding occur on the fifth day of the story, contradicting 2:1.

R tends to make cross references to other parts of the gospel, as in 11:2, 12:9, and 15:20a. The incident mentioned in 11:2, the anointing of Jesus by Mary, is referred to in the past tense, but it does not occur until later (12:3).

Although the redactor employs sources but little compared with the editor, he uses some of E's techniques. Sometimes he repeats elements he found at hand in the gospel, including "on the morrow" and "Behold, the Lamb of God" in 1:29 and the remark that Jesus ranks ahead of John in 1:30. R, as well as E, can restate the material; in 13:34 he restates 15:12. R, too, adds "again" at times to unify the account. A clear example is in 12:39b, required by the additional quotation R inserted in the preceding verse. R, too, can use catchwords as a basis for connecting material. The catchword is "Father" in 5:17-19, "eat" in 6:54, and "clean" in 15:2-3.

Nevertheless, the redactor has not systematically attempted to imitate the style of the gospel, for many linguistic differences remain between his style and that of the other writers. Our report of his traits has shown this. Also, he did not systematically revise the style of the gospel to unify it or to make it conform to his own style. When R adds a citation from Scripture to support a story, he does not change the story to make the vocabulary agree with that in Scripture. In his citation in 19:36 the verb for "break" is *suntribō*, but his own verb in his story is *katagnumi* (19:31-33). In the gospel passage in 19:23-24a and in the Old Testament citation R inserted in 19:24b, different verbs are used for "cast lots" and different nouns for the clothing; yet R allowed the terms to remain as he found them.

Did the redactor transpose some passages in the gospel? It would be hard to prove either that he did or did not. Perhaps he did, for the editor's beginning at 7:19 seems to belong with his expansion in chapter 5 of the story of the healing of the sick man. On the other hand, there is no valid evidence to support Wilkens' claim that the pericopes about the cleansing of the temple, the institution of the Eucharist, and the anointing at Bethany have been transposed.

As for the redactor's ideas, they definitely reflect some of the problems in the church in the first half of the second century. Christian deification of Jesus created the Jewish charge of blasphemy, and E dealt with it weakly in 10:33-38. R in 5:18-23 tries to use a passage in G (or possibly R's own source) as an answer: Jesus (and Christians) has not made himself equal to God, for the Son is dependent on the Father. Judas' betrayal still embarrasses the church, and R denounces him repeatedly. R will not permit the Judas who says something good to be "the Iscariot" in 14:22b. Christian acceptance of the Jewish law and the Old Testament in general is well established in R's community, so he does not reject the law by calling it "your law" as E has done, and he ascribes circumcision (which he rejects) to the Jewish fathers, not to Moses (7:22b). Unlike E, R is no longer enthusiastic about the notion that the Baptist is a witness to Jesus (5:36a). His anti-Jewish attitude is apparent in 7:22b and 8:39b.

In R the bread and wine of the Eucharist are literally the flesh and blood of the divine Jesus--a notion based on the sacred meal in some pagan mystery cults, for it too bestows immortality on those who consume it. This doctrine is present too in 6:51c-53, which may be a source used by R.

R transforms the "beloved disciple" from the man raised from the dead (in S, 11:3, 36) to a disciple who reclined on Jesus' breast (13:23, 25) and wrote the gospel (21:20-24).

CHAPTER 12

THE LITERARY STRUCTURE

The discovery of the number of writers involved in the composition of the Gospel of John and the determination of who wrote what, are the primary goals of this research. The results of the quest are presented in this chapter in which my literal translation of the Greek text is separated according to the work of each writer. A literal translation is not so readable as a modern idiomatic translation, but it enables the reader to grasp some of the variation in style among the writers. No translation is an adequate substitute for the Greek text, however. The word order in the translation is approximate, but to avoid awkwardness the order in the Greek text has been strictly followed only when it is a criterion, mainly with the verb "answer." Words implied but not expressed in the Greek are given in parentheses. The translation is punctuated according to the present text of the gospel, not according to the earlier strata. All Greek verbs have personal endings, and therefore a pronoun is not needed to express a pronoun subject; for example, "I say" can occur as legō (verb only), or as egō legō (pronoun and verb). Accordingly, when the editor or redactor inserted a name as the subject of a verb in the third person, he did not have to change the verb ending unless he changed the number (singular or plural). Thus legei, "he says," is translated as "Jesus says" when the name Jesus is inserted as its subject.

The present research could hardly have been accomplished before 1962, when the publication of P^{66} and P^{75} was completed. The distinction between arthrous and anarthrous personal names is a basic tool in this investigation, and P^{66} and P^{75} are the two earlier of the four main manuscripts (Codices B and S are the other two) necessary for determining the original text. When the presence or absence of the article with personal names is a variant, a decision has been made as to which is the original reading, and the manuscript evidence is given in brackets. In the citations of textual evidence, "B" represents Codex B; "S" indicates Codex Sinaiticus; "P^5," "P^{22}," "P^{45}," "P^{60}," "P^{66}," and "P^{75}" are the symbols of the early papyri cited. The first four papyri consist of only a few verses, and P^{75} is not extant after John 15:8. "Lac." means that there is a lacuna; that is, that portion of the text is missing because the manuscript is in fragmentary condition. An asterisk indicates the original reading in a manuscript, and a "c" appended to the manuscript symbol indicates the reading made by a later "corrector." "Except in" in a citation indicates the reading in the other three of the four main manuscripts.

The analysis of the structure of the gospel is based largely on objective linguistic criteria. These criteria are listed in the Appendix, which the reader should examine before proceeding with the present chapter. The evidence in the Greek text which is not apparent in English translation is given in brackets in this chapter, with Greek words transliterated into English letters. When no Greek term is given for "see," the Greek verb is horaō. When the Greek is not given for "with," the term is meta. Catchwords that the editor or redactor used as a basis for connecting passages from sources with each other or with his own composition are printed in capital letters (e.g., "SEE" in 1:50-51).

The following abbreviations are used in the translation:

acc.	accusative
an.	anarthrous
an. comp.	anarthrous compound name
an. def.	anarthrous name made definite by phrase in apposition to it
art. rep.	article repeated
arth.	arthrous
arth. comp.	arthrous compound personal name
attrib. pos.	attributive position
demon. pron.	demonstrative pronoun
fem.	feminine gender
gen.	genitive
lac.	lacuna
lit.	literally
masc.	masculine gender
neut.	neuter gender
part. gen.	partitive genitive
pl.	plural
poss. adj.	possessive adjective
prep.	preposition
pres. t.	present tense
prob.	probable
rep. obj.	repeated object
rep. subj.	repeated subject
s.	singular
tr.	translated

The Gospel of John

CHAPTER 1:

Jewish Poem

1 In the beginning was the Word, and the Word was with God, and the Word was God.

E

2 This one was in the beginning with God. [E restates v. 1.]

Jewish Poem

3 All things came to be [egeneto] through it, and without it nothing came to be [egeneto]

Christian Gnostic Hymn

which had come to be [gegonen].

Jewish Poem

4 In it was life, and the life was the light of men.
5 And the light shines in the darkness, and the darkness did not overcome it.

E

6 There was [egeneto] a man sent [apostellō] from [para] God, the name to him (was) John [an.].
7 This one came for a testimony, in order that he might testify about the Light, in order that all might believe through him.
8 That one was not the LIGHT, but (he came) in order that he might testify about the Light.

Christian Gnostic Hymn

9 He was the true LIGHT, who enlightens every man,

E

coming into the world [cf. 12:46].
10 He was in the world, and the world came to be through him, and the world did not know him [restatement of v. 3 and G in 17:25].

Jewish Poem

11 It came to its own, and its own did not receive it.

Christian Gnostic Hymn

12 But as many as received him, he gave to them authority to become children of God,

E

to those believing on his name,

Christian Gnostic Hymn

13 who were begotten, not from bloods nor from the will of the flesh nor from the will of man, but from God. 14 And the Word became flesh and tented among us, and we have beheld his glory, glory as the only-begotten from the Father, full of grace and truth.

E

15 John [an.] testifies about him and cried out saying, "This one was whom I said, 'The one coming after me was ahead of me [in rank] because he was first of me [in time].'"

Christian Gnostic Hymn

16 So that from his fullness we all received, even grace on grace.

Later Gloss

17 So that the law was given through Moses; grace and truth came to be through Jesus Christ [an. comp.].

E

that one [demon. pron. as rep. subj.]

Christian Gnostic Hymn

has declared (him).

S

19 And this is the testimony of John [arth.] when [E inserted "the Jews"] they sent [apostellō] priests and Levites

E

from [ek] Jerusalem [an., pl.]

S

in order to ask him, "WHO ARE YOU?"

E

20 And he confessed and did not deny [restatement of v. 20b].

S

And he confessed that "I am not the Christ." 21 And they asked him, "What, then? Are you Elijah [an. O. T. name]?" And he says, "I am not." "Are you the Prophet?" And he answered, "No."

E

22 Then they said [eipan] to him, "WHO ARE YOU?, in order that we may give an answer to those having sent [pempō] us. What do you say about yourself?" 23 He said, "I (am) 'the voice of one crying in the wilderness, Make straight the way of the Lord,' even as Isaiah [an. def.] the prophet said."

S

24 And they were sent [apostellō] from the Pharisees. 25 And they asked him and said [eipan] to him, "Then why do you baptize if you are not the Christ nor Elijah [an.] nor the Prophet?" 26 Answered them John [arth.] saying, "I baptize in water; in your midst stands one whom you do not know,

E

27 the one coming after me, of whom I am not worthy that I should untie the thong of his sandal."

R

28 These things happened in Bethany on the other side of the Jordan, where John [arth.] was baptizing. 29 On the morrow he sees [blepō] Jesus [arth.] coming to [pros] him, and he says, "Behold [ide] the Lamb of God who takes away the sin of the world [expansion of v. 36] 30 This one is (he) about whom I said, 'After me comes a man who was ahead of me because he was first of me.' ["On the morrow" spoils the three-day chronology in S: 1:19, 35; 2:1.]

S

31 And I did not know him, but in order that he might be manifested to Israel, on account of this I came BAPTIZING IN WATER."

E

32 And John [an.] testified, saying that I saw [theaomai] the Spirit descending as a dove from [ek] heaven, and it was staying upon him. 33 And I did not know him, but the one having sent

[pempō] me to BAPTIZE IN WATER, that one [demon. pron. as rep. subj.] said to me, 'Upon whomever you see the Spirit descend and remain upon him, this one [demon. pron. as rep. subj.] is the one baptizing in the Holy Spirit.' 34 And I have seen and have testified that this one is the Son of God."

S

35 On the morrow ["again" is not in P^{75}] John [arth.] stood and two of his disciples [comp. subj., s. verb], 36 and looking at [emblepō] Jesus [arth.] walking, he says, "Behold [ide] the Lamb of God." 37 The two disciples heard him speak and followed Jesus [arth.]. 38 Jesus [arth.] turned, and

E

seeing [theaomai] them following,

S

says to them, "What do you seek?" And they said [eipan] to him, "Rabbi,"--which says being interpreted "Teacher"--"where are you staying?" 39 He says to them, "Come and see." Then they came and saw [eidan] where he stays, and with him they stayed that day. The hour was about [hōs] the tenth. 40 One of the two

E

having heard from John [an.] and having followed him was Andrew [an.], the brother of Simon Peter [an. comp.]. 41 This one

S

finds first his own brother [art. rep.] Simon [an. def.] and says to him, "We have found the Messiah"--which being interpreted is "the Anointed One" [i.e., "the Christ"]. 42 He led him to Jesus [arth.]. Looking at [emblepō] him, Jesus [arth.] said, "You are Simon [an. def.; prob. arth. in S, and E omitted art. when he made the name def.].

E

the son of John [an.];

S

you shall be called Cephas"--which is interpreted "Rock" [i.e., "Peter"].

E

43 On the morrow [spoils S's three-day chronology] he wanted to go out into Galilee, and he finds Philip [an.].

S

And Jesus [arth.] says to him, "Follow me." 44 And Philip [arth.] was from [apo] Bethsaida,

E

from [ek] the city of Andrew [an.] and Peter [an.]. 45 Philip [an.; E inserted "Philip" for clarity]

S

he finds Nathanael [arth.] and says to him, "Him whom Moses [an. O.T. name] in the law and the prophets wrote [comp. subj., s. verb], we have found, Jesus [an. def.], son of Joseph [arth.], the one FROM [apo] NAZARETH."

E

46 Nathanael [an.] said to him, "Can anything good be FROM [ek] NAZARETH?" Philip [an. in P^{66*}, P^{75}, S] says to him, "Come and see [suggested by v. 39]."

S

47 Jesus [arth. in P^{66}, P^{75}, S] saw Nathanael [arth.] coming to [pros] him and says about him, "Behold [ide] truly an Israelite, in whom there is not guile."

E

48 Nathanael [an.] says to him, "How do you know me?" Answered Jesus [an.] and said to him, "Before Philip [an.] called you, when you were under the fig tree, I saw you." 49 Answered him Nathanael [an.],

S

(Nathanael says to him,) "Rabbi, you are the Son of God; you are the King of Israel!"

E

50 Answered Jesus [an.] and said to him, "Because I said to you [s.] that I saw you [s.] under the fig tree, do you [s.] believe?

Greater things than these you [s.] shall SEE." 51 And he says to him,

G

"Truly, truly, I say to you [pl.], you [pl.] shall SEE heaven opened and the angels of God ascending and descending upon the Son of Man."

CHAPTER 2:

S

1 And on [no prep.] the third day [art. rep. in P66, P75, S]
there was a wedding in Cana of Galilee, and the mother of Jesus
[arth.] was there. 2 And Jesus [arth.] also was invited to the
wedding, and his disciples [comp. subj., s. verb]. 3 And when
the wine failed, the mother of Jesus [arth.] says to him, "They
do not have wine." 4 Jesus [arth.] says to her, "What (is that)
to me and to you?

E

Woman, my hour has not yet [oupō] come."

S

5 His mother says to the servants, "Whatever he tells you, do."
6 And six stone jars were standing there,

E

for the purification (rites) of the Jews,

S

holding up to two or three measures. 7 Jesus [arth.] says to
them, "Fill the jars with water." And they filled them to the top.
8 And he says to them, "Now [nun] draw (some) and carry (it) to
the headwaiter." And they carried (it). 9 And [R inserts "when"]
the headwaiter tasted the water having become wine

R

and he did not know whence it is,--but the servants, the ones having drawn the water, knew--the headwaiter calls the bridegroom
10 and says to him, "Every man serves first the good wine, and when they (the guests) are drunk, the inferior (wine). You have kept the good wine until now [arti]."

S

11 This beginning of his signs Jesus [arth.] did in Cana of Galilee [E inserts "and manifested his glory,"] and his disciples believed on him. 12 After this he himself went down into Capernaum, and his mother and brothers and his disciples [comp. subj., s. verb], and they stayed there not many days.

R

13 And the Passover of the Jews was near.

S

And Jesus [arth.] went up into Jerusalem [an., s.]. 14 And he found in the temple those selling cattle and sheep and doves,

E

and the money-changers [kermatistēs] sitting.

S

15 And having made a whip of cords, he cast out all from the temple, both [te] the sheep and the cattle, and poured out the coins of the money-changers [kollubistēs, from Mark or Matt.] and overturned the tables. 16 And he said to those selling the doves, "Take these things away from here. Do not make my Father's house a HOUSE of trade."

E

17 His disciples remembered that it is having been written, "The zeal of your HOUSE shall consume me." 18 Answered the Jews and said [eipan] to him, "What sign do you show, that you do these things?" 19 Answered Jesus [an.] and said to them, "Destroy this TEMPLE, and in three days I will raise it." 20 Then the Jews said [eipan], "Forty-six years this temple was being built, and you will raise it in three days?" 21 But that one was talking about the temple of his body. 22 Then when he was raised from the dead, his disciples remembered that he was saying this,

R

and they believed the Scripture and the word [logos] which Jesus [arth.] said. 23 And when he was in Jerusalem [arth., pl.] at the Passover at the feast,

E

many believed on his name, seeing [theōreō] his signs which he did. 24 But Jesus [an.] himself did not trust himself to them on account of he himself knew all things, 25 and because he did not have need that anyone should testify about man, for he himself knew what was in man.

CHAPTER 3:

E

1 And there was

S

a man of the Pharisees

E

Nicodemus [an.] (was) the name to him, an official of the Jews;
2 this one

S

came to [pros] him at night and said to him, "Rabbi, we know that you have come (as) a teacher from [apo] God. For no one can do these signs which you do unless God is with him." [E now drops S's story and substitutes his own.]

E

3 Answered Jesus [an.] and said to him, "Truly, truly, I say to you [s.],

G

unless a person has been BORN FROM ABOVE [anōthen], he cannot see the kingdom of God."

E

4 Nicodemus [an. in P^{66}, P^{75}, B] says to him, "How can a man being old be born (again)? Can he enter into the womb of his mother a second time and be born?"
5 Answered Jesus [an. in P^{66}, P^{75}, B], "Truly, truly, I say to you, unless a person has been BORN FROM

R

water and [cf. R in 19:34]

E

THE SPIRIT, he is not able to enter into the kingdom of God. 6
The (thing) having been born from the flesh is flesh, and the (thing)
having been born from the Spirit is spirit. 7 Do not marvel that
I said to you [s.]

G

'It is necessary (that) you [pl.] be BORN FROM ABOVE [anōthen].'

E

8 The Spirit blows where it wills, and you [s.] hear its voice, but
you [s.] do not know whence it comes or where it goes [hupagō].
Thus is everyone having been BORN FROM THE SPIRIT." 9
Answered Nicodemus [an.] and said to him, "How can these
things be?" 10 Answered Jesus [an.] and said to him, "Are you
[s.] a teacher of Israel and do not know these things? 11 Truly,
truly, I say to you [s.] that what we know we speak and what we
have seen we testify (to), and you [pl.--E now preaches against
Jews] do not receive our testimony. 12 If I tell you [pl.] earthly
things and you [pl.] do not believe, how will you [pl.] BELIEVE
if I tell you [pl.] HEAVENLY things?"

G

13 And no one has ascended into HEAVEN except the one who has
descended from [ek] heaven, the Son of Man. 14 And even as
Moses [an. O.T. name] lifted up the snake in the wilderness,
thus it is necessary the SON of Man be lifted up, 15 in order that
everyone BELIEVING IN [en in P^{75}, B; epi in P^{66}] HIM may have
LIFE ETERNAL."

G ?

16 For God thus loved [agapaō] the world that [hōste; only in-
stance in John] he gave the only-begotten SON [art. rep.], in
order that everyone BELIEVING ON [epi in P^{75}] HIM might not
perish but have LIFE ETERNAL. [G's "God gave" the Son induced E to insert below one of his themes: God "sent" Jesus. "Judgment" in v. 19 suggested E's theme that Jesus did not come to judge.]

E

17 For God did not send [apostellō] the Son into the world in order
that he might JUDGE the world, but in order that the world might
be saved through him. 18 The one BELIEVING ON [eis] him is
not judged; the one not believing has already been judged because
he has not believed on [eis] the name of the only-begotten Son of
God.

G ?

19 And this is the JUDGMENT, that the Light has come into the world and men loved [agapaō] the Darkness [skotos] rather than the Light, for their works were wicked. 20 For everyone committing evil hates the Light and does not come to [pros] the Light, in order that his works may not be exposed. 21 But the one doing the Truth comes to [pros] the Light in order that his works may be manifested that they have been worked in God.

R

22 After these things

S

Jesus [arth.] came and his disciples [comp. subj., s. verb] into the land Judea, and there he tarried with them and WAS BAPTIZING.

R

23 And John [arth. in P^{66}, B] WAS BAPTIZING in Ainon near Salim because much water was there, and they were arriving and being baptized. 24 For John [arth. in P^{66}, P^{75}, S^{c}] had not yet been cast into prison.

S

25 Then there was a dispute by the disciples [E inserts "of John [an.]"] with a Jew about purification. 26 And they came to John [arth.] and said [eipan] to him, "Rabbi, [Again E drops the story in S and substitutes his own writing, which has nothing to do with purification.]

E

he who was with you across the Jordan, to whom you have testified, behold [ide] this one [demon. pron. as rep. subj.] BAPTIZES and all are coming to him. 27 Answered John [an.] and said, "A man is able to receive nothing unless it has been given to him from [ek] heaven. 28 You yourselves testify that I said that 'I am not the Christ, but that I am (he) having been sent [apostellō] ahead of that one.'

G

29 The one having the bride is the bridegroom. But the friend of

the bridegroom , the one standing and hearing him, rejoices with joy on account of the voice of the bridegroom. Then this, my joy [art. rep. with poss. adj.] has been filled.

E

30 It is necessary (that) that one increase, but (that) I decrease.

G

31 THE ONE COMING FROM ABOVE [anōthen] is above all things; the one being from [ek] the earth is from [ek] the earth and from [ek] the earth he speaks. [The spiritual man is contrasted with the earthly man, as in Gnosticism; this does not fit the Baptist, especially the last clause.]

E

THE ONE COMING FROM [ek] HEAVEN, 32 what he has seen and heard, this [demon. pron. as rep. obj.] he testifies, and no one receives his testimony. 33 The one receiving his testimony sealed that God is true. 34 For whom God sent [apostellō] speaks the words [rēma, pl.] of God, for not by measure does he give the Spirit.

G ?

35 The Father loves [apostellō] the Son and has given all things into his hand. 36 The one believing on the Son has life eternal. But the one disbelieving the Son shall not see life, but the wrath of God remains upon him." [Connecting link with passage above: idea that some do not receive testimony, or believe]

CHAPTER 4:

E

1 Then when

Later Gloss

the Lord knew

S

the Pharisees heard that . . .

E

Jesus [an.] is making more disciples and baptizing (more) than

John [an.], [Again E substitutes the subordination of John to Jesus for the matter in S.]

Later Gloss

2 --and yet [kaitoi ge; only instance in N.T.] Jesus [an.] himself did not baptize, but his disciples (did)--

S

3 he left Judea and went away again into Galilee. 4 But it was necessary for him to pass through Samaria. 5 Then he comes into a city of Samaria [R inserts "being called Sychar"] near the piece of land which Jacob [an. O.T. name] gave to his son [R inserts "Joseph [arth. O.T. name]"]. 6 And a spring [pēgē] [R inserts "of Jacob [arth. O.T. name; suggested by v. 12]"] was there. Then Jesus [arth.], having become weary from the journey, sat down thus by the SPRING [pēgē]. The hour was about [hōs] the sixth.

G ?

7 A woman of Samaria comes to draw water. Jesus [arth.] says to her, "Give to me (water) to drink."

R

8 For his disciples had gone away into the city in order to buy food [trophē]. [R inserted this to explain why Jesus did not ask his disciples to give him a drink.]

G ?

9 The Samaritan woman [art. rep.] says to him, "How do you, being a Jew, ask [aiteō] to drink from me, being a Samaritan woman?"

E

10 For Jews do not associate with Samaritans. Answered Jesus [an.] and said to her, "If you knew the gift of God and who is the one saying to you, 'Give to me (water) to drink,' you would have asked [aiteō] him and he would have given to you LIVING WATER [an.]."

G ?

11 She says to him, "Lord, you do not have a drawing bucket, and

the WELL [phrear] is deep. Then whence do you have LIVING WATER [art. rep.; cf. 7:38] ? 12 Are you greater than our father Jacob [an. O.T. name], who gave to us the well [phrear], and he himself drank from it and his sons and his livestock [comp. subj., s. verb] ?"

E

13 Answered Jesus [an.] and said to her, "Everyone drinking from this water will thirst again; 14 but whoever drinks from the water which I will give to him, will not thirst forever, but the water which I will give to him will become in him a SPRING [pēgē, from v. 6] leaping up for LIFE eternal." 15 The woman says to him, "Lord, give to me this water in order that I may not thirst nor come here to draw." [Note abrupt change in theme between vv. 15 and 16.]

S

16 He says to her, "Go [hupagō], call your husband and come here." 17 Answered the woman and said ["to him" is not in Codex S], "I do not have a husband." Jesus [arth.] says to her, "Rightly you said that 'I do not have a husband.' 18 For you have had five husbands, and whom you have now [nun] is not your husband. This you said (is) true." 19 The woman says to him, "I see [theōreō] that you [s.] are a prophet."

G ?

20 "Our fathers worshiped on this mountain, and you [pl.] say that in Jerusalem [an., pl.] is the place where it is necessary to worship." 21 Jesus [arth.] says to her, "Believe me, woman, that the hour comes when neither on this mountain nor in Jerusalem [an., pl.] you [pl.] will worship the Father. 22 You [pl.] worship what you do not know; we worship what we know, because salvation is from the Jews. 23 But the hour comes [E inserts "and now [nun] is"] when the true worshipers will worship the Father in SPIRIT and truth. For such the Father seeks worshiping [i.e., to worship] him.

E

24 God (is) SPIRIT, and it is necessary (for) the ones worshiping him to worship in spirit and truth." [E restates v. 23.]

S

25 The woman says to him, "I [in P^{66*}, B, S] know that Messiah comes, the one called Christ; when that one comes, he will announce to us all things." 26 Jesus [arth.] says to her, "I am (he), the one speaking to you [s.]." 27 And upon this the disciples came, and they marveled that he was talking with a woman. Nevertheless, no one said, "What do you want?" or "Why are you talking with her?" 28 Then the woman left her water jar and went away into the city and says to men, 29 "Come, see a man who told me all things which I did. Perhaps this is the Christ."

E

30 They went out from [ek] the city and were coming to [pros] him.

S

31 In the meanwhile the disciples were asking [erōtaō] him, saying, "Rabbi, eat [esthiō]." 32 But he said to them, "I have MEAT [brōsis] to eat [esthiō] which you do not know (I have)." 33 Then the disciples were saying to each other, "Has anyone brought to him (meat) to eat [esthiō]?" [Connecting link with G below: idea of food]

G

34 Jesus [arth.] says to them, "My FOOD [brōma] is that I will do the will of the one having sent [pempō] me and I will complete [teleioō] his work. 35 Do you not say, "There are four months, and the harvest comes'? Behold [idou], I say to you, raise your eyes and see [theaomai] the fields, that they are already white for HARVEST.

E

36 The one HARVESTING receives wages and gathers fruit for life eternal, in order that the one sowing and the one harvesting may rejoice together. 37 For in this the saying [logos] is true that the one sowing is one [lit.: other] and the one harvesting is another. 38 I sent [apostellō] you to harvest what you have not labored (for). Others have labored, and you have entered into (the rewards of) their labor." [Note shift in thought from harvest (judgment day) is at hand (G) to "harvesting" which is missionary work.]

R

39 And from [ek] that city many of [part. gen.] the Samaritans believed ["on him" is not in S*] on account of the word [logos] of the woman testifying that "He told me all things which I did [suggested by vv. 29, 40]."

S

40 Then when the Samaritans came to [pros] to him, they asked [erōtaō] him to stay with them. And he stayed there two days.

R

41 And many more believed on account of his word [logos].

S

42 And [te] to the woman they were saying that "No longer on account of your speech we believe. For we ourselves have heard and we know that this one is truly the Savior of the world [typical S usage of 'truly']." 43 And after two days he went out from there INTO GALILEE.

E

44 For Jesus [an.] himself testified that a prophet does not have honor in his OWN FATHERLAND.

R

45 Then when he came INTO GALILEE, the Galileans welcomed him, having seen all the things which he did in Jerusalem [an., pl.] at the feast. [R refers to his own statement in 2:23.] For they themselves also came to [eis] the feast. 46 Then he came again into Cana [arth.] of Galilee, where he made the water wine [R's cross-reference to 2:1-10].

S

And there was a certain royal official whose son was sick in Capernaum [an.].

E

47 This one having heard that Jesus [an.] had come from Judea into Galilee [suggested by 4:54],

S

he went away [E inserts "and asked [erōtaō, from Luke 7:3]"] that he might come down and heal his son.

E

For he was about to die [from Luke 7:2].

R

48 Jesus [arth.] said to him, "Unless you see signs and wonders, you will not believe."

S

49 The royal official says to him, "Lord, come down before my little child [paidion, from Matt. 8:6] dies." 50 Jesus [arth.] says to him, "Go [poreuomai]. Your son lives."

R

The man believed the word [logos] which Jesus [arth.] said, and he went.

S

51 And already when he went down his servants met him, saying that his son lives. 52 Then he inquired that hour in which he had better (health). They said [eipan] to him that "Yesterday (at) the seventh hour the fever left him." 53 Then the father knew that (it was) at that hour in which Jesus [arth.] said to him, "Your son lives."

E

And he himself believed and his whole house [suggested by Acts 16:3; 18:8]. 54 Again

S

Jesus [arth.] did this second sign having come from Judea into Galilee. [That in S this is only the "second" sign shows that 2:23 and 4:45 were not in S.]

CHAPTER 5:

R

1 After these things there was a feast of the Jews, and

E

Jesus [an. in P66, P75, B]

S

he went up into Jerusalem [an., s.].

R

2 And there is in Jerusalem [arth., pl.] by the sheep gate a pool, the one being called in Hebrew Bethsaida, having five porticoes. 3 In these were lying a multitude of the sick, blind, lame, paralyzed.

Very Late Gloss

4 [Omitted here because it is so late that it is not in the earlier manuscripts.]

S

5 And there was a certain man there, having (been) in his illness thirty-eight years. 6 Jesus [arth.], seeing this man lying there, and knowing that he already has (been ill) much time, says to him, "Do you want to become well?" 7 Answered him the sick man, "Lord, I do not have a man, that whenever the water is stirring, he may throw me into the pool. And while I am coming, another goes down before me." 8 Jesus [arth.] says to him, "Arise, PICK UP YOUR BED and walk." 9 The man becomes well, and picked up his bed and walked.

E

And it was the Sabbath [an.] on [prep.] that day. 10 Then the Jews were saying to the one having been healed, "It is the Sabbath [an.] and it is not lawful for you to PICK UP YOUR BED." 11 And he [lit.: "who"] answered them, "The one having made me well, that one [demon. pron. as rep. subj.] said to me, 'Pick up your bed and walk.'" 12 They asked him, "Who is the man, the one having said to you 'Pick up and walk'?" 13 And the one having been healed did not know who it is.

R

For Jesus [arth.] had withdrawn (since) a crowd was [s.] in the place. 14 After these things

S

Jesus [arth. in P^{66}, P^{75}, S] finds him in the temple and said to him, "Behold [ide] you have chosen well. Sin no longer, in order that something worse may not happen to you."

E

15 The man went away and proclaimed to the Jews that Jesus [an.] is the one having MADE him well.

R or S ?

16 And on account of this the Jews were persecuting Jesus [arth.], because he DID these things on the Sabbath [an.].

G ?

17 And he answered [middle voice] them, "MY FATHER works until now [arti], and I WORK." [Connecting link between verses 15, 16, 17, 18, and 19 is idea of Jesus' activity. Except in 17, it is the same Greek verb, poieō, which means either "do" or "make."]

R

18 On account of this the Jews were seeking the more to kill him, because he not only was breaking the Sabbath [arth.], but also he was saying (that) God (is) his own FATHER, MAKING himself equal to God.

G ?

19 Then he ["Jesus" is not in P^{75}, B] answered [middle voice] and was saying to them, "Truly, truly, I say to you, the Son can DO nothing from [apo] himself, except what he sees [blepō] the FATHER doing.

E

For whatever that one does, these things [demon. pron. as rep. obj.] also the Son DOES likewise [E's restatement of vv. 19a, 20].

G ?

20 For the Father loves [phileō] the Son and shows to him all things which he himself does, and greater works than these he will show to him in order that you may marvel. 21 For just as the Father raises the dead and makes (them) alive, thus also the

Son makes ALIVE whom he wishes. 22 For the Father judges no one, but has given all JUDGMENT to the Son, 23 in order that all may honor the Son even as they honor the Father. The one not honoring the Son does not honor the Father, the one having sent [pempō] him.

G

24 Truly, truly, I say to you that the one HEARING my word [logos] and believing the one having SENT [pempō] me has life eternal and does not come into JUDGMENT, but has passed from death into LIFE.

E

25 Truly, truly, I say to you that the hour comes and now is when the dead will HEAR the voice of the Son of God, and having heard, will LIVE [restatement of vv. 24 and 28-29].

G ?

26 For just as the Father has life in himself, thus also he has given to the Son to have LIFE in himself. 27 And he has given to him authority to make judgment, because he is (the) Son of Man [an.; only time in John "Son of Man" is an. or associated with the resurrection]. 28 Do not marvel at this, because the hour comes in which all the ones in the tombs will HEAR his voice, 29 and the ones having done good will go forth into the resurrection of LIFE, the ones having committed evil (will go forth) into the resurrection of JUDGMENT.

G

30 I can do nothing from [apo] myself; even as I hear, I judge, and and my JUDGMENT [art. rep. with poss. adj.] is just, because I do not seek my will [art. rep. with poss. adj.] but the will of the one having sent [pempō] me. 31 If I testify about myself, my testimony is not true. 32 There is another, the one testifying about me, and I know that true is the testimony which he TESTIFIES about me. [In G v. 37 followed v. 32; cf. 8:12-18.]

E

33 You sent [apostellō] to John [an.], and he has TESTIFIED to the truth.

R

34 But I do not receive TESTIMONY from man, but I say these things in order that you may be saved.

E

35 That one [John] was a burning and shining lamp, and you wanted to rejoice for an hour in his light.

R

36 But I have a testimony greater than John [arth.]. For the works which the Father has given to me in order that I will complete [teleioō] them [from 4:34], these works which I do TESTIFY about me that the Father has sent [apostellō] me [cf. 10:25].

G

37 And the Father having sent [pempō] me, [E inserts "that one [demon. pron. as rep. subj.]"] has TESTIFIED about me. Neither his voice have you ever heard nor his form have you seen, 38 and HIS WORD [logos] YOU DO NOT HAVE STAYING IN YOU,

E

because whom that one sent [demon. pron. as rep. obj.] YOU DO NOT BELIEVE. 39 You search the Scriptures [pl.] because you think (that) in them you have life eternal, and those are the ones TESTIFYING about me. 40 And you do not want to come to [pros] me in order that you may have life. 41 I do not receive glory from men. 42 But I know that you do not have the love of God in yourselves. 43 I have come in the name of my Father, and you do not receive me. If another should come in his own name, that one [demon. pron. as rep. obj.] you will receive. 44 How can you believe, receiving glory from one another, and you do not seek the glory, the one from [para] the only (God)? 45 Do not think that I will accuse you to the Father. The one accusing you is Moses [an. O.T. name], on whom you hope. 46 For if you believed Moses [an.], you would believe me. For that one wrote about me. 47 And if you do not believe the Scriptures [pl.] of that one, how will you believe my words [rēma]?"

CHAPTER 6:

R

1 After these things

S

Jesus [arth.] went away across the Sea of Galilee

R

of Tiberias [R inserts to explain the earlier name, Sea of Galilee; cf. R in 21:1].

E

2 And a large crowd followed [s.] him because they saw the signs which he was doing on the ones being sick. 3 And Jesus [an. in P^{66}, P^{75}, B, S*] went up into the mountain, and there he sat down with his disciples.

R

4 And the Passover, the feast of the Jews, was near.

S

5 Then Jesus [arth.],

E

lifting (his) eyes and seeing [theaomai] that a large crowd is coming [s.] to [pros] him,

S

says [E inserts "to Philip [an.]"], "Whence will we buy loaves in order that these (people) may EAT [esthiō] ?"

E

6 But he was saying this testing him, for he himself knew what he was about to do.

S

7 Answered him Philip [arth. in P^{66}, S], "Loaves of two hundred denarii (worth) would not be enough that each may receive a little." 8 One of his disciples says to him,

E

Andrew [an. def.], the brother of Simon Peter [an. comp.],

S

9 "There is a small boy here who has five barley loaves and two

fish, but what are these among so many?" 10 Jesus [arth.] said, "Make the men [anthrōpos] recline." And there was much grass in the place. Then the men [anēr, from Mark 6:44] reclined, (in) number about [hōs] five thousand. 11 Then Jesus [arth.] took the loaves and, having given thanks, he distributed to the ones reclining, likewise also from the fish, as much as they wanted. 12 And when they were full, he says to the disciples, "Gather the fragments left over, in order that they may not be lost." 13 Then they gathered, and they filled twelve baskets of fragments from the five loaves of barley, which were left over by the ones having eaten [bibrōskō, only instance in N.T.]. 14 Then the men [anthrōpos], seeing the sign which he did, were saying that "This one is truly the Prophet, the one coming into the world."

E

15 Then Jesus [an.] knew that they were about to come and to seize him in order that they may make (him) king, he himself withdrew again into the mountain alone.

S

16 And when evening came, his disciples went down to the sea, 17 and getting into a boat [ploion] they came across the sea into Capernaum. And it was already darkness [skotia], and Jesus [arth. in P^{75}, B; lac. in P^{66}] not yet had come to [pros] them. 18 And [te] the sea rose when a strong wind blew. 19 Then having rowed about [hōs] twenty-five or thirty stadia, they see [theōreō] Jesus [arth.] walking on the sea and coming near the boat [ploion], and they were afraid. 20 And he says to them, "I am. Do not be afraid." 21 Then they wanted to take him into the boat [ploion], and immediately the boat [ploion] was at the land to which they were going [hupagō]. 22 On the morrow the crowd,

E

the one having stood [s.] on the other side of the sea,

S

saw [pl.] that

R

another small boat [ploiarion] was not there except one, and that [R tries to make it more explicit that there was only one boat and

Jesus was not in it, so he must have walked on the water.]

S

Jesus [arth.] did not get into the boat [ploion] with his disciples, but his disciples went away alone.

Later Gloss

23 But boats [ploion in P^{75}, B, S; lac. in P^{66}] from [ek] Tiberias came near the place where they ate [esthiō] the bread when the Lord gave thanks.

E

24 Then when the crowd saw [s.] that Jesus [an.] is not there, nor his disciples,

R

they themselves got into the small boats [ploiarion] and

S

they came [pl.] into Capernaum seeking Jesus [arth.]. 25 And finding him on the other side of the sea, they said [eipon] to him, "Rabbi, when did you come here?"

G

26 Answered them Jesus [arth.] and said, "Truly, truly, I say to you, [G's word order in "answered . . . said"]

E

you seek me not because you saw signs, but because you ATE [esthiō] from the loaves and were filled." [E substitutes this for the answer in S to the question in v. 25; the idea of food in S's story of the miraculous feeding and in G in v. 27 is the connecting link in E's mind.]

G

27 Do not work for the MEAT [brōsis] the one perishing, but for the one remaining for life eternal, which the Son of Man will give to you. For God the Father sealed this. 28 Then they said [eipon] to him, "What should we do in order that we may WORK the WORKS OF GOD?"

E

29 Answered Jesus [an. in P^{45}, S; lac. in P^{66}] and said to them, "This is the WORK OF GOD, that you believe on whom that one sent [apostellō]." [E substitutes this for Jesus' answer in G.]

G

30 Then they said [eipon] to him, "What sign do you do, in order that we may see and believe you? What do you WORK?

E

31 Our fathers ate [esthiō] manna in the wilderness, even as it is having been written, 'BREAD FROM HEAVEN he gave to them to eat [esthiō].'"

G

32 Then Jesus [arth.] said to them, "Truly, truly, I say to you,

E

Moses [an. O.T. name] has not given to you the BREAD FROM [ek] HEAVEN, but

G

my Father gives to you the true BREAD [art. rep.] FROM [ek] HEAVEN.

E

33 For the BREAD of God is the one COMING DOWN FROM [ek] HEAVEN and giving LIFE to the world [E's restatement of parts of vv. 32 and 51]."

G

34 They said [eipon] to him, "Lord, give to us always this bread." 35 Jesus [arth.] said to them, "I am the bread of LIFE. The one coming to [pros] me will not hunger, and the one BELIEVING on me will never thirst.

E

36 But I said to you that you have even seen me and you do not BELIEVE.

G

37 Everything [neut.] which the Father gives to me will COME TO
[pros] ME,

E

and the one [masc.] COMING TO [pros] ME I will not cast outside,

G

38 because I have COME DOWN FROM [apo] HEAVEN not in order
that I may do my will [art. rep. with poss. adj.] but the will of the
one having sent [pempō] me, 39 that everything [neut.] which he
has given to me I will not lose (any) of it, but I WILL RAISE IT
[neut.] ON [no prep. in P^{66}, P^{75}, B] THE LAST DAY.

E

40 For this is the will of my Father, that everyone [masc.] seeing
[theōreō] the Son and believing on him may have life eternal, and
I WILL RAISE HIM [masc.] ON [prep. in P^{66}, S] THE LAST DAY
[E's restatement of v. 39]." 41 Then the Jews murmured about
him because he said, "I am the bread the one having COME DOWN
FROM [ek] HEAVEN." 42 And they were saying, "Is this not
Jesus [an. def.], the son of Joseph [an.], whose father and mo-
ther we know? How does he now [nun] say that 'I have come down
from [ek] heaven'?" 43 Answered Jesus [an. in P^{75}, B, S] and
said to them, "Do not murmur with [meta] one another. 44 No
one [masc.] is able to COME TO [pros] ME unless the Father,
the one having sent [pempō] me, should draw him, and I will
RAISE HIM [masc.] ON [prep. in P^{66*}, B] THE LAST DAY. 45
It is having been written in the Prophets, 'And all will be taught
by God.' Everyone having heard and learned from [para] the
Father COMES TO [pros] ME. 46 Not that anyone has seen the
Father, except the one being from [para] God, this one [demon.
pron. as rep. subj.] has seen the Father. 47 Truly, truly, I say
to you, the one believing has life eternal. 48 I AM THE BREAD
OF LIFE. 49 Your fathers ate [esthiō] manna in the wilderness
and died. 50 This is the bread, the one coming down from [ek]
heaven, that anyone may eat [esthiō] of it and may not die.

G

51 I AM THE LIVING BREAD [art. rep.], the one coming down
from [ek] heaven. If anyone EATS [esthiō] of this bread, he will

live forever.

R Source or G ?

And also the bread which I will give is my flesh (given) in behalf of the life of the world." 52 Then the Jews were disputing with [pros] one another saying, "How is this one able to give to us flesh to eat [esthiō] ?" 53 Then Jesus [arth. in P^{75}, S] said to them, "Truly, truly, I say to you, unless you EAT [esthiō] the FLESH of the Son of Man and DRINK his BLOOD, you do not have life in yourselves.

R

54 The one EATING [trōgō; cf. R in 13:18] my FLESH and DRINKING my BLOOD has life eternal, and I will raise him on [no prep.] the last day. 55 For my flesh is true meat [brōsis], and my blood is true drink. 56 The one eating [trōgō] my flesh and drinking my blood stays in me and I in him. 57 Even as the living Father sent [apostellō] me and I live because of the Father, also the one eating [trōgō] me, that one [demon. pron. as rep. subj.] will live because of me.

G

58 This is the bread, the one having come down from [ek] heaven, not even as the fathers ate [esthiō] and died.

R

The one eating [trōgō] this bread will live forever." 59 These things he said in the synagogue (while) teaching in Capernaum.

S

60 Then many of his disciples, having heard, said [eipan], "This saying [logos] is hard. Who is able to hear it?"

G

61 But Jesus [arth.], KNOWING in himself that his disciples were murmuring about this, said to them, "Are you offended at this? 62 Then (what) if you should see [theōreō] the Son of Man ascending where he was formerly?

E

63 The Spirit is the thing making alive; the flesh profits nothing. The words [rēma, pl.] which I have spoken to you are spirit and

life. 64 But there are some of you who do NOT BELIEVE."

R

For Jesus [arth.] KNEW from the beginning there are certain ones, the ones NOT BELIEVING, and there is a certain one, the one (who) will be betraying him.

E

65 And he was saying, "On account of this I have said to you that no one is able to come to [pros] me unless it has been given to him by the Father." [E reinterprets G in v. 37.]

S

66 From [i.e., after] this many of his disciples went back behind and no longer walked with him. 67 Then Jesus [arth.] said to the twelve, "Do you not also want to GO [hupagō] ?"

E

68 Answered him Simon Peter [an. comp.], "Lord, to whom will we GO? You have the words [rēma, pl.] of life eternal; 69 and we have believed and we have known that you are the Holy One of God." [E substituted this for the twelve's reply, as "them" in v. 70 shows.]

S

70 Answered them Jesus [arth. in P^{75}, B], "Have I not chosen you the twelve, and one of you is a devil?" 71 And he was speaking of Judas [arth.], (son) of Simon Iscariot [an. comp.],

E

--for this one was about to betray him--

S

one of the twelve.

CHAPTER 7:

R

1 After these things

S

Jesus [arth.] was walking in Galilee.

E

For he did not want to walk in Judea, because the Jews were seeking to kill him.

R

2 And near was the feast of the Jews, the Tabernacles.

S

3 Then his brothers said [eipon] to him, "Pass from here and go [hupagō] into Judea, in order that your disciples also may see [theōreō] your WORKS which you do. 4 For no one does anything in secret and seeks it to be in public. If you do these things, manifest yourself to the WORLD."

E

5 For not even his brothers believed on him.

S

6 Then Jesus [arth.] says to them,

G

"MY TIME [art. rep. with poss. adj.] is not yet present, but your time [art. rep. with poss. adj.] is always ready. 7 THE WORLD is not able to hate you, but it hates me because I testify about it that its WORKS are evil.

S

8 You go up to the feast.

E

I am not yet going up to this feast, because MY [attrib. pos.] TIME has not yet been fulfilled.

S

9 Saying these things to them, he stayed in Galilee. 10 But when his brothers went up to THE FEAST, then he himself also went up, not visibly but as in secret.

E

11 Then the Jews were seeking him at THE FEAST and were say-

ing, "Where is that one?" 12 And there was much murmuring about him in the crowd. Some were saying that "He is a good (man)." Others were saying, "But no, he leads the crowd astray." 13 Nevertheless, no one was speaking publicly about him on account of the Jews. 14 And already in the midst of the feast Jesus [an.] went up into the temple and was TEACHING. 15 Then the Jews marveled saying, "How does this one know letters, not having been taught?"

G

16 Then answered them Jesus [arth. in P66; lac. in P75] and said [G's word order], "My TEACHING is not mine but of the one having sent [pempō] me. 17 If anyone wills to do his will, he shall know about the teaching, whether it is from [ek] God or I speak from [apo] myself. 18 The one speaking from [apo] himself seeks his own glory [art. rep.]. But the one seeking the glory of the one having sent [pempō] him,

E

this one [demon. pron. as rep. subj.]

G

is true and unrighteousness is not in him.

E

19 Has not Moses [an. O.T. name] given you the law? And no one of you does the law. Why do you seek to kill me?" 20 The crowd answered [s.], "You have a demon! Who seeks to kill you?" 21 Answered Jesus [an.] and said to them, "One work I did and you all marvel. 22 On account of this Moses [an.] has given to you circumcision

R

--not that it is from Moses [arth. O.T. name], but from the fathers--

E

and on the Sabbath [an.] you circumcize a man. 23 If a man receives circumcision on the Sabbath [an.] in order that the law of Moses [an. in B, prob. in P75] may not be broken, are you angry with me because I made a whole man well on the Sabbath [an.]?

24 Do not judge according to appearance, but judge (with) righteous judgment." 25 Then some of the Jerusalemites were saying, "Is not this one he whom they were seeking to kill? 26 And behold [ide], he speaks publicly, and they say nothing to him. Have not the authorities truly known that this one is the Christ? 27 But we know whence [from Galilee] this one is; but when the Christ comes, no one will KNOW WHENCE he is."

G

28 Then Jesus [arth. in P^{66}, B*, S] cried out (while) teaching in the temple and saying, "And you KNOW me and you KNOW WHENCE [from heaven] I am. And I have not come from [apo] myself, but the one having sent [pempō] me is true,

E

whom you do not KNOW. 29 I know him, because I am from [para] him and that one has sent [apostellō] me." 30 Then they were seeking to seize him, and no one laid a hand on him because his hour had not yet come. 31 But many of the crowd believed on him, and they were saying, "When the Christ has come, will he not do more signs than this one has done?" 32 The Pharisees heard the crowd murmuring [s.] these things about him, and

S

the chief priests and the Pharisees sent [apostellō] servants in order that they might seize him.

G

33 Then Jesus [arth.] said,

E

"Still a little time I am with you, and I go [hupagō] to [pros] the one having sent [pempō] me. [Not in G, for not mentioned in G's repetition in v. 36.]

G

34 You will seek me and not find; where I am you will not be able to come." 35 Then the Jews said [eipon] to themselves, "Where is this one about to go [poreuomai], that we will not find him? Is he about to go [poreuomai] into the Diaspora of the Greeks and to teach the Greeks? 36 What is this word [logos] which he said,

"You will seek me and you will not find' and 'where I am you are not able to COME'?"

G

37 On [prep.] the last day

R

the great one [cf. R in 19:31]

G

of the feast Jesus [arth.] stood and cried out saying, "If anyone thirsts, let him COME to [pros] me and drink. 38 The one believing on me, even as the Scripture said, 'Rivers of living water [an.; cf. 4:10-11] will flow from his belly.'"

E

39 And he said this about the Spirit which the ones believing on him were about to receive. For the Spirit was not yet (given), because Jesus [an.] was not yet glorified [E's cross-reference to 20:22].

S

40 Then some of the crowd having heard these words [logos, pl.] were saying, "This one is truly the Prophet." 41 Others were saying, "This one is the Christ." And they were saying, "For the Christ does not come FROM GALILEE. 42 Did not the Scripture say that the Christ comes from the seed of David and from [apo] Bethlehem, the village where David was?" 43 Then there was a schism in the crowd on account of him. 44 Then some of them wanted to seize him, but no one laid a hand on him. 45 Then the servants came to [pros] the chief priests and Pharisees, and those say [pres. t. in P^{66}, S] to them, "Why did you not bring him?" 46 The officers answered, "Never a amn spoke thus!" 47 Answered them the Pharisees, "Have you also been led astray? 48 Have any from the authorities or from the Pharisees believed on him? 49 But this crowd, the one not knowing the LAW, are accursed [pl.]."

E

50 Says to them Nicodemus [an.], the one coming to [pros] him first, being one of them, 51 "Does our LAW not judge a man unless it first hears from him and knows what he does?" 52 They

answered and said [eipan] to him, "Are you also from Galilee? Search (the Scriptures) and see that a prophet is not to rise FROM GALILEE."

[7:53-8:11 is a very late insertion, not appearing in any known N.T. manuscript before the 5th century.]

CHAPTER 8:

E

12 Then again to them

G

Jesus [arth. in P^{66}, S] spoke saying, "I am the Light of the world. The one following me will not walk in Darkness [skotia], but will have the Light of life." 13 Then the Pharisees said [eipon] to him, "You are TESTIFYING ABOUT YOURSELF; your TESTIMONY IS NOT TRUE [cf. 5:31-32]."

E

14 Answered Jesus [an.] and said to them, "And if I TESTIFY ABOUT MYSELF, my TESTIMONY IS TRUE, because I know whence I came and where I am going [hupagō]. You do not know whence I come or where I am going [hupagō]. 15 You judge according to the flesh; I JUDGE no one [cf. 3:17-18]. 16 But even if I judge,

G

and my JUDGMENT [art. rep. with poss. adj.] is true because I am not alone, but I and the one having sent [pempō] me. 17 And even in your law [art. rep. with poss. adj.] it has been written that the testimony of two men is true. 18 I am the one testifying about myself; the FATHER having sent [pempō] me also testifies about me."

E

19 Then they were saying to him, "Where is your FATHER?" Jesus [an.] answered, "You know neither me nor my Father; if you knew me, my Father also you would know." 20 He spoke these words [rēma, pl.] in the treasury (while) teaching in the temple. And no one seized him, because not yet had his hour come. 21 Then he said again [cf. 7:34-36] to them, "I am going

away [hupagō], and you will seek me, and you will die in your sin. Where I am going [hupagō], you are not able to come." 22 Then the Jews were saying, "He isn't going to kill himself, is he, that he says "Where I am going [hupagō], you are not able to come'?" 23 And he was saying to them, "You are from [ek] below; I am from [ek] above. You are from [ek] this world; I am not from [ek] this world. 24 I said to you that you will die in your sins. For if you do not believe that I AM [egō eimi], you will die in your sins." 25 They were saying to him, "Who are you?" Jesus [an. in P66c, P75, B] said to them, "Whatever I also told you (at) the beginning. 26 I have many things about you to speak and to judge, but the one having sent [pempō] me is true, and I, what I have heard from [para] him, THESE THINGS [demon. pron. as rep. subj.] I SPEAK to the world." 27 They did not know that he was speaking to them (about) the Father.

G

28 Then Jesus [arth.] said that "Whenever you have lifted up the Son of Man, then you will know that I AM [egō eimi] and I do nothing from [apo] myself, but even as the Father has taught me, THESE THINGS I SPEAK. 29 And the one having sent [pempō] me is with me; he has not left me alone, because I always do the things pleasing to him."

E

30 When he SPOKE THESE THINGS, many BELIEVED on him.

G

31 Then Jesus [arth.] was saying to the Jews having BELIEVED him, "If you remain in my word [logos; art. rep. with poss. adj.] you are truly my disciples, 32 and you will know the truth, and the truth will make you free." 33 They answered him, "We are seed of Abraham [an. O.T. name], and we have never been ENSLAVED to anyone. How do you say that 'You will BECOME FREE'?"

E

34 Answered them Jesus [an. in P66, P75, B], "Truly, truly, I say to you that everyone doing sin is a SLAVE of sin. 35 But the slave does not remain in the house forever; the Son remains forever. 36 Then if the Son makes you free, you will really BE FREE.

G

37 I know that you are seed of Abraham [an.], but

E

you seek to kill me because

G

my WORD [logos; art. rep. with poss. adj.] has no place in you.

E

38 What I have seen with the Father, I SPEAK; then also what you have heard from [para] the Father, do." 39 They answered and said [eipan] to him, "Our father is ABRAHAM [an.]."

R

Jesus [arth, in P^{66}, P^{75}, S] says to them, "If you were children of ABRAHAM [arth. O.T. name], you would do the works of Abraham [arth.]. [Based on vv. 40–41 and substituted for E's introduction to it.]

E

40 But now [nun] you seek to kill me, a man who has spoken the truth to you, which I heard from [para] God. Abraham did not do this. 41 You do the works of your father." They said [eipan] to him, "We have not been born from fornication; we have one father, God." 42 Jesus [an. in P^{66}, B] said to them, "If God were your father, you would love [agapaō] me, for

G

I CAME forth FROM [ek] God, and I have come. For I have not COME FROM [apo] myself,

E

but that one sent [apostellō] me.

G

43 Why do you not know MY SPEECH [art. rep. with poss. adj.]? (It is) because you are not able to hear my word [logos; art. rep. with poss. adj.].

E

44 You are from (your) father the Devil, and you want to do the desires of your father. That one was a murderer from the beginning and did not stand in the truth, because the truth is not in him. Whenever he speaks a lie, he speaks from his own (nature), because he is a liar and his father (is) [comp. subj., s. verb]. 45 But because I SPEAK the truth, you do not believe me. 46 Does any of you convict me of sin? If I speak truth, why do you not believe? 47 The one being from [ek, from v. 47b] God hears the words [rēma, pl.] of God.

G

On account of this you do not listen, that you are not from [ek] God.

E

48 Answered the Jews and said [eipan] to him, "Do we not rightly say that you are a Samaritan and you have a demon?" 49 Jesus [an.] answered, "I do not have a demon, but I honor mt Father, and you dishonor me. 50 And I do not seek my glory. There is one seeking and judging.

G

51 Truly, truly, I say to you, if anyone will keep my word [logos; art. rep. with poss. adj. in P66], he will not see [theōreō] death forever."

E

52 The Jews said [eipan] to him, "Now [nun] we know that you have a demon. Abraham [an.] died and the prophets [comp. subj., s. verb], and you say, 'If anyone will keep my word [logos], he will not taste death forever.' 53 Are you greater than OUR FATHER ABRAHAM [an. O.T. name], who died and the prophets (who) died? What do you yourself do?" 54 Jesus [an.] answered, "If I will glorify myself, my glory is nothing. My Father is the one glorifying me, whom you say that he is your God; 55 and you do not know him, but I know him. And if I said that I do not know him, I would be a liar like you. But I know him and I keep his word [logos].

G

56 ABRAHAM [an. def.] YOUR FATHER rejoiced that he would SEE my day [art. rep. with poss. adj.], and he saw and was glad."

E

57 Then the Jews said [eipan] to him, "You are not yet fifty years old, and have you SEEN ABRAHAM [an.]?" 58 Jesus [an. in P^{75}, B] said to them, "Truly, truly, I say to you, before Abraham [an.] was born, I am [egō eimi]." 59 Then they picked up stones in order that they might throw them at him. But Jesus [an.] was hidden and went out from the temple.

CHAPTER 9:

S

1 And passing by he saw a man blind from birth. 2 And his disciples asked him, saying, "Rabbi, who sinned, this one or his parents, that he was born blind?"

E

3 Jesus [an.] answered, "Neither this one sinned nor his parents, but (he was born blind) in order that the WORKS of God may be manifest in him. [E substitutes his own answer to the disciples' question.]

G

4 It is necessary that we work the WORKS of the one having sent [pempō] us [as in P^{66}, P^{75}, S*] while it is DAY; night comes when no one is able to work.

E

5 When I am in the world, I am the LIGHT of the world [connecting link with v. 4: idea of light].

S

6 (After) saying these things, he spat on the ground and made clay from the spittle and spread clay on his eyes, 7 and he said to him, "Go [hupagō], bathe in the pool of Siloam"--which is interpreted, "Having been sent [apostellō]." Then he went away and bathed and came (back) seeing [blepō].

E

8 Then the neighbors and the ones seeing [theōreō] him (who) formerly that was a beggar, were saying, "Is not this the one sitting and begging?" 9 Others were saying that "He is this one." Others were saying, "No, but he is like him." That one was saying that "I am (he)." 10 Then they were saying to him, "How were your eyes opened?" 11 That one answered, "A man [R inserts "the one being called Jesus [arth.]"] made clay and anointed my eyes, and he said to me, 'Go [hupago] into Siloam and bathe.' Then going away and bathing, I regained (my) sight." 12 And they said [eipan] to him, "Where is that one?" He says, "I know not."

S

13 They lead him to the Pharisees, the one once blind. 14 And it was the Sabbath [an.] on the day Jesus [arth.] made the clay and opened his eyes. 15 [E inserts "Again also"] then the Pharisees asked him how he regained sight. And he said to them, "He put clay on my eyes, and I bathed, and I see [blepō]." 16 Then some of the Pharisees were saying, "This man is not from [para] God,

R

because he does not keep the Sabbath [arth.]."

S

Others were saying, "How is a man, a sinner, able to do such signs?" And there was a schism among them. 17 Then they say [E or R inserts "again"] to the blind (man), "What do you say about him, since he opened your eyes?" And the (man) said that "He is a prophet."

E

18 Then the Jews did not believe about him that he was blind and regained sight, until they called the parents of him, the one having regained sight 19 and asked them saying, "Is this your son, whom you say that he was born blind?

R

Then how does he see [blepō] now [arti]?"

E

20 Then his parents answered and said [eipan], "We know that

this one is our son and that he was born blind. 21 But how he now [nun] sees [blepō] we do not know, or who opened his eyes we do not know. Ask him; he himself is of age; he himself will speak about himself." 22 His parents said [eipan] these things because they feared the Jews. For already the Jews had agreed that if anyone should confess him (to be) the Christ, he would be (banned) from the synagogue. 23 On account of this his parents said [eipan] that "He is of age; ask him."

R

24 Then for the second time they called the man who was blind and said [eipan] to him, "Give the glory to God. We know that this man is a sinner. 25 Then that one answered, "If he is a sinner, I do not know. One thing I do know; that being blind (formerly), now [arti] I see [blepō]." 26 Then they said [eipan] to him, "What did he do to you? How did he open your eyes?" 27 He answered them, "I told you already and you did not listen. Why do you want to hear (it) again? Do you also want to become his disciples?" 28 And they reviled him and said [eipan], "You are a disciple of that one, but we are disciples of Moses [arth. O.T. name in P^{75}, B, S].

E

29 We know that God has spoken to Moses [an.], but we do not know whence this one is." 30 The man answered and said to them, "For in this is the wonder, that you do not know whence he is, and he opened my eyes. 31 We [1st p. pl.: E's "preaching"] know that God does not hear sinners, but whoever is a worshiper and does his will, he (God) hears him. 32 From the beginning of time it has not been heard that anyone opened the eyes of a (man) born blind. 33 If this one were not from [para] God, he would be able to do nothing." 34 They answered and said [eipan] to him, "You were born wholly in sins, and would you teach us?" And they threw him out. 35 Jesus [an.] heard that they threw him out, and finding him he said, "Do you believe on the Son of Man?" 36 "And who is he, Lord," he said, "in order that I shall believe on him?" 37 Jesus [an. in P^{66}] said to him, "You even see him, and the one speaking with you is that one. [Omit vv. 38-39a, a late gloss, not in P^{75} and S*] 39b For judgment I came into this world, in order that the ones not seeing [blepō] may see [blepō], and the ones seeing [blepō] may become blind." 40 (Some) of the Pharisees,

the ones being with him, heard and said [eipan] to him, "Are we also blind?" 41 Jesus [an. in P66, P75, B] said to them, "If you were blind, you would not have sin. But now [nun] you say that 'We see [blepō]'; your sin remains."

CHAPTER 10:

G

1 "Truly, truly, I say to you, the one not entering through the door into the fold of the sheep,

E

but climbing over at some other place, that one [demon. pron. as rep. subj.]

G

is a thief and a robber. 2 But the one entering through the door is the shepherd of the sheep. 3 The doorkeeper opens to this one, and the sheep hear his voice, and he calls his own sheep by name and he leads them out. 4 Whenever he takes out all his own, he goes [poreuomai] ahead of them, and the sheep follow him because they know his voice. 5 But a stranger they do not follow, but will flee from him because they do not know the voice of strangers." 6 Jesus [arth.] spoke to them this figure (of speech), but those did not know what the things were which he was speaking to them. 7 Then Jesus [arth. except in B] said, "Truly, truly, I say to you, I am the shepherd of the sheep. 8 All who came ["before me" is not in P^{45}, P^{75}, S*] are thieves and robbers, but the sheep did not hear them. 9 I am the door. If anyone enters through me, he will be saved, and he will go in and go out and find pasture. 10 The thief does not come except in order to steal and to slaughter and to destroy. I came in order that they may have life and have it more abundantly. 11 I am the good shepherd [art. rep.]. The GOOD SHEPHERD [art. rep.] lays down his life in behalf of the sheep.

E

12 The hired man, being NOT EVEN A SHEPHERD, whose sheep are not his own, sees [theōreō] the wolf coming and leaves the sheep and flees

R

--and the wolf snatches and scatters them--

E

13 because he is a hired man and it is not a concern to him about the sheep.

G

14 I am the good shepherd [art. rep.], and I know mine [poss. adj.], and mine [poss. adj.] know me, 15 even as the Father knows me and I know the Father, and I LAY DOWN MY LIFE in behalf of the SHEEP.

E

16 And other SHEEP I have which are not of this fold. And it is necessary (for) me to lead those, and they will hear my voice, and there will be one flock, one shepherd. 17 On account of this the Father loves [agapaō] me, because I LAY DOWN MY LIFE, in order that I may take it up again.

G

18 No one took it from [apo] me, but I lay it down from [apo] myself. I have authority to lay it down, and I have authority to take it up again.

E

This commandment I received from [para] my Father." 19 There was a schism again among the Jews on account of these words [logos, pl.; S influence ?--cf. 7:40]. 20 And many of them were saying, "He has a demon and is mad. Why listen to him?" 21 Others were saying, "These are not the words [rēma, pl.] of a demon-possessed (person). Is a demon able to open the eyes of the blind?"

R

22 Then it was the Consecration [i.e., feast of the Dedication of the temple] in Jerusalem [arth., pl.]; it was winter. 23 And Jesus [arth. in P^{66}, P^{75}, S] was walking in the temple in the portico of Solomon [arth. O.T. name in P^{66}, P^{75}, B].

E

24 Then the Jews surrounded him and were saying to him, "Until when do you take away our life [fig. for "How long will you keep us in suspense?"]? If you are the Christ, tell us plainly."

G

25 Jesus [arth. in P^{66}, P^{75}, S] answered,

E

"I told you, and YOU DO NOT BELIEVE. The works which I do in the name of my Father, these [demon. pron. as rep. subj.] testify about me. 26 But

G

YOU DO NOT BELIEVE because you are not from my sheep [art. rep. with poss. adj.]. 27 My sheep [art. rep. with poss. adj.] hear my voice, and I know them, and they follow me, 28 and I give them life eternal, and they will not perish forever, and no one will snatch them from my hand. 29 The Father who has given (them) to me is greater than all, and no one is able to snatch (them) from the hand of the Father. 30 I and the Father are one [neut., not masc.; thus it means not that Jesus and the Father are one person, but as one, united]."

E

31 The Jews picked up stones again [refers to 8:59] in order that they might stone him.

G

32 Answered them Jesus [arth.], "Many good WORKS I have shown to you from [ek] the Father.

E

For which WORK of them do you stone me?" 33 Answered him the Jews, "We stone you not about a good work, but about blasphemy, and because you, being a man, make yourself a god." 34 Answered them Jesus [an. in P^{45}, P^{66}, B], "Is it not written in your law that 'I said, You are gods'? 35 If he [God] said [i.e., called] gods those to whom the word of God came,

R

--and the Scripture [s.] is not able to be broken--

E

36 do you say whom the Father sanctified and sent [apostellō] into the world that 'You blaspheme,' because I said, 'I am the Son of God [cf. 5:18]? 37 If I do not do the works of my Father, do not believe me. 38 But if I do and you do not believe me, believe the works, in order that you may know and understand that the Father (is) in me and I (am) in the Father." 39 They were seeking to seize him, and he went out from their hand. [In G the basis of blasphemy is in v. 30; in E it is in v. 36.]

S

40 And he went away [E's insertion: "again"] across the Jordan

E

to the place where John [an.] was baptizing at first,

S

and he stayed there. 41 And many came to [pros] him and

E

were saying that John [an.] did no sign, but all things whatever John [an.] said about this one were true. 42 And many

S

believed on him there.

CHAPTER 11:

S

1 And there was a certain (man) from [apo] Bethany, being sick,

E

Lazarus [an.], from [ek] the village of Mary [an. in P66, P75, B] and Martha [an. def.], her sister. [E associates this story with the Anointing in chap. 12 because both are located in Bethany; E got name "Mary" from 12:3.]

R

2 And Mary [arth. in P45] was the one having anointed the Lord

with ointment and having wiped his feet with her hair, whose brother Lazarus [arth.] was sick [cross-reference to 12:3].

S

3 Then the sisters sent [apostellō] to him, saying, "Lord, behold [ide], he whom you LOVE [phileō] is sick." 4 And having heard, Jesus [arth.] said, "This sickness is not to death, but for the sake of the glory of God, in order that the Son of God may be glorified through it."

R

5 And Jesus [arth.] LOVED [agapaō] Martha [arth.] and her sister and Lazarus [arth.].

S

6 Then when he heard that he is sick, then [tote men] he stayed in the place in which he was two days [cf. 4:40]. 7 Next after this he says to the disciples, "Let us GO [agō] into Judea again." 8 The disciples say to him, "Rabbi, . . .

E

now [nun] the Jews are seeking to stone you, and are you GOING [hupagō] there again?" 9 Jesus [an.] answered [connecting link with G: idea of motion (go, walk)],

G

"Are there not twelve hours of the day? If anyone WALKS in the day, he does not stumble, because he sees [blepō] the light of this world. 10 But if anyone walks in the night, he stumbles, because the light is not in him."

E

11 He said these things, and

S

after this he says to them, [E inserts "Lazarus [an. def.]"] our friend has fallen asleep, but I am going [poreuomai] in order that I will awaken him." 12 Then the disciples said [eipan] to him, "Lord, if he has fallen asleep, he will awaken [in P^{75}]. 13 But Jesus [arth.] had spoken about his death, but those thought that he is speaking about the sleep of slumber. 14 Then [tote oun]

Jesus [arth. in P^{75}, B, S^c] said to them plainly, [E inserts "Lazarus [an.]"] "he died, 15 and I rejoice for the sake of you, that I was not there, in order that you may believe. But let us go to him."

E

16 Then said Thomas [an.], [R inserts "the one being called 'Twin' [cf. 21:2],"] "Let us go also in order that we may die with him."

R

18 And Bethany was near Jerusalem [arth., pl.] about [hōs apo] fifteen stadia.

S

19 And many of the Jews had come to [pros] Martha [arth.] [E inserts "and Mary [an.]"] in order that they might console them [prob. "her" in S] about the brother. 20 Then Martha [arth.] met him

E

when she heard that Jesus [an.] is coming, but Mary [an.] sat in the house.

S

21 Then Martha [arth.] said to Jesus [arth. in P^{45}, P^{66}, P^{75}], "Lord, if you had been here, my brother would not have died.

E

22 And now [nun] I know that whatever you ask [aiteō] God, God will give to you. [Does not fit the context in S.]

S

23 Jesus [arth.] says to her, "Your brother will arise." 24 Martha [arth.] says to him, "I know that he will arise in the resurrection [E inserts "on [prep.] the last day"]. 25 Jesus [arth.] said to her, "I am the resurrection ["and the life" is not in P^{45}]. He who believes on me, even should he die, will live; 26 and everyone living and believing on me, should not die forever. [Vv. 25b-26 may have been composed by E.] Do you believe this?" 27 She says to him, "Yes, Lord. I have believed that you

are the Christ, the Son of God, the one coming into the world."

E

28 And having said this, she went away and called Mary [an. def.], her sister, saying secretly, "The Teacher is here and calls (for) you." 29 And when that one heard, she rose quickly and came to [pros] him.

R

30 And Jesus [arth.] had not yet come into the village, but was still in the place where Martha [arth.] had met him. 31 Then the Jews, the ones being with her in the house and consoling her [cross-reference to v. 19 in S], seeing Mary [arth.] that she rose quickly and went out, followed her, having supposed that she is going [hupagō] to [eis] the tomb in order that she may WEEP there. 32 Then Mary [arth.]

E

when she came where Jesus [an.] was, having seen him, fell at his feet, saying to him, "Lord, if you had been here, my brother would not have died." [E repeats v. 21 from S.] 33 Then Jesus [an.], when he saw her WEEPING,

R

and the Jews having come with her WEEPING,

E

was agitated in spirit and disturbed (in) himself. 34 And he said, "Where have you laid him?" They say to him, "Lord, come and see."

S

35 Jesus [arth.] WEPT. 36 Then the Jews were saying, "Behold [ide], how he was loving [phileō] him."

E

37 But certain of them said [eipan], "Was not this one [demon. pron. as rep. subj.], the one having opened the eyes of the blind, able to accomplish that also this one might not die?" 38 Then Jesus [an.], again agitated in himself, comes

R

to [eis] the tomb. And it was a cave, and a stone lay on it.

S

39 Jesus [arth.] says, "Take away the stone." Martha [arth.],

Later Gloss

the sister of the deceased [teleutaō--only occurrence in John],

S

says to him, "Already he stinks, for he is (dead) four days." 40 Jesus [arth. in B, S; lac. in P^{75}] says to her, "Did I not say to you that if you would believe, you will see the glory of God? 41 Take away the stone."

G

And Jesus [arth.] lifted up (his) eyes and said, "Father, I give thanks to you because you HEARD me. [From a source, for in the present context Jesus has not addressed the Father.]

E

42 But I knew that you always HEAR me, but I said (this) on account of the crowd, the one standing by, in order that they may believe [pl.] that you sent [apostellō] me." 43 And having said these things,

S

he cried out with a loud voice, [E inserts "Lazarus [an. voc.],"] come out." 44 The dead (man) came out, (his) feet and hands bound with bandages, and his faced wrapped with a handkerchief. Jesus [arth.] says to them, "Loose him and let him go [hupagō]."

E

45 Then many of the Jews, the ones

R

having come to [pros] Mary [arth.; cross-reference to v. 31] and

E

having seen [theaomai] what he did, BELIEVED ON HIM.

S

46 And certain of them went away to the Pharisees and told [eipan] them what Jesus [arth. in S; lac. in P75] had done. 47 Then the chief priests and the Pharisees gathered the Sanhedrin, and were saying, "What shall we do, because this man does many signs? 48 If we permit him thus, everyone will BELIEVE ON HIM, and the Romans will come and destroy both our place and our nation [refers to Roman destruction of Jerusalem, A.D. 70]." 49 But a certain one of them

E

Caiaphas [an.], being high priest that year [drawn from S in 18:13]

S

said to them, "You know nothing. 50 You do not understand that it is advantageous for you that one man should die IN BEHALF OF the people and not that the whole NATION perish."

E

51 And he did not say this from [apo] himself, but being high priest that year, he prophesied that Jesus [an.] was about to die IN BEHALF OF THE NATION, 52 and not only in behalf of the nation, but also in order that the dispersed children of God may be gathered together into one. [E restates and reinterprets S in v. 50.] 53 Then from that day they resolved that they should kill him.

S

54 Then Jesus [arth.] no longer walked about openly among the Jews, but he went away from there into the region near the wilderness, [R inserts "into a city being called Ephraim,"] and there he stayed with the disciples.

R

55 And the Passover of the Jews was near.

S

And many went up into Jerusalem [an., s.] from the region before the Passover, in order that they might purify themselves.

R

56 Then they were seeking Jesus [arth.] and were talking with each other (while) standing in the temple, "What do you think? That he may not come to the feast?"

S

57 And the chief priests and the Pharisees had given orders that if anyone knew where he is, he should reveal (it), so that they might seize him.

CHAPTER 12:

S

1 Then Jesus [arth.], six days before the Passover, came into Bethany

E

where Lazarus [an.] was [suggested by 11:1], whom Jesus [an. in P^{66}, B, S*; lac. in P^{75}] raised from the dead.

S

2 Then they made for him a supper there,

R

and Martha [arth. in B, S; lac. in P^{75}] served. And Lazarus [arth.] was one of those reclining with [sun] him.

S

3 Then Mary [arth.], having taken a litra of pure, costly nard ointment, anointed the feet of Jesus [arth. in P^{66}, S; lac. in P^{75}] and wiped his feet with her hair. And the house was filled with the aroma of the ointment. 4 And says one of [part. gen.] his disciples,

R

Judas [an. def.] the Iscariot, the one being about to betray him,

S

5 "Why was this ointment not sold for three hundred denarii and given to the poor?"

R

6 But he said this not because about the poor was a concern to him, but because he was a thief and having the moneybox, he used to take the things put (into it).

S

7 Then Jesus [arth.] said, "Permit her, in order that she may keep it for the day of my burial. 8 For the poor you always have with you, but me you do not always have." 9 Then a large crowd of the Jews

R

knew [s.] that he is there, and they came not on account of Jesus [arth.] only, but also in order that they might see Lazarus [arth.] whom he raised from the dead [repeats from E in v. 1]. 10 And the chief priests resolved that they would kill Lazarus [arth.] also, 11 because on account of him many of [part. gen.] the Jews

S

were going [hupagō, pl.] and were believing [pl.] on Jesus [arth.]. 12 On the morrow a great crowd

R

the one coming [s.] to [eis] the feast,

S

having heard [pl.] that Jesus [arth. in P66, P75, B] is coming into Jerusalem [an., s.], 13 took [pl.] branches of palms and went out [pl.] to meet him, and cried out [pl.], "Hosanna! Blessed be the one coming in the name of the Lord, even the King of Israel." 14 And Jesus [arth.], having found a little donkey, sat upon it

E

even as it is having been written: 15 "Fear not, daughter of Zion. Behold, your king comes, seated on a colt of a donkey." 16 His disciples did not know these things at first, but when Jesus [an. except in P66c] was glorified, then they remembered that these things were having been written about him and they did these things to him. 17 Then the crowd was testifying [s.]

R

the one being with him when he called Lazarus [arth.] from the
tomb and raised him from the dead [cross-reference to v. 9]. 18
On account of this also the crowd met [s.] him, because

S

. . . (the crowd) heard [pl.] that he himself had done this sign.
19 Then the Pharisees said [<u>eipan</u>] to themselves, "You see
[<u>theōreō</u>] that you accomplish nothing. Behold [<u>ide</u>], the world
has gone off after him." 20 And there were certain Greeks among
the ones going up in order that they might worship at the feast.
21 Then these came [E inserts "to Philip [an.]"]

R

the one from Bethsaida [from S, 1:44] of Galilee,

S

and were asking [<u>erōtaō</u>] [E inserts "him"] saying, "Lord, we
want to see Jesus [arth.]." 22 Philip [arth. in P^{66}, P^{75}, B]
comes and tells Andrew [arth.];

E

Andrew [an.] comes, and Philip [an.],

S

and they tell Jesus [arth.].

G

23 And Jesus [arth.] answers them saying, "The HOUR has come
that the Son of Man should be glorified. 24 Truly, truly, I say to
you, if a kernel of wheat, falling into the earth, does not die, it
itself remains alone. But if it dies, it bears much fruit. 25 The
one loving [<u>phileō</u>] his life loses it, and the one hating his life in
this world preserves it for life eternal. 26 If anyone would serve
me, let him follow me; and where I am, there also my servant
[art. rep. with poss. adj.] will be. If anyone serves me, the
Father will honor him.

E

27 Now [<u>nun</u>] my soul is disturbed, and what should I say--Father,
save me from this HOUR? But on account of this I came into this

hour. 28 Father, glorify your name." Then a voice came from [ek] heaven, "I have glorified and I will glorify (it) again." 29 The crowd, the one standing and having heard, was saying [s.], "It was thunder." Others were saying, "An angel has spoken to him." 30 Answered Jesus [an.; "and said" is not in S], "This voice came not for the sake of me, but for the sake of you. 31 Now [nun] is the judgment of this world; now [nun] the ruler of this world will be cast out.

G

32 And if I am LIFTED UP from the earth, I will draw all things [neut.] to myself."

E

33 And he was saying this signifying by what death he was about to die. 34 Then answered [s.] him the crowd, "We have heard from the law that the Christ remains forever, and how do you say that it is necessary (that) the Son of Man be LIFTED UP? Who is this Son of Man? [E is dealing with the controversy between Christians and Jews over whether the Son of Man would ascend to heaven, a Christian belief contrary to Jewish belief.]

G

35 Then Jesus [arth.] said to them,

E

"Still a little time THE LIGHT is among you.

G

WALK while you have THE LIGHT, in order that DARKNESS [skotia] may not seize you.

E

And the one WALKING in the DARKNESS [skotia] knows not where he is going [hupagō].

G

36 While you have the Light, BELIEVE IN THE LIGHT, in order that you may become Sons of Light."

E

Jesus [an. in P^{66}, B] spoke these things, and going away was hidden from them. 37 But (though) he had done so many signs before them, they did not BELIEVE ON HIM,

R

38 in order that the word [logos] of Isaiah [an. def.] the prophet might be fulfilled which he said: "Lord, who has believed our report? And to whom has the arm of the Lord been revealed [cf. R in 15:25]?" 39 On account of this they were unable to BELIEVE,

E

because [R inserts "again"] Isaiah [an. O.T. name] said, 40 "He has blinded their eyes and hardened their heart, in order that they may not see with their eyes and understand with (their) heart, and change, and I would heal them." 41 Isaiah [an.] said these things because he saw his glory, and he has spoken about him. 42 Nevertheless, though, many even of the leaders BELIEVED ON HIM, but on account of the Pharisees they did not confess (it), in order that they might not be banned from the synagogue. 43 For they loved [agapaō] the glory of men rather than the glory of God [cf. 5:44]. 44 And Jesus [an.] cried out and said,

G

"The one BELIEVING ON ME, believes not on me but on the one having sent [pempō] me, 45 and the one seeing [theōreō] me sees the one having sent [pempō] me.

E

46 I have come as Light into the world, in order that the one BELIEVING ON ME may not remain in Darkness [skotia]. 47 And if anyone hears my words [rēma, pl.] and does not keep them, I do not judge him. For I did not come in order that I may judge the world, but in order that I may save the world. 48 The one rejecting me and not receiving my WORDS [rēma, pl.] has him who JUDGES (him).

R

The WORD [logos, s.] which I have spoken, that one [demon. pron. as rep. subj.] will JUDGE him on [no prep. in P^{66}] the last day.

G

49 Because I have not spoken from [ek] myself, but the Father having sent [pempō] me has himself given commandment to me what I said and what I will speak. 50 And I know that his commandment is life eternal. Therefore what things I speak , even as the Father told me, thus I speak." [In G v. 49 followed v. 45.]

CHAPTER 13:

R

1 And before the feast of the Passover

G

Jesus [arth.], seeing that his hour had come that he should pass from [ek] this world to the Father,

E

having loved [agapaō] his own in the world, he loved [agapaō] them to (the) end. 2 And when it was suppertime, when the Devil had already put (it) into (his) heart that Judas Iscariot [an. comp.], (son) of Simon [an.], should betray him,

G

3 knowing that the Father had given to him all things into (his) hands,

R

and that he went forth from [apo] God and that he is going [hupagō] to [pros] God,

E

4 he got up from supper and laid aside (his) garments, and taking a linen cloth he girded himself. 5 Next he cast water into a basin and began to wash the feet of the disciples and to wipe (them) with the linen cloth with which he was girded. 6 Then he comes to [pros] Simon Peter [an. comp.]. He says to him, "Lord, do you wash my feet?" 7 Answered Jesus [an.] and said to him, "What I do you do not know

R

now [arti], but you will after these things."

E

8 Peter [an.] says to him, "You may never wash my feet." Jesus [an.] answered him, "If I do not wash you [s.], you [s.] have no part with me." 9 Simon Peter [an. comp.] says to him, "Lord, not my feet only, but also (my) hands and head."

R

10 Jesus [arth. except in B] says to him, "The one having bathed does not have need to wash, but is wholly clean. And you [pl.] are clean, but not all." 11 For he knew the one betraying him. On account of this he said that "You [pl.] are not all clean."

E

12 Then after he washed their feet, he took his garments and reclined again. He said to them, "Do you know what I have done for you? 13 You call me 'Teacher' and 'Master (or 'Lord'),' and you say well, for I am. 14 Then if I, (your) MASTER and Teacher, washed your feet, you also ought to wash the feet of one another. 15 I have given an example to you in order that even as I have done, you also should do.

G

16 Truly, truly, I say to you, a slave is not greater than his MASTER (or 'LORD'), nor an apostle than the one having sent [pempō] him. 17 If you know these things, you will be blessed if you do them. [In vv. 12-15 the master is not greater than those he teaches; in vv. 16-17 the slave is not greater than the master--a different idea. E inserts the latter on the basis of the catchword "master" in spite of the disparity in thought.]

R

18 I am not talking about all of you; I know whom I have chosen. But in order that the Scripture may be fulfilled: 'The one eating [trōgō; esthiō in LXX] my bread lifted his heel against me.' 19 From now [arti] on I tell you before (it) happens, in order that when (it) happens you may believe that I am [egō eimi].

G

20 Truly, truly, I say to you, the one receiving anyone I will send [pempō], receives me, and the one receiving me, receives the one having sent [pempō] me."

E

21 Having said these things, Jesus [an. except in P^{66c}] was disturbed in spirit and testified and said, "Truly, truly, I say to you that one of you will betray me." 22 The disciples looked at [blepō] each other, being uncertain about whom he is speaking. 23 There was reclining one of his disciples

R

on the breast of Jesus [arth.], whom Jesus [arth. in P^{66c}, S; lac. in P^{75}] loved [agapaō].

E

24 Then Simon Peter [an. comp.] nods to this one and says to him, "Say who (it) is about whom he speaks." 25 That one,

R

lying thus on the breast of Jesus [arth.],

E

says to him, "Lord, who is (it)?" 26 Jesus [an. in P^{66}, B; lac. in P^{75}] answers, "That one (it) is to whom I will dip a piece of bread and give (it) to him." Then having dipped a piece of bread, he takes and gives (it) to Judas Iscariot [an. comp.], (son) of Simon [an. in P^{66}].

R

27 And then after the piece of bread Satan entered into that one. Then Jesus [arth. in P^{66}, S; lac. in P^{75}] says to him, "What you do, do quickly." 28 No one of the ones reclining (to eat) knew for what (reason) he said this to him. 29 For some thought, since Judas [arth. in P^{66}; lac. in P^{75}] had the money box, that Jesus [arth. in P^{66}; lac. in P^{75}] says to him, "Buy what we have need of for the feast," or in order that he might give something to the poor.

E

30 Then taking the piece of bread, that one went out immediately. And it was night. 31 Then when he went out, Jesus [an. in P^{66}, B, S; lac. in P^{75}] says, "Now [nun] the Son of Man has been glorified, and God has been glorified by him, 32 and God will glorify him by him, and immediately he will glorify him. 33 Little

children, still a little (while) I am with you. You will seek me, and even as I said to the Jews, 'Where I am going [hupagō] you are not able to come,'

R

also I say to you now [arti]. 34 A new commandment I give to you, that you love [agapaō] one another; even as I have loved [agapaō] you, that you also may love [agapaō] one another. 35 By this all will know that you are my disciples, if you have love for one another." [Cf. 15:12-17.]

E

36 Simon Peter [an. comp.] says to him, "Lord, where are you going [hupagō] ?" Jesus [an. in P^{66}, B; lac. in P^{75}] answered, "Where I am going [hupagō], you are not able to follow me now [nun], but you will follow later."

R

37 Peter [arth. in P^{66}, B; lac. in P^{75}] says to him, "Why can I not follow you now [arti] ?

E

. . . I will lay down my life for you." 38 Jesus [an.] answers, "Will you lay down your life for me? Truly, truly, I say to you, the cock will not crow until you deny me thrice [refers to G in 18:27]."

CHAPTER 14:

G

1 "Let not your [pl.] heart [s.] be disturbed; you believe on God, believe on me also. 2 In the house of my Father there are many rooms; and if (there were) not, I would have told you. I AM GOING [poreuomai] to prepare a place for you. 3 And if I go [poreuomai] and prepare a place for you, I am coming again and will take you to myself, in order that where I am, you also may be.

E

4 And where I AM GOING [hupagō], you know the way." 5 Thomas [an.] says to him, "Lord, we do not know where you are going [hupagō]; how do we know THE WAY?" 6 Jesus [an. in P^{66}, S; lac. in P^{75}] says to him,

G

"I am THE WAY and the Truth and the Life. No one comes to [pros] the FATHER except through me.

E

7 If you had known me, my FATHER also you would have KNOWN.

R

From now [arti] (on) you KNOW and have SEEN HIM."

E

8 Philip [an.] says to him, "Lord, show to us the Father, and it will be sufficient for us." 9 Jesus [an. in P^{66}] says to him, "So much time I am with you, and you do not know me, Philip [an.]? The one having seen me has SEEN THE FATHER [cf. 12:45]. How do you say, 'Show to us the Father'? 10 Do you not believe that

G

I am in the Father and the Father is in me?

E

The words [rēma, pl.] which I say to you

G

I do not speak from [apo] myself. But the Father staying in me does the works themselves. 11 Believe me that I am in the Father and the Father in me; if not, BELIEVE on account of the WORKS.

E

12 Truly, truly, I say to you, the one BELIEVING on me, the WORKS which I do, that one [demon. pron. as rep. subj.] also will do, and greater than these he will do because I am going [poreuomai] to the Father. 13 And whatever you ASK [aiteō] IN MY NAME, this [demon. pron. as rep. obj.] I will do, in order that the Father may be glorified by the Son. [E here restates G material.]

G

14 If you ASK [aiteō] me anything IN MY NAME, I will give (it).

E

15 If you love [agapaō] me,

G

you will keep MY COMMANDMENTS [art. rep. with poss. adj.].

E

16 And I will ASK [erōtaō] the Father, and another Paraclete he will give to you, in order that it may be with you forever, 17 the Spirit of Truth, which the world is not able to receive, because it neither sees [theōreō] nor knows it. You know it, because it stays with you and will be in you. 18 I will not leave you orphaned; I am coming to [pros] you. 19 Still a little (while) and the world will no longer see [theōreō] me, but you will see [theōreō] me, because I live and you will live. 20 On [prep.] that day you will know that I (am) in my Father and you in me and I in you. 21 The one having MY COMMANDMENTS and keeping them, that one [demon. pron. as rep. subj.] is the one loving [agapaō] me. And the one loving [agapaō] me will be kept by my Father, and I will love [agapaō] him and will reveal myself to him. 22 Says to him Judas [an.], [R inserts "--not the Iscariot [arth.]"] "Lord, what happened that [i.e., why] you are about to reveal yourself to us and not to the world?" 23 Answered Jesus [an.] and said to him, "If anyone loves [agapaō] me, he will keep my WORD [logos, s., from v. 24b], and my Father will love [agapaō] him, and we will come to [pros] him and will make a dwelling place with him. 24 The one not loving [agapaō] me does not keep my words [logos, pl.; G influence].

G

And the WORD [logos] which you hear is not mine, but of the Father having sent [pempō] me. 25 I have spoken these things to you (while) staying with you. 26 And the Paraclete, the Holy Spirit, which the Father will send [pempō] in my name [E inserts "that one [demon. pron. as rep. subj.]"] WILL TEACH YOU ALL THINGS

E

and WILL REMIND YOU OF ALL THINGS which I told you. [E reinterprets G's preceding statement in an effort to solve the problem created by Christians who claimed that Jesus had uttered apostolic preaching which originated after Jesus' death.]

G

27 PEACE I leave with you; my peace I give to you; not as the world gives I give to you.

E

Let NOT your heart be DISTURBED nor be timid [E's restatement of 14:1, suggested by "peace" in v. 27a]. 28 You have heard that I said to you, 'I am going [hupagō] away and I am coming to [pros] you.' If you loved [agapaō] me, you would have rejoiced that I am going [poreuomai, from G material in v. 12] to [pros] the Father, because the Father is greater than I. 29 And now [nun] I have told you before it happens, in order that when it happens, you may believe. [E is trying to convince the doubters that Jesus is still alive and has ascended to heaven.] 30 I will no longer speak much with you, for the ruler of the world is coming, and he has nothing in me; 31 but in order that the world may know that I love [agapaō] the Father, and even as the Father has commanded me, thus I do.

G

Arise, let us go from here."

CHAPTER 15:

G

1 "I am the true vine [art. rep.], and my Father is the farmer. 2 Every branch in me not bearing fruit, he takes it away, and everything [neut.] bearing fruit, he CLEANS [i.e., prunes] it in order that it may BEAR MORE FRUIT.

R

3 Already you are CLEAN on account of the word [logos] which I have spoken to you.

G

4 Remain in me, and I in you; even as the branch is not able to bear fruit from [apo] itself except it remain in the vine, thus neither you (can) unless you REMAIN IN ME. 5 I am the vine; you are the branches.

E

The one REMAINING IN ME and I in him, this one [demon. pron.

as rep. subj.] BEARS MUCH FRUIT, because without me you are not able to do anything [E restates v. 4].

G

6 If a person does not remain in me, he is cast out as a branch and is withered, and they gather and throw them into the fire, and they are burned. 7 If you remain in me

E

and my words [rēma, pl.] remain in you,

G

ask [aiteō] whatever you wish and it shall be to you.

E

8 By this my Father is glorified, that you BEAR MUCH FRUIT and become my disciples. 9 Even as the Father loved [agapaō] me, I also LOVED [agapaō] you.

G

REMAIN IN MY LOVE [art. rep. with poss. adj.].

E

10 If you keep my commandments, you REMAIN IN MY LOVE, even as I have kept the commandments of the ["my" is not in P^{66}, S; lac. in P^{75}] Father and I remain in his love.

G

11 These things I have spoken to you in order that my joy [art. rep. with poss. adj.] may be in you and your joy may be filled. 12 This [refers to v. 9c] is my commandment [art. rep. with poss. adj.]

E

that you love [agapaō] one another even as I LOVED [agapaō] you. 13 Greater love than this has no one, that he lays down his life for the sake of his FRIENDS.

G

14 You are my FRIENDS if you do what I COMMAND YOU.

E

15 No longer I call you slaves, for the slave does not know what his master does; but I called you FRIENDS because all things which I heard from [para] my Father I made known to you [different basis for being "friends" than in v. 14].

G

16 You did not choose me, but I chose you and appointed you

E

in order that you may go [hupagō] and BEAR FRUIT and your fruit remain [E's insertion creates a double purpose]

G

in order that whatever you ask [aiteō] the Father in my name, he may give to you.

E

17 These things I COMMAND YOU in order that you may love [agapaō] one another.

G

18 If the world hates you, know that it has hated me first. 19 If you were from [ek] the world, the world would love [phileō] its own; but because you are not from [ek] THE WORLD,

E

--but I chose you from [ek] THE WORLD, on account of this--

G

the world hates you.

R

20 Remember the WORD [logos] which I said to you, 'A slave is not greater than his master [R's cross-reference to 13:16].'

E

If they persecuted me, you also they will persecute. If they kept my WORD [logos], yours also they will keep. 21 But all these things they will do to you on account of my name, because they do not know the one having sent [pempō] me. 22 Unless I came and spoke to them, they would not have sin. But now [nun] they do not have an excuse for their sin.

G

23 The one HATING ME also hates my Father.

E

24 If I did not do the works among them which no one other did, they would not have sin. But now [nun] they have both seen and have both seen and have HATED ME and my Father.

R

25 But (it is) in order that the word [logos] may be fulfilled, the one having been written in their law that 'They HATED ME without a cause [cf. R in 12:38].'

E

26 Whenever the Paraclete comes which I will send [pempō] to you from [para] the Father, the Spirit of Truth which proceeds from [para] the Father, that one [demon. pron. as rep. subj.] will testify about me. 27 And you also testify, because from the beginning you are with me." [E's theme: Jesus has many kinds of testimony.]

CHAPTER 16:

E

1 I HAVE SPOKEN THESE THINGS to you in order that you may not stumble [i.e., commit apostasy]. 2 They will ban you from the synagogues. But the hour comes that everyone killing you will think he offers service to God. 3 And they will do these things because they know neither the Father nor me. 4 But I have spoken these things to you in order that whenever the hour has come, you will remember them, because I told you. 5 And now [nun] I go [hupagō] to [pros] the one having sent [pempō] me, and no one of you asks me, 'Where are you going [hupagō; cf. 13:36]?'

G

6 But because I HAVE SPOKEN THESE THINGS TO YOU, sorrow has filled your heart. 7 But I say the truth to you: it is advantageous for you that I go away [aperchomai]. For if I do not go away

[aperchomai], the Paraclete will not COME to [pros] you; but if I go [poreuomai], I will send [pempō] it to you.

E

8 And COMING that one will convict the world about sin and about righteousness and about judgment. 9 About sin because they do not believe on me; 10 and about righteousness because I am going [hupagō] to [pros] the Father and no longer you will see [theōreō] me; 11 and about judgment because the ruler of this world has been judged.

G

12 I have still many things to say to you, but you are not able to bear (them) now [arti]. 13 But whenever that one comes, the Spirit of Truth, it will guide you into all truth. For it will not speak from [apo] itself, but whatever it hears it will speak, and the coming [i.e., future] things it will proclaim to you. 14 That one will glorify me, because IT WILL RECEIVE FROM ME AND PROCLAIM TO YOU.

E

15 All things whatsoever the Father has are mine. On account of this I say that IT RECEIVES FROM ME AND PROCLAIMS TO YOU. 16 A little (while) and no longer you will see [theōreō] me, and again a little (while) and you will see [horaō] me." 17 Then some of his disciples said [eipan] to one another, "What is this which he says to us, 'A little (while) and no longer you will see [theōreō] me, and again a little (while) and you will see [horaō] me,' and 'because I am going [hupagō] to [pros] the Father'?" 18 Then they were saying, "What is this, 'a little (while)'? We do not know." 19 Jesus [an. in P^5, P^{66}, B; lac. in P^{75}] knew that they wanted to ask him, and he said to them, "About this are you deliberating with one another because I said, "A little (while) and you will not see [theōreō] me, and again a little (while) and you will see [horaō] me'? 20 Truly, truly, I say to you that you will weep and you will lament, but the world will rejoice; you will be sorrowful, but your sorrow will become into joy. 21 Whenever a woman is in travail, she has sorrow because her hour has come; but when she has given birth to the child, she no longer remembers the anguish on account of the joy that a man has been born into the world. 22 Then you also now [nun] have sorrow; but again I will

see [horaō] you and your heart will rejoice, and your joy no one takes from you. 23 And ON [prep.] THAT DAY YOU WILL not ASK [erōtaō] me anything.

G

Truly, truly, I say to you, whatever you ASK [aiteō] the Father, he will give to you in my name. 24 Until now [arti] you have not asked [aiteō] anything in my name. Ask [aiteō], and you will receive, in order that your joy may be filled. 25 These things in figures (of speech) I have spoken to you; the hour comes when no longer in figures I will speak to you, but in plainness about the Father I will proclaim to you. 26 ON [prep.] THAT DAY in my name YOU WILL ASK [aiteō]

E

and I do not say to you that I will ask [erōtaō]

G

the Father ["about you" is not in P^5 (P^{66} ?)]. 27 For the Father himself loves [phileō] you, because you have loved [phileō] me

E

and have believed that I came forth from [para] God.

G

28 I came forth from [ek] the Father and have come into the world. Again, I am leaving the world and going [poreuomai] to the Father."

E

29 His disciples say, "Behold [ide], now [nun] you speak in plainness, and you do not say a figure (of speech). 30 Now [nun] we know that you know all things and do not have need that anyone ask you;

R

by this we believe that you came forth from [apo] God."

E

31 Answered them Jesus [an. in P^{22}, P^{66}, B; lac. in P^{75}], . . . [R substitutes his own composition.]

R

"Now [arti] do you believe? 32 ["Behold" is not in P^{66}.] The hour comes and has come that you will be scattered, each to his own (home), and will leave me ALONE.

G

And I am not ALONE, because the Father is with me. 33 THESE THINGS I HAVE SPOKEN to you in order that you may have peace in me. In the world you have affliction, but have courage: I have conquered the world."

CHAPTER 17:

E

1 These things Jesus [an. in B, S; lac. in P^{66}, P^{75}] spoke, and

G

having lifted up his eyes to heaven, he said, "Father, the hour has come; glorify your Son in order that the Son may glorify you. 2 Even as you gave to him authority over all flesh, in order that everything [neut.] which you have given to him, he may give to them LIFE ETERNAL.

Later Gloss

3 And this is ETERNAL LIFE [only instance in John of word order "eternal life"], that they may know you, the only true God and whom you sent [apostellō], Jesus Christ [an. comp.; only other occurrence of "Jesus Christ" is in 1:17].

G

4 I GLORIFIED you on earth, having completed [teleioō] the work which YOU HAD GIVEN TO ME in order that I should do.

E

5 And now [nun] GLORIFY me, Father, with yourself with the glory which I had with you before the world was [suggested by v. 24]. 6 I manifested your name to the men whom YOU GAVE TO ME from [ek] the world. Yours they were and to me you gave them, and your word [logos] they have kept. 7 Now they know that all things whatsoever you have given to me are from [para] you, 8 because the words [rēma, pl.] which you gave to me, I have given to them, and they themselves received, and they know

truly that from [para] you I came forth, and they believed that you sent [apostellō] me. 9 I ask [i.e., pray; erōtaō] for them; not for the world I ask [erōtaō], but for those whom you have given to me, because they are yours; 10 all my things are yours, and yours (are) mine, and I have been glorified by them. 11 And no longer I am in the world, and they themselves are in the world, and I am coming to [pros] you. Holy Father, keep them in your name which you have given to me, in order that they may be one even as we (are). 12 When I was with them, I kept them in your name and guarded (them), and no one of them is lost

R

except the Son of Destruction, in order that the Scripture may be fulfilled.

E

13 And now [nun] I am coming to [pros] you and

G

I speak these things in the world in order that they may have my joy [art. rep. with poss. adj.] filled in themselves. 14 I have given to them your word [logos], and the world hated them because they are not FROM [ek] THE WORLD even as I am not from [ek] the world.

E

15 I do not ask [erōtaō] that you take them FROM [ek] THE WORLD, but (that) you keep them from evil. 16 From [ek] the world they are not, even as I am not from the world [restatement of v. 14b].

G

17 Sanctify them in the truth. Your WORD [logos; art. rep. with poss. adj.] is truth.

E

18 Even as you sent [apostellō] me into the world, I also sent [apostellō] them into the world.

G

19 And in behalf of them I sanctify myself, in order that they themselves also may be sanctified in truth.

E

20 And not about these only do I ask [erōtaō], but also about the ones believing on me through their WORD [logos], 21 in order that all may be one.

G

Even as you, Father, (are) in me and I in you, in order that they themselves also may be in us,

E

in order that the world may believe that you sent [apostellō] me. [E creates a different purpose by inserting a favorite theme of his.] 22 And the glory which you have given to me, I have given to them, in order that they MAY BE ONE even as we (are) one,

G

23 I in them and you in me, in order that they MAY BE COMPLETED [teleioō] INTO ONE,

E

in order that the world may know that you sent [apostellō] me and loved [agapaō] them even as you loved [agapaō] me. [Again E adds a different purpose.]

G

24 Father, what [neut.] you have given to me, I wish that where I am, those also may be with me, in order that they may see [theōreō] my glory [art. rep. with poss. adj.] which you have given to me

E

because you loved [agapaō] me

G

before the foundation of the world. 25 Righteous Father, even the world did not know you, but I KNEW you.

E

And these KNEW that you sent [apostellō] me. 26 And I made known to them, and will make known, your name, in order that the love with which you loved [agapaō] me may be in them, and I in them."

CHAPTER 18:

E

1 Having said these things, Jesus [an. in B, S; lac. in P^{66}, P^{75}]

S

he went out

R

with [sun] his disciples [redundant--stated at end of this v.] on the other side of the wady Kedron,

S

where there was a garden, into which he himself entered and his disciples [comp. subj., s. verb].

E

2 And Judas [an.], the one betraying him, also knew the place, because Jesus [an.] often there with [meta] his disciples.

S

3 Then Judas [arth.], taking a cohort and servants from the chief priests and Pharisees [cf. 7:32, 45], comes there with [meta] lanterns, torches, and weapons.

E

4 Then Jesus [an.], knowing all the things coming upon him [i.e., would happen to him], came forth and

S

he says to them, "Whom do you seek?" 5 They answered him, "Jesus [an. def.] the Nazoraean." He says to them, "I am (he)."

E

And Judas [an.], the one betraying him, was also standing with them [does not fit v. 3, where Judas is the leader].

S

6 Then when he said to them "I am," they drew back and fell to the ground.

E

7 Then again he asked them, "Whom do you seek?" And they said [eipan], "Jesus [an. def.] the Nazoraean." 8 Jesus [an.] answered, "I told you that 'I am.' Then if you seek me, permit them to go [hupagō]."

R

9 --in order that might be fulfilled the word [logos] which he said, that "of those whom you have given to me, I lost from them no one [cross-reference to 6:39; cf. 17:12]."

E

10 Then Simon Peter [an. comp.; prob. anonymous in S, as in synoptics]

S

having a sword, drew it and struck the slave of the high priest and cut off his right ear [art. rep.].

E

And the name to the slave was Malchos [an.; same construction in E in 1:6].

R

11 Then Jesus [arth.] said to Peter [arth.], "Put the sword into the sheath. The cup which the Father has given to me, should I not drink it?"

S

12 Then the cohort and the tribune

E

and the servants of the Jews

S

seized Jesus [arth.] and bound him. 13 And they led (him) to

E

Annas [an.] first, for he was the father-in-law of [E tries to harmonize with Luke 3:2 and Acts 4:6]

S

Caiaphas [arth.; E changed art. from acc. to gen.], who was the high priest of that year.

E

14 And Caiaphas [an.] was the one having counseled the Jews that it is advantageous (for) one man to die in behalf of the people [E refers to his own insertion in 11:49].

G

15 And following Jesus [arth.] was [E inserts "Simon Peter [an. comp.] and"] another disciple

E

And that disciple was known to the high priest;

G

and he entered with Jesus [arth.] into the court of the high priest, 16 but Peter [arth.] stood outside at the door. Then went out the other disciple [art. rep. in B, S; lac. in P^{75}],

E

the one known by the high priest,

G

and he talked to the doorkeeper [fem.], and she led in Peter [arth.]. 17 Then the maid, the doorkeeper [art. rep.], says to Peter [arth.], "Are you not also of the disciples of this man?" That one says, "I am not." 18 And the slaves and the servants had stood, having made a charcoal fire because it was cold, and were warming (themselves). And Peter [arth.] was also with them standing and warming (himself). [In G v. 25b followed this.]

S

19 Then the high priest asked Jesus [arth.] about his disciples and about his teaching.

E

20 Answered him Jesus [an. in P^{66}, B, S; lac. in P^{75}], "I openly have spoken to the world; I always taught in a synagogue and in a temple, where all the Jews come together, and in secret I spoke

nothing. 21 Why do you ask me? Ask the ones having heard what I spoke to them. Behold [ide], these know what things I said." [E substitutes for Jesus' answer in S.]

S

22 And when he said these things, one of [part. gen.] the servants standing by gave a slap to Jesus [arth.], saying, "Thus do you answer the high priest?"

E

23 Answered him Jesus [an.], "If I spoke wrongly, testify about the wrong; but if well, why do you strike me?"

R

24 Then Annas [arth.] sent [apostellō] him bound to Caiaphas [an. def.], the high priest.

E

25 And Simon Peter [an. comp.] was standing and warming (himself). [E repeats 18:18b as a connecting link.]

G

Then they said [eipon] to him, "Are you not also of his disciples?" That one denied and said, "I am not." 26 Says one of the slaves of the high priest,

E

being a relative (of him) whose ear Peter [an.] had cut off,

G

"Did I not see you in the garden with him?" 27 Then again Peter [arth. in S; lac. in P^{66}, P^{75}] denied, and immediately a cock crowed. 28 Then they lead Jesus [arth.] from Caiaphas [arth.] into the praetorium. And it was early. And they themselves did not enter into the praetorium, in order thay they might not be defiled but might eat [esthiō] the Passover. 29 Then Pilate [arth.] went outside to them and says, "What accusation do you bear against this man?"

E

30 They answered and said [eipan] to him, "Unless this one was

doing wrong, we would not have delivered him to you." [E censored the charge against Jesus by substituting v. 30 for it.]

G

31 Then Pilate [arth. in S, prob. in P^{66}; lac. in P^{75}] said to them, "You take him and according to your law judge (him)." The Jews said [eipon] to him, "It is not lawful for us to kill anyone."

R

32 --in order that the word [logos] of Jesus [arth.] might be fulfilled which he said signifying by what death he was about to die. [R derived this from E in 12:33.]

G

33 Then Pilate [arth.] entered again into the praetorium and called Jesus [arth.] and said to him, "Are you the king of the Jews?" [Refers to the Jewish charge E censored in v. 30.] 34 Jesus [arth. in S; lac. in P^{75}] answered, "Do you say this from [apo] yourself, or did others tell [eipon] you about me?" 35 Pilate [arth.] answered, "I am not a Jew, am I? Your nation [art. rep. with poss. adj.] and the chief priests delivered you to me. What did you do?"

E

36 Jesus [an.] answered,

G

"My kingdom [art. rep. with poss. adj.] is not from [ek] this world. If my kingdom [art. rep. with poss. adj.] was from [ek] this world, my servants [art. rep. with poss. adj.] would fight in order that I might not be delivered to the Jews. But now [nun] my kingdom [art. rep. with poss. adj.] is not from here." 37 Then Pilate [arth.] said to him, "So you are a king?" Jesus [arth. in B, S; lac. in P^{75}] answered, "You say (rightly) that I am a king. For this I have been born, and for this I have come into the world, in order that I may testify to the truth. Everyone who is from the truth hears my voice." 38 Pilate [arth.] says to him, "What is truth?"

R

And having said this, he went out again to the Jews and says to them, "I find no guilt in him. 39 And it is a custom for you that I release to you one (man) at the Passover. Then do you wish that I should release to you the king of the Jews?" 40 Then they cried out again saying, "Not this one, but Barabbas [arth.]." And Barabbas [arth.] was a robber.

CHAPTER 19:

S

1 Then [tote oun] Pilate [arth.] took Jesus [arth.] and scourged (him). 2 And the soldiers having woven a crown of thorns, placed it on (his) head, and put on him a purple robe. 3 And they were coming to [pros] him and were saying, "Hail, king of the Jews!" and they gave to him blows. 4 Pilate [arth.] went outside [R inserts "again"] and says to them, "Behold [ide], I am leading him outside to you in order that you may know that I find no guilt in him." 5 Then Jesus [arth.] came outside, wearing the thorny crown and the purple robe.

R

And he [Pilate) says to them, "Behold [idou] the man!" 6 Then when the chief priests and servants saw [eidon] him, they cried out, "Crucify, crucify!" Pilate [arth.] says to them, "You take him and crucify (him), for I do not find guilt in him." 7 The Jews answered, "We have a law, and according to that law he ought to die because he made himself Son of God [only time "Son of God" is an.]." 8 Then when Pilate [arth.] heard this word [logos], he was more afraid.

G

9 And he entered into the praetorium [R inserts "again"] and says to Jesus [arth.], "Whence are you?" But Jesus [arth.] gave no answer to him. 10 Pilate [arth.] says to him, "You are not speaking to me? Do you not know that I have authority to release you and authority to crucify you?" 11 Answered him Jesus [arth.], "You would not have any authority over me unless it had been given to you from above.

R

On account of this the one having betrayed me to you has greater sin."

S

12 Upon this Pilate [arth.] was seeking to release him. But the Jews cried out saying, "If you release this one, you are not a friend of Caesar. Everyone making himself a king opposes Caesar." 13 Then Pilate [arth.], having heard these words [logos, pl.], led Jesus [arth.] outside and sat on the judgment seat in the place called "Stone Pavement"

R

and in Hebrew "Gabbatha [Aramaic, not Hebrew]." 14 And it was the Preparation of the Passover.

S

The hour was about [hōs] the sixth. And he says to the Jews, "Behold [ide] your king!" 15 Then those cried out, "Take (him) away! Take (him) away! Crucify him!" Pilate [arth.] says to them, "Shall I crucify your king?" The chief priests answered, "We do not have a king except Caesar." 16 Then [tote oun] he delivered him to them in order that he might be crucified. 17 Then they took Jesus [arth.], and bearing his own cross, he went out into the place called "Skull,"

R

which is called in Hebrew "Golgotha [Aramaic, not Hebrew],"

S

18 where they crucified him, and with him two others, one on each side and Jesus [arth.] in the middle. 19 And Pilate [arth.] wrote also a title and put (it) on the cross. And it was having been written, "Jesus [an. comp.] the Nazoraean, the king of the Jews."

R

20 Then many of [part. gen.] the Jews read this title, because the place where Jesus [arth.] was crucified was near the city, and (the title) was having been written in Hebrew, Latin, Greek.

S

21 Then the chief priests of the Jews were saying to Pilate [arth.], "Write not 'the king of the Jews,' but that that one said, 'I am king of the Jews.'" 22 Pilate [arth.] answered, "What I have written, I have written." 23 Then the soldiers, when they cruci-

fied Jesus [arth.], took his garments and made four parts, a part for each soldier, and (they took his) tunic. But the tunic was seamless, woven from the top through the whole (tunic). 24 Then they said [eipan] to each other, "Let us not split it, but choose about it by lot whose it shall be,"

R

in order that the Scripture might be fulfilled, "They divided my garments among them, and for my clothing they cast lots." 25 Then the soldiers did these things.

S

And stood beside the cross of Jesus [arth.] his MOTHER, and the sister of his mother, Mary [an. def.] the (wife) of Clopas [arth.], and Mary [an. def.] the Magdalene.

E

26 Then Jesus [an.], seeing (his) MOTHER, and a disciple [R inserts "whom he loved [agapaō]"] standing nearby, says to (his) mother, "Woman, behold [ide in B; lac. in P^{66}, P^{75}] your son!" 27 Next he says to the disciple, "Behold [ide] your mother!" And from that hour the disciple took her into his own (home).

S

28 After this Jesus [arth.], knowing that already all things had been COMPLETED [teleō],

R

in order that the Scripture might be COMPLETED [teleioō],

S

says, "I thirst." 29 A vessel full of vinegar was sitting there; then having put on hyssop a sponge full of vinegar, they held (it) to his mouth. 30 Then when he was receiving the vinegar, he said, "It is completed [teleō]"; and having bowed his head, he gave up (his) spirit.

R

31 Then the Jews, since it was the Preparation, in order that the bodies might not remain on the cross on the Sabbath [arth.]-- for it was the great day of that Sabbath [arth.]--, asked [erōtaō]

Pilate [arth.] that their legs might be broken and (that) they might be taken away. 32 Then the soldiers came and broke the legs of the first and of the other one crucified with him. 33 But having come to [epi] Jesus [arth.], when they saw [eidon] him having already died, they did not break his legs. 34 But one of [part. gen.] the soldiers pierced his side with a spear, and immediately came out blood and water. 35 And the one having seen has testified, and true is his testimony, and that one knows that he says true, in order that you also may believe [cf. 21:24]. 36 For these things happened in order that the Scripture might be fulfilled, "Not a bone of him shall be broken." 37 And again another Scripture says, "They shall look on whom they pierced."

R

38 And after these things

S

Joseph [an. def.] from [apo] Arimathea

E

--being a disciple of Jesus [an. in B; lac. in P^{66}, P^{75}], but having been hidden on account of fear of the Jews--

S

asked [erōtaō] Pilate [arth.] that he might take away the body of Jesus [arth.]. ["And Pilate [arth.] gave permission" is not in P^{66}.] Then he came and took away his body.

E

39 And Nicodemus [an.], the one having come to [pros] him first at night, came also carrying a mixture of myrrh and aloes, about [hōs] a hundred pounds.

S

40 Then they took the body of Jesus [arth.] and bound it in linen cloths with spices, even as it is the custom with Jews to bury. 41 And in the place where he was crucified there was a garden, and in the garden a new tomb

E or R ?

in which no one had yet been laid [from Luke 23:53].

S

42 Then there,

R

on account of the Preparation of the Jews,

S

because the tomb was near, they laid Jesus [arth.].

CHAPTER 20:

P^1 ?

1 And on the first (day) of the week Mary [an. def.] the Magdalene comes to [eis] the tomb early, it being still dark, and she sees [blepō] the stone having been taken away from the tomb.

E

2 Then she runs and comes to [pros] Simon Peter [an. comp.] and to [pros] another disciple [cf. 18:15-16]

Later Gloss

whom Jesus [arth.] loved [phileō],

E

and says to them, "They have taken the Lord from the tomb, and we do not know where they laid him [restatement of v. 13]."

P^1 ?

3 Then Peter [arth.] went forth and another disciple [comp. subj., s. verb], and they were coming to [eis] the tomb. 4 And the two were running together. And the other disciple ran faster than Peter [arth.] and came first to [eis] the tomb. 5 And having stooped (down), he sees [blepō] lying (there) the linen cloths;

E

nevertheless, he did not go in. 6 Then comes also Simon Peter [an. comp.] following him, and he went into the tomb. And he sees [theōreō] the linen cloths lying (there), 7 and the napkin which was on his head, not lying with the linen cloths but rolled up in a place by itself. [E tries to counteract the idea in the source that the other disciple is superior to Peter: although in P^1 the other disciple gets to the tomb first, in E only Peter goes in.]

P^1 ?

8 Then [tote oun] went in [E inserts "also"] the other disciple,

R

the one having come first to [eis] the tomb,

P^1 ?

and he saw [horaō] and believed. [Was it understood in P^1 that Peter did not believe until later when he had a vision of Jesus ?]

R

9 For not yet did they know the Scripture that it is necessary (for) him to rise from the dead.

E

10 Then the disciples went away again to [pros] them [i.e., their homes]. 11 And Mary [an.] stood at the tomb WEEPING.

P^2 ?

Then when she was WEEPING, she peered into the tomb, 12 and she sees [theōreō] two angels in white sitting, one at the head and one at the feet, where the body of Jesus [arth.] had lain. 13 And those say to her, "WOMAN, WHY DO YOU WEEP ?" She says to them, "Because they have taken away my Lord, and I do not know where they laid him." 14 Having said these things, she turned back and sees [theōreō] Jesus [arth.] standing.

E

And she did not know that it is Jesus [an.]. 15 Jesus [an.] says to her, "WOMAN, WHY DO YOU WEEP ? Whom do you seek ?" That one, having supposed that he is the gardener, says to him, "Lord, if you removed him, tell me where you laid him, and I will take him away."

P^2 ?

16 Jesus [arth. in S; lac. in P^{66}, P^{75}] says to her, "Mary [an. voc.]." Having turned, that one says to him [R inserts "in Hebrew"], "Rabbouni [Aramaic, not Hebrew]," which says [i.e., means] "Teacher." 17 Jesus [arth. in S; lac. in P^{66}, P^{75}] says to her, "Touch me not, for not yet have I ascended to [pros] the Father; but go [poreuomai] to [pros] my brethren

and tell them and tell them, 'I am ascending to [pros] my Father and your Father

E

and my God and your God.'" 18 Mary [an. def.] the Magdalene comes announcing to the disciples that "I have seen [horaō] the Lord," and (that) he said these things to her.

P^1 ?

19 Then when it was evening on that day, the first (day) of the week,

E

and when the doors had been closed where the disciples were on account of fear of the Jews, [E reinterprets v. 26, where the motif is only that the risen Jesus is supernatural and goes through closed doors.]

P^1 ?

Jesus [arth.] came and stood in (their) midst and says to them, "Peace to you."

E

20 And having said this, he showed (his) hands and side to them.

P^1 ?

Then the disciples rejoiced (at) seeing [horaō] the Lord.

E

21 Then he ["Jesus" [arth.] is not in S; lac. in P^{66}, P^{75}] said to them again, "Peace to you [repetition from v. 19]. Even as the Father sent [apostellō] me, I also send [pempō] you." 22 And having said this,

P^1 ?

he breathed on them and says to them, "Receive the Holy Spirit. 23 If you forgive the sins of any, they are forgiven to them; if you retain (the sins) of any, they have been retained."

E

24 And Thomas [an.], one of the twelve,

R

the one being called "Twin [cf. 21:2],"

E

was not with them when Jesus [an.] came. 25 Then the other disciples were saying to him, "We have seen [horaō] the Lord." And he said to them, "Unless I see [horaō] in his hands the place of the nails and put [ballō] my finger in the place of the nails and put [ballō] my hand into his side, I will not believe." [E expands the story by restating material in v. 27.]

P^1 ?

26 And after eight days [E inserts "again"] his disciples were inside, and Jesus [arth.] comes when the doors had been closed and stood in (their) midst and said, "Peace to you." 27 Next he says to Thomas [arth.], "Put [pherō] your finger here and see [horaō] my hands, and put [pherō] your hand (here)

E

and put [ballō] (it) into my side,

P^1 ?

and be not unbelieving, but BELIEVING."

E

28 Answered Thomas [an. in P^{66}, B; lac. in P^{75}] and said to him, "My Lord and my God." 29 Jesus [an. in P^{66}, B; lac. in P^{75}] says to him, "Because you saw [horaō] me, have you believed? Blessed (are) the ones not having seen [horaō] and (yet) having BELIEVED."

S

30 Then many other signs Jesus [arth.] did in the presence of the disciples, which are not having been WRITTEN in this book.

E

31 But these things have been WRITTEN in order that you may BELIEVE that Jesus [an.] is the Christ, the Son of God, and in order that believing you may have life in his name.

CHAPTER 21:

R

1 After these things Jesus [arth.] manifested himself again to the disciples by the Sea of Tiberias. And he manifested (himself) thus.

SOURCE: STORY OF CATCHING FISH

2 There were together Simon Peter [an. comp.] and Thomas [an.],

R

the one being called "Twin,"

SOURCE: STORY OF CATCHING FISH

and Nathaniel [an.],

R

the one from [apo] Cana of Galilee [R gives location of cities], and the (sons) of Zebedee [arth.],

SOURCE: STORY OF CATCHING FISH

and two others of his disciples. 3 Simon Peter [an. comp.] says to them, "I am going away to fish." They say to him, "We also are coming with [sun] you." They went out and got into the boat [ploion], and during that night they caught nothing.

SOURCE: STORY OF MEAL

4 And just as it becomes morning Jesus [an.] stood on the beach, although the disciples did not know that it is Jesus [an.]. 5 Then Jesus [an.] says to them, "Little children, do you not have any relish (to eat)?" They answered him, "No."

SOURCE: STORY OF CATCHING FISH

6 He says [in S*] to them, "Cast the net on the right side of the boat [ploion] and you will find." Then they cast, and they were not strong enough to haul it in because [apo] of the abundance of fish [ichthus].

R

7 Then that disciple whom Jesus [arth.] loved [agapaō] says to Peter [arth.], "It is the Lord." Having heard that it is the Lord,

SOURCE: STORY OF CATCHING FISH

then Simon Peter [an. comp.] tied around (himself) an outer garment

R

--for he was naked--

SOURCE: STORY OF CATCHING FISH

and cast himself into the sea. 8 And the other disciples came

R

in the small boat [ploiarion], for they were not far from the land but about [hōs apo] two hundred cubits away--

SOURCE: STORY OF CATCHING FISH

dragging the net (full) of fish [ichthus].

SOURCE: STORY OF MEAL

9 Then when they got up on the land, they see [blepō] a charcoal fire lying (there) and small fish [opsarion] lying on (it) and bread.

R ?

10 Jesus [arth.] says to them, "Bring some of the small fish [opsarion] which you caught now [nun]."

SOURCE: STORY OF CATCHING FISH

11 Then Simon Peter [an. comp.] went up and hauled to the land the net full of 153 large fish [ichthus]; and (though) there were so many, the net was not torn.

SOURCE: STORY OF MEAL

12 Jesus [an. in B; lac. in P^{66}, P^{75}] says to them, "Come, eat." None of the disciples dared to ask him, "Who are you?," knowing that he is the Lord. 13 Jesus [an. in B; lac. in P^{66}, P^{75}] comes and takes the bread and gives (it) to them, and the small fish [opsarion] likewise.

R

14 This already (was) the third (time) Jesus [arth. in S; lac. in P^{66}, P^{75}] was manifested to the disciples, having been raised from the dead. 15 Then when they had eaten, Jesus [arth.] says to Simon Peter [arth. comp.],

SOURCE: STORY OF TRIPLE AFFIRMATION

"Simon [an. def.], (son) of John [an.], do you love [agapaō] me more than these?" He says to him, "Yes, Lord, you know that I love [phileō] you." He says to him, "Feed my lambs." 16 He says to him [R inserts "again"] a second (time), "Simon [an. def.], (son) of John [an.], do you love [agapaō] me?" He says to him, "Yes, Lord, you know that I love [phileō] you." He says to him, "Tend my sheep." 17 He says to him the third (time), "Simon [an. def.], (son) of John [an.], do you love [phileō] me?"

R

Peter [arth.] was grieved that he said to him the third (time), "Do you love [phileō] me?" and he said,

SOURCE: STORY OF TRIPLE AFFIRMATION

"Lord, [R inserts "you KNOW all things"], you KNOW that I love [phileō] you." He says to him, "Feed my sheep.

R

18 Truly, truly, I say to you, when you were younger, you girded yourself and walked around where you wanted; but when you are old, you will stretch forth your hands and another will gird you and will carry you where you do not want (to go)." 19 And he said this signifying by what (kind of) death he will glorify God. And having said this, he says to him, "Follow me." 20 Having turned around, Peter [arth.] sees [blepō] the disciple whom Jesus [arth.] loved [agapaō], who also reclined on his breast at the supper and said, "Lord, who is the one betraying you [R's cross-reference to 13:23-24]?" 21 Then Peter [arth.], seeing [horaō] this one, says to Jesus [arth.], "Lord, but what (about) this one?" 22 Jesus [arth.] says to him, "If I want him to remain until I come, what (is it) to you? You follow me." 23 Then this word [logos] went forth to the brethren that that disciple will not die. But Jesus [arth.] said not to him that he will not die, but "If I want him to remain until I come." 24 This is the disciple, the one testifying about these things and the one having written these things, and we know that his testimony is true.

Later Gloss (not in S*)

25 And there are also many other things which Jesus [arth.] did; if everyone whatsoever were written, I suppose the world itself would not hold the books that would be written!

CHAPTER 13

THE SIGNIFICANCE OF THE DISCOVERY

The discovery of the literary origin of the Gospel of John is significant for its effect on future studies of the gospel and of other ancient literature. It should prepare the way for a more accurate ~~of~~ understanding of that gospel, and for the development of a more scientific approach to the analysis of works written in Greek in the Hellenistic and Roman periods.

Although there are a few passages, especially those labeled with a question mark in the preceding chapter, which are still uncertain as to authorship, I am confident that at least 90% of the material has been identified correctly. It seems clear that four main writers are involved: the authors of two written sources, the editor who used portions of the sources in his composition, and the redactor. In addition, the editor and redactor used a few brief written sources, and a later copyist inserted a few glosses.

The first effect of this knowledge, therefore, should be to settle definitely the old question of whether one author wrote the whole gospel. The evidence for composite authorship is overwhelming. Interpretations of John based on the traditional assumption that one author wrote it all will be obsolete. If anyone wants to defend the old theory, let him explain why the alleged author was so inconsistent in syntax as well as in vocabulary and ideas. Why do patterns of these three types of criteria tend to occur together? Why are the patterns definitely related to the aporia, the breaks in thought and structure? Why are personal names in John sometimes arthrous and sometimes anarthrous? The process of composite authorship explains the phenomena; theories of single authorship have not and cannot.

A second effect on the interpretation of John will be the realization that it is necessary to recognize the individual views of each writer, instead of assuming that a unified view can be found there. The ways in which the editor and redactor operated, with E selecting only portions of his sources, and with E and R often attracted to material on the basis of catchwords instead of agreement with the thought in the whole passage--these demonstrate that E and R did not assimilate into their own thinking all of the source material, not even of the portions they used. Therefore their views cannot be determined by examining the gospel as a whole;

their views are to be found through the examination of what each of them wrote. Interpretations which assume that the editor assimilated all his source material into his own theology only produce misinterpretation, assigning to him ideas he never had. The same principle applies to the redactor.

An obvious effect of the new knowledge is new insight into the literary origin of the gospel. We now have a better understanding of how and why it was produced. The manner in which the editor operated is quite fascinating to analyze. His use of catchwords as a basis for selecting passages from his source G and for writing his own expansion of and reinterpretation of source material reveals how his mind operated. Both the editor and the redactor added the names of persons and places on the basis of their own notions, not on the basis of historical tradition. They were not concerned with real historical accuracy, but only with the appearance of historical accuracy.

The discovery of the literary origin of the Gospel of John and of the linguistic/literary techniques employed should contribute much to the future understanding of Greek literature written in the ancient Mediterranean world. Many ancient works, both biblical and non-biblical, have often been interpreted as unified works by a single author, when actually they are composite works containing different points of view.

Foremost in this area should be a new recognition by biblical scholars and historians of the absolute necessity of the use of an inductive, scientific approach in the analysis and interpretation of ancient writings. Because it has been esteemed as a sacred book, the Bible especially has suffered from misinterpretation. Look back over the past theories of the literary origin of the Gospel of John and see how many, many times a bias of some sort was in control. Observe the ridiculous results that bias produced! Such efforts were not genuine research. They were only dishonest apologetics masquerading as scholarship. With regard to the biased approach vs. the scientific approach, the biblical saying applies: "By their fruits you shall know them." Only a scientific approach can produce the fruit of accurate solution of historical and literary problems, including the problems in understanding the Bible.

It is hoped that the method employed in the present study will contribute to the further development of scientific method for the analysis of other ancient literature. An important tool is the recognition that the use or non-use of the article "the" with personal names was a matter of style with some writers who wrote in Greek. This tool performed a vital role in unraveling the threads in John, because personal names occur often and the editor's practice was the opposite of that of the other three major writers. Recognition of the fact that some editors and redactors used catchwords and restatement of source material as literary devices will also aid in the development of methodology. Fuller recognition of the tendency of later writers to add details will help prevent the error of assuming that details indicate earliness and historical accuracy of the material.

Further, the discovery of the main cause of the use and non-use of the Greek article with personal names in the gospel is important for Greek grammarians. They have observed that usage often did not follow the rules which apparently guided some classical Greek writers, but they seldom have recognized adequately, if at all, that with some writers usage was merely a matter of personal style. The style of some writers went so far as always to use the article, others used it except when the name was already definite, while some writers never used the article with personal names. This fact should be reported in Greek grammars.

Finally, the present investigation opens the door for fresh approaches to old problems relating to the Gospel of John. It also paves the way for the study of new questions.

The few passages to which authorship was assigned with some hesitation in this study deserve further investigation. Perhaps I identified them correctly; if not, perhaps someone else will have new insight into the problem.

A new field of study now is the determination of the beliefs and general thought of each of the four main writers in the gospel. Precise studies were not possible without an accurate identification of the work of each one. Detailed study of the manner in which the editor and the redactor operated is another new area for study, including comparison of their techniques with those of other ancient writers.

The relation of the four main writers to the synoptic gospels also merits further investigation. The author of S definitely used Mark, as the order of events in John 6:5-21 and the vocabulary in many passages show. S contains at least 22 parallels with Mark, ten of which are in neither Matthew nor Luke (1:26; 5:8, 14; 6:5, 7, 9-11; 12:3a, 5, 8; 19:2). G's parallelism with the synoptics is mainly with Matthew (13:16, 20; 15:7, (18 ?); 16:23b; 17:2), except in chapter 18 (verses 15, 17, 18, 25, 37) where all parallels may be from Mark--does this indicate that G is not a source in the Passion story, after all? E exhibits some parallels with all the synoptics, and the editor apparently is the only writer who used Acts (in 4:53b; 18:13). The redactor apparently used Luke, for R has at least two parallels with matter exclusively in Luke (in 3:24; 12:2b).

The knowledge of the literary origin of the Gospel of John raises the question of whether the studies of the use of that gospel in the early church may need some revision. Did the early Christian writers who apparently quote Johannine material really quote the gospel, or did they quote its sources?

The question of the literary origin of 1 John and its possible relation to the gospel also should receive new investigation. J. C. O'Neill's study (1966) is generally sound, but the results of the discovery of the literary structure of John should now be applied to that epistle. The present writer plans to make such a study.

The discovery of its literary origin opens the way for new studies and new understanding of the Gospel of John. Even more fascinating is the probability that the methodology will be developed further and applied to other ancient writings, including other New Testament books.

APPENDIX

(Specific verses are listed only when a writer uses the expression less than six times. Only occurrences in the four main writers and in R's sources are listed.)

SYNTAX	S	G	E	R
'about' (hōs) with nos.	1:39; 4:6; 6:10, 19; 19:14	---	19:39	---
'about' (hōs apo) w. nos.	---	---	---	11:18; 21:8
'about to' (mellō)	---	7:35 (2 times)	8 times	12:4; 18:32
'after this' begins sent.	2:12; 11:7, 11; 19:28	---	---	---
'after these things'	---	---	---	8 times
'and' or'both' (te)	2:15; 4:42; 6:18	---	---	---
'answered' + ind. obj. + n. subj.	6 times	10:32	11 times	---
'answered' + n. subj. + 'and said' + ind. obj.	(4:17 ?)	---	19 times	---
'answered' + ind. obj. + n. subj. + 'and said'	---	6:26; 7:16	---	---
article repeated	2:1; 18:10	40 times	---	---
art. omitted with pers. names [an.]	--- (except def.)	--- (except def.)	all	--- (except in sources)
art. with O. T. pers. names [arth.]	---	---	---	7 times

SYNTAX	S	G	E	R
'ask' (aiteō) as 'pray,' 'request'	11:22	7 times	4:10; 14:13	---
'ask' (erōtaō) as 'pray,' 'request'	4:31,40, 47; 12:21; 19:38	---	7 times	19:31
'behold' (ide)	8 times	---	6 times	1:29 (from S)
'behold' (idou)	---	4:35	---	19:5
'boat' (ploion)	6:17,19, 21,22	---	---	(R source: 21:3, 6)
'boat, little' (ploiarion)	---	---	---	6:22,24; 21:8
'called, being'	---	---	---	9 times
'command-ment'	11:57	6 times	10:18; 13: 34; 14:21	---
'complete' (teleioō)	---	4:34; 17: 4,23	---	5:36; 19:28b
'complete' (teleō)	19:28a, 30	---	---	---
comp. subj., s. verb	6 times	4:12	8:44,52	---
'crowd' + s. verb	---	---	9 times	5:13; 12:9
'crowd' + pl. verb	6 times	---	11:42	---
'darkness' (skotia)	6:17	8:12; 12:35b	12:35c,46	---
'darkness' (skotos)	---	3:19	---	---
'day, on' (prep.)	11:24	7:37; 16:26	5:9; 6:40, 44; 14:20; 16:23	---
'day, on'' (no prep.)	2:1	6:39; 4:35; 19:5	---	6:54; 12:48
demon. pron. ('this,' 'that') as rep. subj. or obj.	---	---	17 times	5:19; 6:57; 12:48

SYNTAX	S	G	E	R
'Devil' [see also: 'Satan']	6:70	---	8:44; 13:2	---
'eat' (bibrōskō)	6:13	---	---	---
'eat' (esthiō)	4:31,32, 33; 6:5	6:51,52, 53,58; 18:28	6:26,31 (2 times),49, 50	---
'eat' (trōgō)	---	---	---	6:54,56,57, 58; 13:18
'even as . . also' (kathōs . . kai)	---	---	13:15; 15:9; 17:18; 20:21	13:33
'even as . . thus' (kathōs . . houtōs)	---	3:14; 12:50; 14:31; 15:4	---	---
'just as . . thus' (hōsper . . houtōs)	---	5:21,26	---	---
'everything' instead of 'everyone'	---	6:37,39; 15:2; 17:2	---	---
'Father, my'	2:16	6 times	16 times	---
'fill' (plēroō) sorrow or joy	---	6 times	---	---
'fulfill' (plēroō) Scripture or Jesus' word	---	---	---	8 times
'from' (apo) a town	1:44,45; 7:42; 11:1a; 19:38	---	---	12:21; 21:2
'from' (ek) a town	---	---	1:19,44, 46; 4:30; 11:1b	4:39
'from' (apo) God/Father	3:2	---	---	13:3; 16:30
'from' (ek) God/Father	---	7:17; 8:42, 47c; 10:32; 16:28	8:47a (from G)	---
'from' (para) God/Father	9:16	---	18 times	---

SYNTAX	S	G	E	R
'from' heaven or world or earth	---	11 times	15 times	---
'from (apo) self'	---	12 times	11:51	---
'go' (hupagō)	7 times	---	22 times	11:31; 13:3
'go' (poreuomai)	4:50; 11:11	8 times	14:12, 28	---
'Hebrew, in'	---	---	---	5:2; 19:13, 17, 20; 20:16
'hide'	---	12:36	8:59; 19:38	---
'hour was about' - number	1:39; 4:6; 19:14	---	---	---
'hour comes and now (nun) is'	---	___	4:23; 5:25	---
'hour comes and has come'	---	---	---	16:32
'Jerusalem' (an., s.)	2:13; 5:1; 11:55; 12:12	---	---	---
'Jerusalem' (an., pl.; tr. as s.)	---	4:20, 21	1:19	4:45
'Jerusalem' (arth., pl.; tr. as s.)	---	---	---	2:23; 5:2; 10:22; 11:18
'Judas (arth.), (son) of Simon Iscariot' (an. comp.)	6:71	---	---	---
'Judas Iscariot (an. comp.), (son) of Simon' (an.)	---	---	13:2, 26	---
'Judas (an. def.) the Iscariot'	---	---	---	12:4; 14:22
'love' (verb, agapaō)	---	3:16, 19	26 times	8 times (R source: 21:15, 16)

SYNTAX	S	G	E	R
'love' (verb, phileō)	11:3, 36	5:20; 12:25; 15:19; 16:27 (twice)	---	21:17b (R source: 21: 15, 16, 17 (twice)
'my' (emos) in attrib. p. --art. not rep.	---	7:16	5:47; 7:8; 14:27; 17: 10	---
'name, believe on' (eis) Jesus'	---	---	1:12; 2:23; 3:18	---
'name, in' (en) Jesus'	---	7 times	20:31	---
'name,' Father's	---	---	7 times	---
'near'	6:19; 11:54	---	---	8 times
'necessary, it is'	---	3:14; 4: 20; 9:4	3:7, 30; 4: 24; 10:16; 12:34	20:9
'necessary, it was'	4:4	---	---	---
'never' (pōpote - neg.)	---	5:37; 6: 35; 8:33	---	---
'not . . but in order that'	---	---	6 times	1:31; 13:18
'now' (arti)	---	5:17; 16: 12, 24	---	9 times
'now' (nun)	2:8; 4:18; 11:22	18:36	23 times	21:10 ?
'on account of this' (dia touto)	---	---	9 times	6 times
'others were saying'	7:41; 9:16	---	7:12; 9:9; 10:21; 12: 29	---
part. gen. ('one of,' etc.	18:22	---	---	4:39; 12:4, 11; 19:20
poss. adj., no art.	---	4:34	13:35	---
poss. adj., one art.	7:8	7:16; 14:24, 27; 15:11	5:47; 15:20	---

SYNTAX	S	G	E	R
poss. adj., art. rep.	---	29 times	---	---
'rabbi'	8 times	---	---	---
'remember, disciples'	---	---	2:17, 22; 12:16; 16:4	15:20
'ruler of world'	---	---	12:31; 14:30; 16:11	---
'Sabbath' (an.)	9:14	---	5 times	5:16
'Sabbath' (arth.)	---	---	---	5:18; 9:16; 19:31 (twice)
'said' (eipan, 1st aor. in 3rd p. pl.)	9 times	---	19 times	9:24, 26, 28
'said' (eipon, 2nd aor. in 3rd p. pl.)	6:25; 7:3	8 times	---	---
'Satan' [see also 'Devil']	---	---	---	13:27
'saying, was/were'	13 times	5:19; 8:31	30 times	---
'Scripture (s.) be fulfilled' or 'completed'	---	---	---	13:18; 17:12; 19:24b, 28, 36
'Scripture'(s.), other instances	7:42	7:38	---	2:22; 10:35; 19:37; 20:9
'Scriptures' (pl.)	---	---	5:39, 47	---
'see' (horaō, except eidan, eidon)	11 times	6 times	38 times	6 times
'see' (eidan, 1st aor. in 3rd p. pl.)	1:39	---	---	---
'see' (eidon, 2nd aor. in 3rd p. pl.)	---	---	---	19:6, 33
'see' (theaomai)	---	---	1:32, 38; 4:35; 6:5; 11:45	---

SYNTAX	S	G	E	R
'see' (theōreō)	4:19; 6:19; 7:3; 12:19	6 times	12 times	---
'see, look at' (blepō)	9:7, 15	5:19; 11:9	6 times	1:29; 9:19, 25; 21:20
'see, look at' (emblepō)	1:36, 42	---	---	---
'send' (apostellō)	1:19, 24; 7:32; 9:7; 11:3	---	19 times	5:36; 6:57; 18:24
'send' (pempō)	---	22 times	9 times	---
'Simon'	1:41, 42	---	---	---
'Simon Peter' (an.)	---	---	12 times	(R source: 21:2, 3, 7, 11)
'Simon Peter' (arth.)	---	---	---	21:15
'Peter' (an.)	---	---	1:44; 13:8; 18:26	---
'Peter' (arth.)	---	---	---	6 times
'the Son'	---	12 times	8 times	---
'Son of God' (an.)	---	---	---	19:7
'the Son of God' (arth.)	11:4, 27	---	6 times	---
'Son of Man' (an.)	---	5:27	---	---
'the Son of Man' (arth.)	---	6 times	9:35; 12:34 (twice); 13:31	---
'still,' 'yet' (eti)	---	---	7:33; 12:35; 14:19	11:30; 13:33; 16:12
'then' (tote men)	11:6	---	---	---
'then' (tote oun)	11:14; 19:1, 16	---	---	---
'to' (eis; not as 'into') with 'come'	---	---	---	4:45; 11:38, 56; 12:12
'to' (eis; not as 'into') with 'go'	---	---	---	11:31

SYNTAX	S	G	E	R
'to' (pros) with 'come'	12 times	7 times	14 times	1:29; 11:45
'to' (pros) with 'go'	---	---	7:33; 13:3; 16:5, 10, 17	---
'truly, truly, I say to you' (s.)	---	---	3:3, 5, 11; 13:38	21:18
'truly, truly, I say to you' (pl.)	---	12 times	7 times	---
'walk' in figurative sense	---	8:12; 11: 9, 10; 12: 35 (twice)	---	---
'with' (meta)	11 times	7 times	22 times	---
'with' (sun)	---	---	---	12:2; 18:1 (R source: 21:3)
'word' (logos), Father's	---	5:38; 14:24; 17:6, 14, 17	8:55	---
'word' (logos), God's	---	---	10:35	12:38; 15:25 18:19
'word' (logos), Jesus'	---	6 times	8:52; 14:23; 15:20	6 times
'words' (logos, pl.)	7:40; 19:13	---	10:19; 14:24	---
'words' (rēma, pl.)	---	---	12 times	---
'written, is/was having been'	19:19; 20:30	---	6 times	19:20

NOTES

CHAPTER 1

1. Wellhausen, Evang. Joh., pp. 5-6.
2. Edwards, Disciple Who Wrote, p. 41.
3. Wellhausen, op. cit., p. 4.
4. Morton Scott Enslin, Christian Beginnings (New York: Harper, 1938), p. 446.
5. Schwartz, "Aporien."
6. Fortna, Gospel of Signs, p. 2.

CHAPTER 2

1. Wendt, Gospel St. John, p. 50.
2. Fortna, original diss., p. 9.
3. Cited in Eusebius, Hist. eccl. iii. 39.
4. Herder, Briefe das Studium; cited from Schweitzer, Quest, p. 35.
5. Listed by Moffatt, Introd., 3d. ed., p. 516. Whether these three men based their conclusion on the differences between John and the synoptic gospels is unknown to me. I could not locate Vogel's forename.
6. Howard, Fourth Gospel, 2d ed., p. 67.
7. Bacon, F.G.R.D., 2d ed., p. 528, n. 1.
8. Lützelberger, kirchliche Tradition, pp. 187-88; cited from A. Schweizer, Evang. Joh., p. 58.
9. Cited from Schweitzer, Quest, p. 35.
10. Dodd, Historical Trad., p. 16, n. 2.
11. Parker, "John Son of Zebedee."
12. Dodd, Interpretation, p. 12, n. 2.
13. Works defending close similarity between John and the Scrolls include: F.-M. Braun, "L'arrière-fond judaique du quatrième évangile et la Communauté de l'Alliance," RB 62 (1955): 5-44; Raymond E. Brown, "The Qumran Scrolls and the Johannine Gospel and Epistles," CBQ 17 (1955): 403-19, 559-74 (reprinted in Krister Stendahl, ed., The Scrolls and the New Testament (New York: Harper, 1957), pp. 183-207); Frank Moore Cross, Jr., The Ancient Library of Qumran and Modern Biblical Studies (New York: Doubleday, 1958), pp. 161-62; A. Feuillet, "La littérature de Qumran et les écrits johanniques," Études 3 (1959): 440-56; Karl G. Kuhn, "Johannesevangelium und Qumrantexte," Neotestimentica et Patristica; eine Freundesgabe, Herrn Professor Dr. Oscar

Cullmann zu seinem 60. Geburtstag überreicht (NovTSup 6; Leiden: Brill, 1962), pp. 111-21; Kurt Schubert, The Dead Sea Community: Its Origin and Teachings (London: A. and C. Black, 1959), p. 152; Ethelbert Stauffer, "Probleme der Priestertradition," TLZ 81 (1956): 135-50. Brown still leans in this direction in his commentary, The Gospel according to John. Lucetta Mowry ("The Dead Sea Scrolls and the Background of the Gospel of John," BA 17 (1954):78-97) contends that the differences as well as the similarities indicate that the writer of the gospel was reacting against the Essene sect, which produced the Scrolls; this theory, too, should be rejected, for although the gospel is opposed to Jews and Judaism, there is no evidence that the author or authors had the Qumran sect in mind. James H. Charlesworth, "A Critical Comparison of the Dualism in 1QS iii, 13-iv, 26 and the 'Dualism' contained in the Fourth Gospel," NTS 15 (1969):389-418, observes similarities in terminology and differences in the meaning and use of the terms. He concludes that these differences are the result of John's reinterpretation of the Essenes' vocabulary, and thus at least the first draft of the gospel was probably written in Palestine.

14. W. F. Albright, "Recent Discoveries in Palestine and the Gospel of St. John," The Background of the New Testament and Its Eschatology, ed. by W. D. Davies and D. Daube (Cambridge: University Press, 1956), pp. 153-71--especially pp. 169-71.

15. Works which reject the claims include: Millar Burrows, More Light on the Dead Sea Scrolls (New York: Viking, 1958), pp. 123-30; Dodd, Historical Trad., p. 15, n. 3; F. C. Grant, Gospels, pp. 175-76; Haenchen, "Aus der Literatur," pp. 313, 323-24; Wayne A. Meeks, The Prophet-king: Moses Traditions and the Johannine Christology (Leiden: Brill, 1967), pp. 11-12; H. M. Teeple, "Qumran and the Origin of the Fourth Gospel," NovT 4 (1960):6-25.

16. F. C. Grant, op. cit., p. 175.

17. Dodd, Historical Trad., p. 13.

18. See Sanders, Fourth Gospel; also Melvyn R. Hillmer, "The Gospel of John in the Second Century," a doctoral dissertation at Harvard University, 1966.

19. William Temple, Readings in St. John's Gospel (London: 1945), p. x.

20. As pioneers Keim and Hilgenfeld deserve more fame than they have received.

21. Cited from Watkins, Modern Criticism, p. 247.

22. In Eusebius Hist. eccl. iii. 23; iii. 39; v. 8. For arguments against the theory that there were two Johns, see Bacon, Gospel of Hellenists, chaps. 4-5.

23. Carpenter, Johannine Writings, p. 218.

24. Harnack, Chronologie, 1:656ff. Harnack suggests that in Asia (Ephesus) John the Presbyter was thought to have been a disciple of Jesus, and thus the church identified the two Johns with each other. Cf. Weisse's opinion in 1838 that the author of the present gospel used John's written memoirs as a source and that he, the author, may have been the Elder of the Ephesian church (evang. Geschichte, 1:99).

25. The group includes Hugo Delff (1890), Percy Gardner (1915), B. H. Streeter (1924), A. H. McNeile (1927), G. H. C. Macgregor (1928), and J. H. Bernard (1929).

26. Sanday, Criticism, p. 16. For recent discussions of "the beloved disciple" as the author, see Schnackenburg, "Zur Herkunst," and Kragerud, Lieblingsjünger, listed in the bibliography of this book. Kragerud thinks that the beloved disciple has symbolic meaning.

27. Bousset, "Einheit," pp. 3, 5, 7; Schweitzer, op. cit., pp. 118, 229; Howard, op. cit., pp. 75, 109.

28. Schmiedel, Johannine Writings, p. 202.

29. Dodd, Historical Trad., p. 3.

30. See Schweitzer, op. cit., pp. 220, 254-55, 322.

CHAPTER 3

1. David Friedrich Strauss, Ulrich von Hutten, 3. Teil (Leipzig: Brockhaus, 1860), p. xliv. The citation in Howard (Fourth Gospel, 2nd ed., p. 258) is confusing, for it gives the source as Vorrede zu den Gesprächen von Ulrich von Hutten, as though the Vorrede ("Foreword") were a separate publication. Strauss' statement is in the Vorrede, but the Vorrede is only the preface of Gespräche von Ulrich von Hutten, which in turn is Part 3 of Strauss's Ulrich von Hutten. Howard's citation comes from the 7th edition in which the Vorrede is published as an appendix to Parts 1 and 2 of Ulrich von Hutten.

2. Meyer, Ursprung, 1:316, 321.

3. Barrett, Gospel St John, pp. 6-8.

4. E. Schweizer, Ego Eimi, pp. 82-112, especially 105, 108.

5. Ruckstuhl, lit. Einheit, pp. 203-19.

6. Cf. Smith, Composition and Order, pp. 64, 70. For Fortna's test of the method of Schweizer and Ruckstuhl, see his Gospel of Signs, pp. 203-18.

7. Smith, op. cit., p. 71.

8. Jeremias, "Literarkritik," p. 35.

9. Haenchen, "Johan. Probleme," p. 52.

10. Cited from A. Schweizer, Evang. Joh., p. 10.

11. Bacon, F.G.R.D., 2d ed., p. 200.

12. Hirsch, "Stilkritik," p. 135; Mendner, "Joh. Literarkritik," pp. 418-34.

13. Fortna, original diss., p. 27.

14. Howard, Fourth Gospel, 2d ed., p. 121.

15. Brooke, Com. Joh. Epistles, p. xvi; Streeter, Four Gospels, p. 460.

16. Smith, op. cit., p. 108.

17. A. H. McNeile, An Introduction to the Study of the New Testament, 2d ed., rev. by C. S. C. Williams (Oxford: Clarendon Press, 1953), p. 273.

18. Windisch, "joh. Erzählungsstil"; Lightfoot, St. John's Gospel, pp. 19-21; Weisse, evang. Geschichte, 1:117; John L. McKenzie, Dictionary of the Bible (Milwaukee: Bruce, 1965), p. 446.

19. Strachan, Fourth Gospel, 3d ed., p. 81, n. 2; Lightfoot, op. cit., p. 21.

20. Moffatt, Introd., 3d ed., p. 558.

21. Streeter, op. cit., p. 377.

22. K. F. Th. Schneider, Die Aechtheit des Johanneischen Evangeliums nach den Quellen neu untersucht (Berlin: Wiegandt und Grieben, 1854), p. 2; cited from Wellhausen, Evang. Joh., p. 3.

23. Cited from Goguel, Introd. au N.T., II, pp. 44-45.

24. Cited from Wellhausen, op. cit., p. 5.

25. Renan, Life Jesus, p. 55; Albertz is cited from Fortna, original diss., p. 10, n. 11.

26. Moffatt, op. cit., p. 552.

27. Strachan, op. cit., p. 81.

28. Barrett, op. cit., p. 20.

29. Schmiedel, Johannine Writings, p. 203.

30. Price, "Search," p. 15.

31. Eric L. Titus, "Did Paul Write I Corinthians 13 ?," JBR 27 (1959):299-302.

32. Bauer, Johannesev., pp. 229, 241.
33. Howard, op. cit., p. 115.
34. F. C. Grant, Gospels, p. 178.
35. Barrett, op. cit., p. 20.
36. Bousset, "Einheit," p. 64; Heitmüller and Fridrichsen cited from Krister Stendahl, The School of St. Matthew (Uppsala: Almquist & Wiksells, 1954), p. 31, n. 4.
37. Renan, op. cit., pp. 54-58.
38. Price, op. cit., p. 11.
39. Faure, "alttest. Zitate," p. 117.
40. Howard, op. cit., p. 133.
41. Strachan, op. cit., p. 81; Wilkens, Entstehungsgeschichte, p. 172; Grundmann, Zeugnis u. Gestalt, pp. 6-7; Smith, op. cit., p. 239.

CHAPTER 4

1. For an account of the influence of rationalism on early "lives" of Jesus, see Schweitzer, Quest, chaps. 3-6.
2. Ibid., pp. 80-84.
3. Cited from Watkins, Modern Criticism, p. 247; Moffatt, Introd., 3d ed., p. 559.
4. A. Schweizer, Evang. Joh., p. 9.
5. Weisse, evang. Geschichte, 1:106-27; 2:184, 195.
6. Cited from Watkins, op. cit., p. 248; Bousset, "Einheit," pp. 4-5; A. Schweizer, op. cit., pp. 12-21.
7. Translated from A. Schweizer, ibid., p. 22.
8. Translated from ibid., p. 98.
9. Bousset, op. cit., p. 3; Schweitzer, op. cit., p. 127.
10. A. Schweizer, "Johannesev."
11. Cited from Bousset, op. cit., p. 4.
12. Ibid., p. 5.
13. Wendt, Teaching, 1:24.
14. Drummond, Inquiry, p. 16; Strachan, Fourth Gospel, 3d ed., p. 16.
15. Goguel, Introd. au N.T., II, pp. 78-79.
16. For Goguel's discussion of the evangelist's treatment of his sources, see ibid., chap. 11.
17. Bacon, F.G.R.D., 2d ed., p. 480.
18. Bultmann, Gospel John, p. 11.
19. See Easton, "Bultmann's RQ," for a reconstruction of the text in English of the Revelation Speeches (in Authorized Version!).

20. Käsemann, "R. Bultmann," p. 188.
21. Colwell, Greek of Fourth Gospel.
22. See Hartke, Vier urchr. Parteien, 1:142, for the list of signs.
23. Morton and Macgregor, Structure, p. 55.
24. Fortna, original diss., p. 64.
25. S. Temple, "Key," p. 232.
26. Teeple, "Grundschrift in the Fourth Gospel?"
27. S. Temple, op. cit., p. 221.
28. Fortna, Gospel of Signs, pp. 226-28.
29. Ibid., pp. 3-8.

CHAPTER 5

1. Raney, Relation of Fourth Gospel, p. 77.
2. Adapted from Becker's summary in his Reden Johan., pp. 9-10.
3. Dodd, Interpretation, p. 115.
4. Ibid., pp. 122-23.

CHAPTER 6

1. Blinzler, Joh. u. Synoptiker, pp. 16-60; this is a more comprehensive survey of works on this subject than I am presenting here.
2. Ibid., p. 50.
3. Cited from ibid., p. 16.
4. Cited from Stephen Neill, The Interpretation of the New Testament 1861-1961 (New York: Oxford University Press, 1964), p. 26.
5. For a fuller presentation of the evidence that the evangelist used Mark and Luke see Bernard, Com. St. John, 1:xciv-cii; Barrett, Gospel St John, pp. 34-37; John M. Creed, The Gospel according to St. Luke (London: Macmillan, 1953), pp. 318-21; Feine-Behm-Kümmel, pp. 144-45.
6. Gardner-Smith, John and Synoptic G., p. xii.
7. Ibid., p. x.
8. Ibid., p. 89.
9. Ibid., p. 90.
10. Ibid., pp. 92-96.
11. Ibid., pp. 96-97.
12. Neill, op. cit., p. 319.
13. Dodd, Historical Trad., p. 8, n. 2.

14. Haenchen, "Aus der Literatur," p. 303.
15. Dodd, Apostolic Preaching, p. 25.
16. Ibid., p. 75.
17. Dodd, Interpretation, pp. 449-53. Note his approving reference to Gardner-Smith's book on p. 449, n. 2.
18. Dodd, Historical Trad., p. 8.
19. Ibid., p. 424.
20. Ibid., p. 428.
21. Bultmann, "johan. Tradition."
22. Fortna, original diss., pp. 45-46, n. 38.
23. Brown, Gospel John, 1:xxxiv-xxxix.
24. Robinson, "Recent Research," pp. 247-52; Smith, Composition and Order, pp. 95-96.
25. Haenchen, op. cit., p. 302; tr. by Teeple.
26. For a balanced view of form criticism as only one literary method among many, see Güttgemanns' work listed in the bibliography of this book.
27. Teeple, "Oral Tradition."
28. Bernard, op. cit., 1:xcvi. He states that John "almost certainly" uses Mark and "most probably he uses Luke, or perhaps we should say uses Q."
29. Goguel, Introd. au N.T., chap. 11, and especially pp. 405-6.
30. Howard, Fourth Gospel, p. 147. Writing later in his "Introduction" to the Gospel of John in The Interpreter's Bible (8:439), he states that the writer of the gospel drew upon the synoptic gospels "to some extent, or else made use of some of the same traditions either in oral or written form."
31. Jeremias, "Literarkritik," p. 46.
32. Bultmann, Gospel John, p. 6.
33. Daube, N.T. and Rab. Judaism, pp. 312-20, 324.
34. See Vincent Taylor, The Gospel according to St. Mark (London: Macmillan, 1952), pp. 649-51, 653-64.
35. Buse, "Marcan Passion Narr.," p. 215 and p. 219, resp.
36. Buse, "Passion Narr. Matt. and Luke," p. 75.
37. See Parker's review in JBL 85 (1966):508-9.
38. Fortna, Gospel of Signs, p. 226.
39. Blinzler, op. cit., pp. 50, 60.

CHAPTER 7

1. Frommann, joh. Lehrbegriff, p. 25.

2. A. Schweizer, Evang. Joh., pp. 10, 57-58. He cites T. A. Seyffarth, Ein Beitrag zur Spezial-Charakteristik der Johanneischen Schriften (Leipzig: Reclam, 1823), pp. 271-74.

3. A. Schweizer, ibid., pp. 55, 60ff. Bousset, "Einheit," p. 3, reports his view on the strata.

4. Cited from Bousset, ibid., p. 5.

5. Ibid., p. 60.

6. Friedrich Wilhelm Blass, Evangelium secundum Johannem cum variae lectionis delectu (Leipzig: Teubner, 1902); cited from Wellhausen, Evang. Joh., p. 5.

7. Schwartz's articles were not available to me; I reconstructed his theory from several reports, mainly Bousset's "Einheit."

8. Wellhausen, op. cit., p. 7; tr. by Teeple.

9. Ibid., p. 6, n. 1.

10. Ibid., p. 102.

11. Spitta, Joh.-Evang., p. v.

12. Bousset, op. cit., pp. 41-42.

13. Spitta, op. cit., p. 404.

14. Ibid., p. 401.

15. Lewis, "Misinterp.," 6:389, 391.

16. Thompson, "Editorial Elements," p. 217.

17. Ibid., p. 218.

18. Mendner, "Tempelreinung," p. 102; tr. by Teeple.

19. For an interpretation of the Gospel of Mark as a Christian Passover Haggadah, see John Bowman, The Gospel of Mark: The New Christian Jewish Passover Haggadah (Leiden: Brill; 1965; "Studia Post-Biblica," 8). The interpretation is unsound.

20. Robinson, "Recent Research," p. 245.

21. Haenchen, "Joh. Probleme," p. 21, n. 1; Fortna, original diss., p. 13, n. 19.

22. Brown, Gospel John, 1:xxxiii.

23. Fortna, op. cit., p. 12.

24. Brown, op. cit., 1:xxxiv-xxxix.

25. Ibid., p. xxxix.

26. Fortna, "Wilhelm Wilkens's Contribution," p. 461.

27. Dodd, Interpretation, p. 431; Barrett, Gospel St John, pp. 479-80; Lightfoot, St. John's Gospel, pp. 38, 338ff.

CHAPTER 8

1. For an example see T. Worden's article in Scripture 16 (1964):5-16.

2. Macgregor, Gospel John, p. 329.

3. In his Vita Christi Evangelicis et scriptoribus orthodoxis excerpta; reported by J. P. Norris in The Journal of Philology 3 (1871):112.

4. Cited from NTA 8 (1963/64):367.

5. Burton, Introd. to Gospels, pp. 117-22, 127.

6. Lewis, Disarrangements, p. 4.

7. Howard, Fourth Gospel, 2d ed., p. 111.

8. Bernard (Com. St. John, 1:xxviii, n. 2) refers to the work of F. J. Paul (1909), A. C. Clark (1914), and J. M. Thompson (1915).

9. Hoare, Original Order, pp. 10-11.

10. Ibid., p. 36.

11. Smith, Composition and Order, pp. 125, 176.

12. Cottam, Fourth Gospel Rearranged, p. 2.

13. Ibid., pp. 112, 118.

14. See Harold H. Oliver, "A Textual Transposition in Codex C," JBL 76 (1957):233-36.

15. Kenyon, Books and Readers, p. 53.

16. Cottam, op. cit., p. 86.

17. Morton and Macgregor, Structure, pp. 32-34.

18. Schnackenburg, "sit. Redestücke," pp. 97-98.

19. Barrett, Gospel St John, p. 20.

CHAPTER 9

1. Teeple, "Methodology," p. 281.

2. Goodenough, "John a Primitive Gospel," p. 153; Dodd, Historical Trad., p. 423.

3. Teeple, "Greek Article," p. 317.

4. In most of the material in Paul's letters personal names are anarthrous. A few of the passages which contain arthrous personal names and which are probably later insertions are Gal. 1:7; "to Cephas" in 2:14; 3:8, 15-18; "Abraham's offspring" in 3:29; 4:24-27; 6:2; 1 Cor. 1:6, 13a, 17; 10:14-22; 2 Cor. 1:5. Often there is other evidence too that these passages are insertions: they break the flow of thought, they intrude to provide scriptural support, or they disagree with other passages. The use and non-use of the Greek article with personal names in Paul's letters is a new field which deserves study. See R. W. Funk's dissertation, listed in the bibliography of this book.

5. Hirsch, "Stilkritik," pp. 133-34. Since he does not recog-

nize an editor, he assigns this "technique of the similar insertion" (Technik des gleichendigen Einsatzes) to "R," the redactor. He states that in this technique, which was used in the Hellenistic period, the insertion ended with an expression corresponding, often verbally, to the one with which R had interrupted the text. As examples he lists 3:31; (4:23); 5:24; 6:36, 56; 8:24, 45; 10:14, 26; 15:12; 17:13; 19:28. I do not find that the insertion always ends with the catchword, however, nor is the insertion always matter which the editor has composed--sometimes it is from a written source.

6. Mark 9:49, in which the verb "salted" represents cleansing by means of punishment ("fire"), and Mark 9:50, in which the noun "salt" represents not punishment, but a personal virtue which should not be lost, as in Matt. 5:13.

7. In the present study the following Greek texts were used:

Novum Testamentum Graece, ed. by Erwin Nestle and Kurt Aland, 25. Aufl. (Stuttgart: Württembergische Bibelanstalt, 1963). Available from the American Bible Society.

The Greek New Testament, ed. by Kurt Aland and others (New York: American Bible Society, 1966).

Synopsis Quattuor Evangelium, ed. by Kurt Aland (Stuttgart: Württembergische Bibelanstalt, 1964).

Papyrus Bodmer II: Evangile de Jean chap. 1-14, ed. by Victor Martin (Cologny-Genève: Bibliotheca Bodmeriana, 1956). Papyrus Bodmer II is P^{66}.

Papyrus Bodmer II: Supplément: Evangile de Jean chap. 14-21, nouvelle ed., ed. by Victor Martin and J. W. B. Barns (Cologny-Genève: Bibliotheca Bodmeriana, 1962). Contains facsimile of whole P^{66}; this is important because there are errors in the transcription of chapters 1-14 published in 1956 listed above.

Papyrus Bodmer XV: Evangile de Jean chap. 1-15, ed. by Victor Martin and Rudolphe Kasser (Cologny-Genève: Bibliotheca Bodmeriana, 1961). Papyrus Bodmer XV is P^{75}.

CHAPTER 10

1. The data in this paragraph are cited from Holtzmann, Evangelium, p. 31.

2. Cited from ibid., p. 32.

3. Cited from ibid.

4. Harnack, "Verhältnis des Prologs," p. 230.

5. See Howard, Fourth Gospel, 2d ed., "Appendix C," for

outline of these and later efforts.

6. Baldensperger, *Prolog*, pp. 3-9.

7. Brown, *Gospel John*, 1:15.

8. Bernard, *Com. St. John*, 1:cxxxix.

9. Bacon, *Gospel of Hellenists*, p. 143.

10. As we observed in chapter 4.

11. Bultmann, *Gospel John*, pp. 17-18.

12. Ibid., p. 35, n. 3; p. 54, n. 2.

13. Käsemann, "Structure and Purpose," p. 148.

14. Ibid., pp. 156-59; p. 166, n. 107.

15. Brown, op. cit., p. 22.

16. Feuillet, *prologue*, pp. 196-203.

17. *Apostellō* instead of *pempō* for "send"; substantive use of *houtos* and *ekeinos*; *martureō peri*; *para theou*; participial phrases; anarthrous personal names.

18. Schnackenburg, "Logus-Hymnus," p. 79.

19. 1:12; 2:23; 3:18c.

20. For comments on parallels in Egyptian temple inscriptions, see K. Haacker, "Eine formgeschichtliche Beobachtung zu Joh 1,3 fin.," *BZ*, N.F., 12 (1968):119-21.

21. Wisd. Sol. 9:1; Philo *De cherub*. 125-27; *alia*. In Philo the Logos was "with" God, though the preposition is *para* (*Quod immut*. 31) instead of *pros*. Philo even calls the Logos "God" (*theos*, without the article) in *De Somn*. i. 228-29; cf. *De conf. ling*. 146. He also characteristically uses the same preposition (*dia*) as the Jewish poem to describe the activity of the Logos as maker of the world (e.g., *Spec. leg*. i. 81); see Schnackenburg, *G. St John*, 1:237.

22. *De opif*. 9.

23. There will be a day of warfare in which God will "bring darkness low and elevate light" (*1 QM* 13:15). There is no sound evidence for the view that the verb *katalambanō* in verse 5 does not carry the notion of conflict between light and darkness.

24. Wisd. Sol. 9:1-2; Philo *Leg. all*. i. 65.

25. Wisd. Sol. 9:10; 10:8; *1 Enoch* 42:1-2.

26. Contrary to Käsemann, op. cit., p. 144.

27. R. M. Grant, *Gnosticism and Early Chr.*, p. 169.

28. Bréhier, *Les idees*, pp. 107-11, 237. Bréhier and Goodenough display a far better understanding of Philo and his background than does Wolfson in his studies of Philo.

29. CH 1:31; cited from the Nock and Festugiere ed.
30. De post. Caini 43.
31. Ibid., 5; Sir. 43:31.
32. CH 1:6; the Logos is luminous.
33. See Dodd, Bible and Greeks, p. 186.
34. Noted by Macgregor, Gospel John, p. 14.
35. Bultmann, op. cit., p. 60, n. 2.
36. Haenchen, "Probleme 'Prologs,'" p. 331.
37. Euripides Ion 693.
38. Plato Timaeus 92c.
39. See Wilfred Knox, Some Hellenistic Elements in Primitive Christianity (London: Oxford University Press, 1944), p. 57.
40. See Goodenough, By Light, pp. 18-19.
41. Apollo: Plato Republic iv. 427c. Serapis: Aelius Aristides 45.
42. Suggested by Schnackenburg (op. cit., 1:194-95), Brown (op. cit., 1:520), and others. The same objection applies to the suggestion that the author of the Hermetic Poimandres may have used John.
43. For example, Carpocrates, the libertine Gnostic. Docetism became the necessary result of the contradiction between the incarnation of a divine Jesus and the gnostic idea that the flesh is inherently evil. This embarrassing contradiction probably was not recognized at first by Christian Gnostics; at least the author of the Prologue hymn is a non-docetic Christian Gnostic. It is doubtful that the gnostic Gospel of Truth is docetic either, for in it the Son has an incorruptible flesh (31:5-8) and men were permitted to taste, smell, and take hold of him (30:28-31). If the Gospel of Truth is not docetic, this is an important point of similarity.
44. Cited from Bréhier, op. cit., p. 107.
45. With my source-within-a-source hypothesis compare Haenchen's theory of the origin of the Prologue: a pagan myth that lamented the world's rejection of Wisdom was adapted to a Jewish hymn in which Wisdom becomes Torah and finds a resting place in Israel; then the Jewish hymn was expanded into a Christian hymn in which the Logos finds a believing community; next, the evangelist added verse 18; finally, the redactor who added chapter 21 added verses 6-8, 12-13, and 15.

CHAPTER 11

1. Jesus' miracles in S are changing water to wine (2:1-12), healing a sick boy (4:48-53), healing a sick man (5:5-9), feeding 5,000 (6:5-14), walking on the sea (6:16-21), healing a blind man (9:1, 6-7, 13, 15-17), and raising a man from the dead (chap. 11). Cf. the general claim in Acts 2:22.

2. Bultmann, Gospel John, p. 6 (cf. Smith, Composition and Order, p. 44); Schnackenburg, G. St John, 1:67.

3. Teeple, "The Historical Beginnings of the Resurrection Faith," in Studies in New Testament and Early Christian Literature, David E. Aune, ed., NovTSup, 33 (Leiden: Brill, 1972), pp. 118-19.

4. Schnackenburg, op. cit.

5. The possessive adjective with one article occurs seven times, four of which are in G (see Appendix).

6. See R. M. Grant, Gnosticism, index (top of p. 251). Marcion is particularly famous for his opposition to the Old Testament with its temperamental, warlike God.

7. Bultmann correctly recognizes that 3:8 "goes back to Gnostic tradition" (Gospel John, p. 143, n. 1). John 3:8 is in E, but the thought is similar.

BIBLIOGRAPHY

The abbreviated title in brackets following some items is the form in which the work is cited in the Notes.

Agourides, Sava. "The Purpose of John 21." In Studies in the History and Text of the New Testament in honor of Kenneth Willis Clark, ed. by Boyd L. Daniels and M. Jack Suggs. (Studies and Documents, 29) Salt Lake City: University of Utah Press, 1967.

Aland, Kurt. "Eine Untersuchung zu Joh 1, 3-4." ZNW 59 (1968): 174-209.

Ammon, Christoph Friedrich von. Johannem evangelii auctorem ab editore huius libri fuisse diversum. Erlangen: Palmsche Verlagshandlung, 1811.

Appel, Heinrich. Die Echtheit des Johannesevangeliums mit besonderer Berücksichtigung der neuesten kritischen Forschungen. Leipzig: Deichert, 1915.

Bacon, Benjamin Wisner. "The Displacement in John xiv." JBL 13 (1894):64-76.

-----. The Fourth Gospel in Research and Debate. New Haven: Moffatt, Yard, 1910. 2d ed., 1918. [F.G.R.D., 2d ed.]

-----. The Gospel of the Hellenists. New York: Holt, 1933. [Gospel of Hellenists]

Bailey, John Amedee. The Traditions Common to the Gospels of Luke and John. (NovTSup, 7) Leiden: Brill, 1963. [Trads. Common to Luke and John]

Baldensperger, Guillaume [D. W.]. Der Prolog des vierten Evangeliums: Sein polemisch-apologetischer Zweck. Freiburg im Breisgau: Mohr, 1898.

Barrett, Charles Kingsley. The Gospel according to St John. London: S.P.C.K., 1955. [Gospel St John]

Bauer, Walter. A Greek-English Lexicon of the New Testament and Other Early Christian Literature. A translation and adaptation of the 4th ed. by William F. Arndt and F. Wilbur Gingrich. Chicago: University of Chicago Press, 1957.

-----. Das Johannesevangelium. 3. Aufl. (HNT, 6) Tübingen: Mohr, 1933. [Johannesev.]

-----. "Johannesevangelium und Johannesbriefe." TR, N.F. 1 (1929):135-60. ["Johannesev. u. Johannesbr."]

Baur, Ferdinand Christian. Kritische Untersuchungen über die kanonischen Evangelien. Tübingen: Fues, 1847.

Becker, Heinz. Die Reden des Johannesevangeliums und der Stil der gnostischen Offenbarungsrede. (FRLANT, N.F., 50) Göttingen: Vandenhoeck & Ruprecht, 1956. [Reden Johan.]

Becker, Jürgen. "Die Abschiedsreden Jesu im Johannesevangelium." ZNW 61 (1970):215-46.

-----. "Aufbau, Schichtung und theologiegeschichtliche Stellung des Gebetes in Johannes 17." ZNW 60 (1969):56-83.

-----. "Wunder und Christologie. Zum literarkritischen und christologischen Problem der Wunder im Johannesevangelium." NTS 16 (1969/70):130-48.

Benoit, Pierre. "Marie-Madeleine et les disciples au tombeau selon Joh 20. 1-18." In Judentum. Urchristentum. Kirche. Festschrift für Joachim Jeremias, ed. by Walther Eltester, pp. 141-52. (BZNW, 26) Berlin: Töpelmann, 1960.

Berger, Klaus. Die Amen-Worte Jesu: Eine Untersuchung zum Problem der Legitimation in apokalyptischer Rede. (BZNW, 39) Berlin: de Gruyter, 1970.

Bernard, John Henry. A Critical and Exegetical Commentary on the Gospel according to St. John. (ICC) 2 vols. London: Clark, 1928. [Com. St. John]

Bertling, Karl Friedrich. "Eine Transposition im Evangelium Johannis." TSK 53 (1880):351-53.

Beyschlag, Willibald. Zur johanneischen Frage: Beiträge zur Würdigung des vierten Evangeliums gegenüber den Angriffen der kritischen Schule. Gotha: Berthes, 1876.

Bible. N.T. English. 1935. Moffatt. The New Testament: A New Translation, by James Moffatt. London: Hodder & Stoughton, 1935.

----------. German. 1906. Die Schriften des Neuen Testaments: neu übersetzt und für die Gegenwart erklärt. 1. Aufl. Göttingen: Vandenhoeck & Ruprecht, 1906. 2. Band, Das Johannes-Evangelium, von Wilhelm Heitmüller. [Heitmüller, Joh.-Evangelium]

----------. John. English. 1956. Revised. St. John's Gospel: A Commentary, by R. H. Lightfoot. Ed. by C. F. Evans. Oxford: Clarendon Press, 1956. [Lightfoot, St. John's Gospel]

----------------------. 1966. Brown. The Gospel according to John. Introd., tr., and notes by Raymond E. Brown. 2 vols. (The Anchor Bible, 29-29A) Garden City, N.Y.: Doubleday, 1966-70. [Brown, Gospel John]

Bible. N.T. John. German. 1890. Delff. Das vierte Evangelium: ein authentischer Bericht über Jesus von Nazareth, wiederhergestellt, übersetzt und erklärt von Hugo Delff. Husum: Delff, 1890.

-------------------------. 1941. Bultmann. Das Evangelium des Johannes. 1. Aufl. (Meyer, 2) Göttingen: Vandenhoeck & Ruprecht, 1941. 17. Aufl., 1963. ET of 17. Aufl.: The Gospel of John: A Commentary. Philadelphia: Westminster Press, 1971. [Bultmann, Gospel John]

Blank, Josef. "Das Johannesevangelium. Der Prolog: Joh 1, 1-18. BL 7 (1966):28-39, 112-27.

-----. Krisis: Untersuchungen zur johanneischen Christologie und Eschatologie. Freiburg im Breisgau: Lambertus-Verlag, 1964.

Blass, Friedrich Wilhelm, and Albert Debrunner. A Greek Grammar of the New Testament and Other Early Christian Literature. A tr. and rev. of the 9th-10th (1960) German ed., by Robert W. Funk. Chicago: University of Chicago Press, 1961.

Blinzler, Josef. Johannes und die Synoptiker: ein Forschungsbericht. (SBS, 5) Stuttgart: Verlag Katholisches Bibelwerk, 1965. [Joh. u. Synoptiker]

Boismard, Marie-Émile. "L'évolution du thème eschatologique dans les traditions johanniques." RB 68 (1961):507-24.

-----. Le prologue de saint Jean. (Lectio Divina, 11) Paris: Éditions du Cerf, 1953.

-----. "Saint Luc et la rédaction du quatrième évangile (Jn 4.46-54)." RB 69 (1962):185-211.

-----. "Les traditions johanniques concernant le Baptist." RB 70 (1963):5-42.

Borgen, Peder. "John and the Synoptics in the Passion Narrative." NTS 5 (1958/59):246-59. ["Passion Narrative"]

-----. "Logos Was the True Light. Contributions to the Interpretation of the Prologue of John." NovT 14 (1972):115-30.

-----. "The Unity of the Discourse in John 6." ZNW 50 (1959): 277-78.

Bornkamm, Günther. "Die eucharistische Rede im Johannes-Evangelium." ZNW 47 (1956):161-69.

Bousset, Johann Franz Wilhelm. "Ist das vierte Evangelium eine literarische Einheit?" ThRu 12 (1909): 1-12, 39-64. ["Einheit"]

Braun, Françoise-Marie. Jean le théologien. 3 vols. Paris: Gabalda, 1959-1966.

Braun, Herbert. "Literar-Analyse und theologische Schichtung im ersten Johannesbrief." ZTK 48 (1951):262-92.

Bréhier, Émile. Les idées philosophiques et religieuses de Philon d'Alexandrie. 3d ed. Paris: Librairie Philosophique J. Vrin, 1950. [Les idées]

Bretschneider, Karl Gottlieb. Probabilia de evangelii et epistolarum Iohannis apostoli indole et origine eruditorum iudiciis modeste subjecit Carolus Theophilus Bretschneider. Lipsiae: Barth, 1820. [Probabilia]

Brooke, Alan England. A Critical and Exegetical Commentary on the Johannine Epistles. (ICC) Edinburgh: Clark, 1912. [Com. Joh. Epistles]

Brown, Raymond Edward. The Gospel according to John. (See: Bible. N.T. John. English. 1966. Brown.)

Bultmann, Rudolf Karl. Das Evangelium des Johannes. (See: Bible. N.T. John. German. 1941. Bultmann)

-----. "Hirsch's Auslegung des Johannes-Evangeliums." EvT 4 (1937):115-42. ["Hirsch's Auslegung"]

-----. "Johannesevangelium." In RGG, 3. Aufl., pp. 840-50. Tübingen: Mohr, 1959. ["Johannesev." in RGG]

-----. "Der religionsgeschichtliche Hintergrund des Prologs zum Johannesevangelium." In Eucharisterion: Studien zur Religion und Literatur des Alten und Neuen Testaments, Herman Gunkel zum 60. Geburtstage, pp. 1-26. (FRLANT, 36, vol. 2) Göttingen: Vandenhoeck & Ruprecht, 1923.

-----. "Zur johanneischen Tradition." TLZ 80 (1955):521-26.

Burch, Vacher. The Structure and Message of St. John's Gospel. London: Hopkinson, 1928.

Burney, Charles Fox. The Aramaic Origin of the Fourth Gospel. Oxford: Clarendon Press, 1922.

Burton, Ernest De Witt. A Short Introduction to the Gospels. Chicago: University of Chicago Press, 1904. [Introd. to Gospels]

Buse, Ivor. "St John and the Marcan Passion Narrative." NTS 4 (1957/58):215-19. ["Marcan Passion Narr."]

-----. "St John and the Passion Narratives of St Matthew and St Luke." NTS 7 (1960/61):65-76. ["Passion Narr. Matt. and Luke"]

Carpenter, Joseph Estlin. The Johannine Writings: A Study of the Apocalypse and the Fourth Gospel. Boston: Houghton Mifflin, 1927. [Johannine Writings]

Colson, Jean. L'Énigme du disciple que Jésus aimait. Paris: Beauchesne, 1969.

Colwell, Ernest Cadman. The Gospel of the Spirit: A Study in the

Fourth Gospel, by Ernest Cadman Colwell and Eric Lane Titus. New York: Harper, 1953.
-----. The Greek of the Fourth Gospel: A Study of Its Aramaisms in the Light of Hellenistic Greek. Chicago: University of Chicago Press, 1931. [Greek of Fourth Gospel]
-----. John Defends the Gospel. Chicago: University of Chicago Press, 1936.
Cottam, Thomas. The Fourth Gospel Rearranged. London: Epworth Press, 1952. [Fourth Gospel Rearranged]
Crossan, Dominic M. The Gospel of Eternal Life: Reflections on the Theology of St. John. Milwaukee: Bruce, 1967.
Cryer, Cecil. "The Prologue of the Fourth Gospel." ExpT 32 (1920/21):440-43.
Curtis, K. Peter G. "Luke xxiv. 12 and John xx. 3-10." JTS, N.S., 22 (1971):512-15.
Dahl, Niels Alstrup. "Die Passionsgeschichte bei Matthäus." NTS 2 (1955/56):17-32.
Daube, David. The New Testament and Rabbinic Judaism. London: Athlone Press, 1956. [N.T. and Rab. Judaism]
Dauer, A. "Das Wort des Gekreuzigten an seine Mutter und den 'Jünger, den er liebte.' Eine traditionsgeschichtliche und theologische Untersuchung zu Joh 19, 25-27." BZ 11 (1967):222-39.
Deeks, D. "The Structure of the Fourth Gospel." NTS 15 (1968/69):107-29.
Dekker, C. "Grundschrift und Redaction im Johannesevangelium." NTS 13 (1966/67):66-80.
Delff, Heinrich Karl Hugo. Neue Beitrage Zur Kritik und Erklärung des vierten Evangeliums. Husum: Delff, 1890.
-----. Das vierte Evangelium . . . (See: Bible. N.T. John. German. 1890. Delff.)
Demke, Christoph. "Der sogenannte Logos-Hymnus im johanneischen Prolog." ZNW 58 (1967):45-68.
De Wette, Wilhelm Martin Leberecht. Lehrbuch der historisch-kritischen Einleitung in die kanonistischen und apocryphischen Bücher des Neuen Testaments. Berlin: Reimer, 1817.
Dibelius, Martin. "The Structure and Literary Character of the Gospels." HTR 20 (1927):151-70. ["Structure & Lit. Character"]
Dodd, Charles Henry. The Apostolic Preaching and Its Developments. London: Hodder & Stoughton, 1936. [Apostolic Preaching]
-----. The Bible and the Greeks. London: Hodder & Stoughton,

1935. [*Bible and Greeks*]

-----. *Historical Tradition in the Fourth Gospel*. Cambridge: University Press, 1963. [*Historical Trad.*]

-----. *The Interpretation of the Fourth Gospel*. Cambridge: University Press, 1953. [*Interpretation*]

Doress, Jean. *The Secret Books of the Egyptian Gnostics: An Introduction to the Gnostic Coptic Manuscripts Discovered at Chenoboskion*. London: Hollis & Carter, 1960. [*Secret Books*]

Drummond, James. *An Inquiry into the Character and Authorship of the Fourth Gospel*. London: Williams & Norgate, 1903. [*Inquiry*]

Duprez, Antoine. *Jésus et les dieux guérisseurs: A propos de Jean, V*. (Cahiers de la Revue Biblique, 12) Paris: Gabalda, 1970.

Easton, Burton Scott. "Bultmann's *RQ* Source." *JBL* 65 (1946): 143-56. ["Bultmann's *RQ*"]

Eckermann, Jacob Christian R. *Theologische Beiträge*. Band 5, *Resultate der bisher über den Ursprung der Evangelien angestellten Untersuchungen*. Altona: Hammerich, 1796.

Edwards, Hubert Edwin. *The Disciple Who Wrote These Things*. London: Clarke, 1953. [*Disciple Who Wrote*]

Edwards, Rowland Alexander. *The Gospel according to St. John: Its Criticism and Interpretation*. London: Eyre & Spottiswoode, 1954.

Eltester, Walther. "Der Logos und sein Prophet: Fragen zur heutigen Erklärung des johanneischen Prologs." In *Apophoreta: Festschrift für Ernst Haenchen*, pp. 109-34. Berlin: Töpelmann, 1964.

Evanson, Edward. *The Dissonance of the Four Generally Received Evangelists, and the Evidence of Their Respective Authenticity Examined*. Ipswich: Jermym, 1792.

Faure, Alexander. "Die alttestamentlichen Zitate im 4. Evangelium und die Quellenscheidungshypothese." *ZNW* 21 (1922):99-121. ["alttest. Zitate"]

Fee, Gordon D. "The Use of the Definite Article with Personal Names in the Gospel of John." *NTS* 17 (1970/71):168-83.

Feine, Paul, and Johannes Behm. *Einleitung in das Neue Testament*. 14. bearb. Aufl. by Werner Georg Kümmel. Heidelberg: Quelle & Meyer, 1965. ET: *Introduction to the New Testament*. Nashville: Abingdon Press, 1966. [ET cited as: Feine-Behm-Kümmel]

Feuillet, Andre. Le prologue du quatrième évangile: Étude de théologie johannique. Paris: Desclee De Brouwer, 1968. [prologue]

Flowers, Harold Joseph. "Interpolations in the Fourth Gospel." JBL 40 (1921):146-58.

Fortna, Robert Tomson. The Gospel of Signs: A Reconstruction of the Narrative Source Underlying the Fourth Gospel. (SNTSMS, 11) Cambridge: University Press, 1970. [Gospel of Signs] Rev. of author's Th.D. diss. at Union Theological Seminary, N.Y., 1965; latter cited as: [original diss.]

-----. "Source and Redaction in the Fourth Gospel's Portrayal of Jesus' Signs." JBL 89 (1970):151-66.

-----. "Wilhelm Wilkens's Further Contribution to Johannine Studies--a Review Article." JBL 89 (1970):457-62. ["Wilhelm Wilkens's Contribution"]

Freed, Edwin D. "The Entry into Jerusalem in the Gospel of John." JBL 80 (1961):329-38.

-----. Old Testament Quotations in the Gospel of John. (NovTSup, 11) Leiden: Brill, 1965.

-----. "The Son of Man in the Fourth Gospel." JBL 86 (1967): 402-9.

-----. "Variations in the Language and Thought of John." ZNW 55 (1964):167-97.

Frommann, Karl. Der johanneische Lehrbegriff in seinem Verhältnisse zur gesammten biblisch-christlichen Lehre. Leipzig: Breitkopf und Härtel, 1839. [joh. Lehrbegriff]

Funk, Robert W. A Greek Grammar . . . (See: Blass, Friedrich Wilhelm)

-----. "The Syntax of the Greek Article; Its Importance for Critical Pauline Problems." Ph.D. diss., Vanderbilt University, 1953.

Gächter, Paul. "Strophen im Johannesevangelium." ZKT 60 (1936):99-120, 402-23.

Gardner-Smith, Percival. Saint John and the Synoptic Gospels. Cambridge: University Press, 1938. [John and Synoptic G.]

Garvie, Alfred Ernest. The Beloved Disciple. London: Hodder & Stoughton, 1922.

Goguel, Maurice. Introduction au Nouveau Testament. Tome II, Le Quatrième Évangile. Paris: Leroux, 1923. [Introd. au N.T., II]

Goodenough, Erwin Ramsdell. By Light, Light. New Haven:

Yale University Press, 1935. [By Light]

-----. "John a Primitive Gospel." JBL 64 (1945):145-82.

Goodwin, Charles. "How Did John Treat His Sources?" JBL 73 (1954): 61-75.

Granskou, David M. "Structure and Theology in the Fourth Gospel: A Study of Literary Features in the Fourth Gospel and Their Relation to Its Theology." Ph.D. diss., Princeton Theological Seminary, 1960.

Grant, Frederick Clifton. The Gospels: Their Origin and Their Growth. New York: Harper, 1957. [Gospels]

Grant, Robert McQueen. Gnosticism: A Source Book of Heretical Writings from the Early Christian Period. New York: Harper, 1961. [Gnosticism]

-----. Gnosticism and Early Christianity. New York: Oxford University Press, 1959; 2d ed., New York: Harper, 1966. [Gnosticism and Early Chr.]

-----. "The Origin of the Fourth Gospel." JBL 69 (1950):305-22.

Gregory, Caspar René. Wellhausen und Johannes. 2. Aufl. Leipzig: Hinrichs, 1910. [Wellhausen und Joh.]

Grundmann, Walter. Zeugnis und Gestalt des Johannesevangeliums: Eine Studie zur denkerischen und gestalterischen Leistung des vierten Evangelisten. Stuttgart: Calwer Verlag, 1961. [Zeugnis u. Gestalt]

Guilding, Aileen. The Fourth Gospel and Jewish Worship. Oxford. Clarendon Press, 1960. [Fourth Gospel]

Güttgemanns, Erhardt. Offene Fragen zur Formgeschichte des Evangeliums: Eine methodologische Skizze der Grundlagenproblematik der Form- und Redaktionsgeschichte. (BEvT, 54) München: Kaiser, 1970.

Haenchen, Ernst. "Aufbau und Theologie des Poimandres." ZTK 53 (1956):149-91.

-----. "Aus der Literatur zum Johannesevangelium 1929-1956." ThRu, N.F. 23 (1955/56):295-335. ["Aus der Literatur"]

-----. "Johanneische Probleme." ZTK 56 (1959):19-54. ["Johan. Probleme"]

-----. "Probleme des johanneischen 'Prologs.'" ZTK 60 (1963): 305-34. ["Probleme 'Prologs'"]

Hahn, Ferdinand. "Der Prozess Jesu nach dem Johannesevangelium: Eine redaktionsgeschichtliche Untersuchung." In Evangelisch-katholischer Kommentar zum Neuen Testament, 2. Zürich: Benziger Verlag; Neukirchener Verlag, 1970.

Harnack, Adolf von. Geschichte der Altchristlichen Literatur bis Eusebius. 2. Teil: Die Chronologie der Altchristlichen Literatur bis Eusebius. Leipzig: Hinrichs, 1897. [Chronologie]

-----. "Über das Verhaltnis des Prologs des vierten Evangeliums zum ganzen Werk." ZTK 2 (1892):189-231.

Harris, James Rendel. The Origin of the Prologue to St. John's Gospel. Cambridge: University Press, 1917.

-----. "The Stoic Origins of St. John's Gospel." BJRL 6 (1921/22): 439-51. ["Stoic Origins"]

Harrison, Everett Falconer. Introduction to the New Testament. Grand Rapids: Eerdmans, 1964.

Hartke, Wilhelm. Vier urchristliche Parteien und ihre Vereinigung zur apostolischen Kirche. 2 vols. (Deutsche Akademie der Wissenschaften zu Berlin. Schriften der Sektion für Altertumswissenschaft, 24) Berlin: Akademie, 1961. [Vier urchr. Parteien]

Hasler, Victor. Amen: Redactionsgeschichtliche Untersuchung zur Einführungsformel der Herrenworte "Wahrlich ich sage euch." Zürich, Stuttgart: Gotthelf-Verlag, 1969.

Heitmüller, Wilhelm. Das Johannes-Evangelium. (See: Bible. N.T. German. 1906.)

Herder, Johann Gottfried von. Briefe das Studium der Theologie betreffend. 4 vols. Weimar: Hoffmann, 1780-1781. [Briefe das Studium]

-----. Von Gottes Sohn, der Welt Heiland: Nach Johannes Evangelium. Riga: Hartknoch in Leipzig, 1797.

Hilgenfeld, Adolf. Historisch-Kritische Einleitung in das Neue Testament. Leipzig: Fues's Verlag, 1875.

Hillmer, Melvyn Raymond. "The Gospel of John in the Second Century." Th.D. diss. at Harvard University, 1966. (Summarized in HTR 59 (1966):446.)

Hirsch, Emanuel. "Stilkritik und Literanalyse im vierten Evangelium." ZNW 43 (1950/51):129-43. ["Stilkritik"]

-----. Studien zum vierten Evangelium. Tübingen: Mohr, 1936.

-----. Das vierte Evangelium in seiner ursprünglichen Gestalt, verdeutscht und erklärt. Tübingen: Mohr, 1936. [Das vierte Evangelium]

Hoare, Frederick Russel. The Original Order and Chapters of St. John's Gospel. London: Burns, Oates, 1944. [Original Order]

Holtzmann, Heinrich Julius. Evangelium, Briefe und Offenbarung des Johannes. 3. Aufl., rev. by W. Bauer. (Hand-Commentar

zum Neuen Testament, 4) Tübingen: Mohr, 1908. [Evangelium]
-----. "Das schriftstellerische Verhältnis des Johannes zu den Synoptikern." Zeitschrift für wissenschaftliche Theologie 12 (1869):62-85, 155-78, 446-56.
Hoskyns, Edwyn Clement. The Fourth Gospel. Ed. by Francis Noel Davey. London: Faber and Faber, 1940; 2d rev. ed., 1947.
Howard, Wilbert Francis. The Fourth Gospel in Recent Criticism and Interpretation. London: Epworth Press, 1921; 2d ed., 1935; 4th ed., rev. by C. K. Barrett, 1955. [Fourth Gospel, 2d ed.]
-----. "Introduction" to the Gospel of John in The Interpreter's Bible, vol. 8. New York: Abingdon-Cokesbury, 1952. ["Introduction"]
Hug, Johann Leonard. Einleitung in die Schriften des Neuen Testaments. 3. Aufl. Stuttgart and Tübingen: Cotta, 1826.
Hurst, George Leopold. The Literary Background of the New Testament. New York: Macmillan, 1928.
Irigoin, Jean. "La composition rhythmique du prologue de Jean (I, 1-18)." RB 78 (1971):501-14.
Jeremias, Joachim. "Joh 6:51c-58--redaktionell?" ZNW 44 (1952/53):256-57.
-----. "Johanneische Literarkritik." TB 20 (1941):33-46. ["Literarkritik"]
-----. Der Prolog des Johannesevangeliums (Johannes 1,1-18). Stuttgart: Calwer Verlag, 1967.
Johnston, Edwin D. "The Johannine Version of the Feeding of the Five Thousand: An Independent Tradition?" NTS 8 (1961/62): 151-54.
Johnston, George. The Spirit-Paraclete in the Gospel of John. Cambridge: University Press, 1970.
Jonas, Hans. The Gnostic Religion: The Message of the Alien God and the Beginnings of Christianity. Boston: Beacon Press, 1958. 2d ed., rev., 1963. [Gnostic Religion]
Käsemann, Ernst. "Aufbau und Anliegen des johanneischen Prologs." In Libertas Christiana; Festschrift für Friedrich Delekat zum 65. Geburtstag, pp. 75-99. München: Kaiser, 1957. ET: "The Structure and Purpose of the Prologue to John's Gospel," in E. Käsemann, New Testament Questions of Today, pp. 138-67. Philadelphia: Fortress Press, 1969. ["Structure and Purpose"]
-----. Jesu letzter Wille nach Johannes 17. Tübingen: Mohr, 1966. ET: The Testament of Jesus: A Study of the Gospel of John in the Light of Chapter 17. Philadelphia: Fortress Press,

1968.
-----. "Rudolf Bultmann, Das Evangelium des Johannes." In Verkündigung und Forschung 3 (1947), Theologischer Jahresbericht, pp. 1942-46. ["R. Bultmann"]
Keim, Karl Theodor. Die Geschichte Jesu von Nazareth. 3 vols. Zürich: Drell, Füssli, 1867-72.
Kenyon, Frederic George. Books and Readers in Ancient Greece and Rome. Oxford: Clarendon Press, 1932. [Books and Readers]
Kragerud, Alv. Der Lieblingsjünger im Johannesevangelium. Oslo: Osloer Universitaetsverlag, 1959. [Lieblingsjünger]
Kümmel, Werner Georg. Introduction to the New Testament. (See: Feine, Paul)
Kundsin, Karl. Character und Ursprung der johanneischen Reden. (Acta Universitatis Latviensis, I, 4) Riga: University of Latvia, 1939.
Kysar, Robert Dean. "The Background of the Prologue of the Fourth Gospel: A Critique of Historical Methods." CJT 116 (1970):250-55.
-----. "The Source Analysis of the Fourth Gospel: A Growing Concensus ?" NovT 15 (1973): 134-52.
Lagrange, Marie-Joseph. Évangile selon Saint Jean. Paris: Gabalda, 1925.
Lee, E. Kenneth. "St Mark and the Fourth Gospel." NTS 3 (1956/57):50-58.
Lewis, Frank Warburton. "Another Disarrangement in the Fourth Gospel." The Interpreter 8 (1911/12):109-10.
-----. Disarrangements in the Fourth Gospel. Cambridge: University Press, 1910.
-----. "Misinterpretations in the Fourth Gospel." The Interpreter 6 (1909/10):384-91; 7 (1910/11):88-97, 201-4. ["Misinterp."]
Lightfoot, Robert Henry. St. John's Gospel. (See: Bible. N.T. John. English. 1956. Revised.)
Lindars, Barnabas. Behind the Fourth Gospel. (Studies in Creative Criticism, 3) London: S.P.C.K.,1971.
-----. "The Composition of John XX." NTS 7 (1960/61):142-47.
-----. New Testament Apologetic: The Doctrinal Significance of the Old Testament Quotations. London: SCM Press, 1961.
Lohse, Eduard. "Wort und Sakrament im Johannesevangelium." NTS 7 (1960/61):110-25.
Loisy, Alfred Firmin. Les Origines du Nouveau Testament. Paris: Nourry, 1936. ET: The Origins of the New Testament.

New York: Macmillan, 1950. [Origins N.T.]

-----. Le Quatrième Évangile. 2d ed. Paris: Nourry, 1921.

Lücke, Friedrich. Commentar über das Evangelium des Johannes. 3 vols. Bonn: Weber, 1820. 2. Aufl., 1833-1834; 3. Aufl. 1840-1843.

Lützelberger, E. C. J. Die kirchliche Tradition über den Apostel Johannes und seine Schriften in ihrer Grundlosigkeit nachgewiesen. Leipzig: Brockhaus, 1840. [kirchliche Tradition]

Macgregor, George Hogarth Carnaby. The Gospel of John. (Moffatt New Testament Commentary) New York: Harper, 1929. [Gospel John]

Malatesta, Edward. "The Literary Structure of John 17." Biblica 52 (1971):190-214.

-----. St. John's Gospel 1920-1965. A Cumulative and Classified Bibliography of Books and Periodical Literature on the Fourth Gospel. (Analecta Biblica, 32) Rome: Pontifical Biblical Institute, 1967.

Manson, Thomas W. "The Life of Jesus: Some Tendencies in Present-Day Research." In The Background of the New Testament: Studies in Honour of C. H. Dodd, ed. by W. D. Davies and D. Daube, pp. 211-21. Cambridge: University Press, 1956.

Martyn, James Louis. History and Theology in the Fourth Gospel. New York: Harper and Row, 1968.

-----. "Source Criticism and Religionsgeschichte in the Fourth Gospel." Perspective 11 (1970): 247-73.

Meeks, Wayne A. "Galilee and Judea in the Fourth Gospel." JBL 85 (1966):159-69.

-----. "The Man from Heaven in Johannine Sectarianism." JBL 91 (1972):44-72.

Mendner, Siegfried. "Johanneische Literarkritik." TZ 8 (1952): 418-34. ["Joh. Literarkritik"]

-----. "Nikodemus." JBL 77 (1958):298-323.

-----. "Die Tempelreinigung." ZNW 47 (1956):93-112. ["Tempelreinigung"]

-----. "Zum Problem 'Johannes und die Synoptiker.'" NTS 4 (1957/58):282-307.

Merlier, Octave. Le quatrième évangile; la question johannique. (Connaissance de la Grèce, 11. Études néo-testamentaires, 2) Paris: Presses Universitaires de France, 1961.

Meyer, Arnold. "Die Behandlung der johanneischen Frage im

letzten Jahrzehnt." ThRu 2 (1899): 255-63, 295-305, 333-45. ["Behandlung"]

Meyer, Eduard. Ursprung und Anfänge des Christentums. 1. Teil: Die Evangelien. Stuttgart: Cotta, 1921. [Ursprung]

Meyer, Paul W. "John 2:10." JBL 86 (1967):191-97.

Michel, Otto. "Der Anfang der Zeichen Jesus." In Die Leibhaftigkeit des Wortes: theologische und seelsorgerliche Studien und Beiträge als Festgabe für Adolf Köberle zum sechzigsten Geburtstag . . ., ed. by Otto Michel and Ulrich Mann. Hamburg: Furche-Verlag, 1958.

Mitton, C. Leslie. "The Provenance of the Fourth Gospel." ExpT 71 (1960):337-40.

Moffatt, James. An Introduction to the Literature of the New Testament. New York: Scribners, 1911. 3d ed., 1918. [Introd. 3d ed.]

-----. The New Testament. (See: Bible. N.T. English. 1935. Moffatt.)

Montgomery, James A. The Origin of the Gospel according to St. John. Philadelphia: Winston, 1923. [Origin]

Morris, Leon. Studies in the Fourth Gospel. Grand Rapids: Eerdmans, 1969.

Morton, Andrew Queen, and G. H. C. Macgregor. The Structure of the Fourth Gospel. Edinburgh: Oliver and Boyd, 1961. [Structure]

Moulton, William Fiddian, and Alfred S. Geden, eds. A Concordance to the Greek Testament according to the Texts of Westcott and Hort, Tischendorf and the English Revisers. 3d ed. Edinburgh: Clark, 1926.

Mussies, G. The Morphology of Koine Greek as Used in the Apocalypse of St. John: A Study in Bilingualism. (NovTSup, 27) Leiden: Brill, 1971.

Nauck, Wolfgang. Die Tradition und der Charakter des ersten Johannesbriefes. Tübingen: Mohr, 1957.

Nicol, W. The Semeia in the Fourth Gospel: Tradition and Redaction. (NovTSup, 32) Leiden: Brill, 1972.

Nicolas, Michel. Études critiques sur la Bible. Nouveau Testament. 2 vols. Paris: Michel-Lévy, 1862-1864.

Noack, Bent. Zur johanneischen Tradition: Beiträge zur Kritik an der literarkritischen Analyse des vierten Evangeliums. København: Rosenkilde og Bagger, 1954.

Norden, Eduard. Agnostos Theos: Untersuchungen zur Formenge-

schichte religiöser Rede. Leipzig: Teubner, 1913.
Norris, J. P. "On the Chronology of St John V. and VI." The Journal of Philology 3 (1871):107-12. ["Chronology"]
Nunn, Henry Preston Vaughan. The Authorship of the Fourth Gospel. Windsor, Berkshire: Alden & Blackwell, 1952.
O'Neill, J. C. "The Prologue to St. John's Gospel." JTS 20 (1969):41-52.
-----. The Puzzle of 1 John: A New Examination of Origins. London: S.P.C.K., 1966.
Osty, Émile. "Les points de contact entre le récit de la passion dans saint Jean." RSR 39 (1951):146-54.
Parker, Pierson. "John the Son of Zebedee and the Fourth Gospel." JBL 81 (1962):35-43. ["John Son of Zebedee"]
-----. "Luke and the Fourth Gospel." NTS 9 (1962/63):317-36.
-----. "Two Editions of John." JBL 75 (1956):303-14. ["Two Editions"]
Peake, Arthur S. A Critical Introduction to the New Testament. London: Duckworth, 1909. [Introd. N.T.]
Porter, Calvin L. "An Analysis of the Textual Variation between Pap 75 and Codex Vaticanus in the Text of John." In Studies in the History and Text of the New Testament in honor of Kenneth Willis Clark, ed. by Boyd L. Daniels and M. Jack Suggs, pp. 71-80. (Studies and Documents, 29) Salt Lake City: University of Utah Press, 1967. ["Analysis of Textual Variation"]
_____. "Papyrus Bodmer XV (P^{75}) and the Text of Codex Vaticanus." JBL 81 (1962):363-76.
-----. "A Textual Analysis of the Earliest Greek Manuscripts of the Gospel of John." Ph.D. diss., Duke University, 1961.
Price, James L. "The Search for the Theology of the Fourth Evangelist." JAAR 35 (1967):3-15. ["Search"]
Raney, W. H. The Relation of the Fourth Gospel to the Christian Cultus. Giessen: Töpelmann, 1933. [Relation of Fourth Gospel]
Reese, James M. "Literary Structure of Jn 13:31--14:31; 16:5-6, 16-33." CBQ 34 (1972):321-31.
Reimarus, Hermann Samuel. Von dem Zwecke Jesu und seiner Jünger. Braunschweig: Lessing, 1778. ET: (1) Reimarus: Fragments. Ed. by Charles H. Talbert; tr. by Ralph S. Fraser. Philadelphia: Fortress Press, 1970. (2) The Goal of Jesus and His Disciples. Introd. and tr. by George Wesley Buchanan. Leiden: Brill, 1970.
Renan, Joseph Ernest. La Vie de Jésus. Paris: Michel Lévy

frères, 1863. ET of 23d final rev. ed.: The Life of Jesus. Boston: Roberts, 1896. [Life Jesus]

Richter, Georg. "Die Fleischwerdung des Logos im Johannesevangelium." NovT 13 (1971):81-126.

-----. "Die Gefangennahme Jesu nach dem Johannesevangelium (18, 1-12)." BL 10 (1969):26-39.

-----. "Ist en ein strukturbilendes Element im Logoshymnus Joh 1, 1ff.?" Biblica 51 (1970):539-44.

-----. "Zur Formgeschichte und literarischen Einheit von Joh 6:31-58." ZNW 60 (1969):21-55.

Ridderbos, Herman. "The Structure and Scope of the Prologue to the Gospel of John." NovT 8 (1966):180-201.

Robinson, James McConkey. "Recent Research in the Fourth Gospel." JBL 78 (1959):242-52. ["Recent Research"]

Robinson, John Arthur Thomas. "The Destination and Purpose of St John's Gospel." NTS 6 (1959/60):117-31.

-----. "The Relation of the Prologue to the Gospel of St John." NTS 9 (1962/63):120-29.

Ruckstuhl, Eugen. Die literarische Einheit des Johannesevangeliums, der gegenwärtige Stand der einschlägigen Erforschung. (Studia Friburgensia, N.F., 3) Freiburg in der Schweiz: Paulus-Verlag, 1951. [lit. Einheit]

Sanday, William. The Criticism of the Fourth Gospel. New York: Scribner's, 1905. [Criticism]

Sanders, Joseph Newbould. The Fourth Gospel in the Early Church: Its Origin and Influence on Christian Theology up to Irenaeus. Cambridge: University Press, 1943. [Fourth Gospel]

Schenkel, Daniel. "Über die neuesten Bearbeitungen des Lebens Jesu." TSK 13 (1840):736-808.

Schlatter, Adolf von. Der Evangelist Johannes. 2. Aufl. Stuttgart: Calwer Verlag, 1948.

Schmiedel, Paul Wilhelm. "John, Son of Zebedee." In Cheyne and Black, Encyclopaedia Biblica. 4 vols. New York: Macmillan, 1899-1903.

-----. Das vierte Evangelium gegenüber den drei ersten. Halle: Volks-Bücher, 1906. ET: The Johannine Writings. London: Black, 1908. [Johannine Writings]

Schnackenburg, Rudolf. Die Johannesbriefe. Freiburg im Breisgau: Herder, 1953; 2. Aufl., 1963.

-----. Das Johannesevangelium. (HTKNT, 4) Freiburg im Breisgau: Herder. 1. Teil, 1965; 2. Teil, 1971; 3. Teil, n.y.p.

ET of 1. Teil: The Gospel According to St John. Vol. 1. New York: Herder and Herder, 1968. [G. St John]
-----. "Logos-Hymnus und Johanneischer Prolog." BZ, N.F., 1 (1957):69-109. ["Logos-Hymnus"]
-----. "Die situationsgelösten Redestücke in Joh 3." ZNW 49 (1958):88-99. ["sit. Redestücke"]
-----. "Zur Herkunst des Johannesevangeliums." BZ, N.F., 14 (1970):1-23. ["Zur Herkunst"]
-----. "Zur Traditionsgeschichte von Joh 4, 46-54." BZ 8 (1964):58-88.
Schneider, Johannes. "Zur Komposition von Joh 18, 12-27." ZNW 48 (1957):111-19.
Schnider, Franz, and Werner Stenger. Johannes und die Synoptiker: Vergleich ihrer Parallelen. München: Kösel, 1971.
Schottroff, Louise. Der Glaubende und die feindliche Welt: Beobachtungen zum gnostischen Dualismus und seiner Bedeutung für Paulus und das Johannesevangelium. (WMANT, 37) Neukirchen-Vluyn: Neukirchener Verlag, 1970.
Schulz, Siegfried. Komposition und Herkunst der Johanneischen Reden. (BWANT, 5 F., 1 [entire series, 81]) Stuttgart: Kohlhammer, 1960. [Komposition und Herkunst]
-----. Untersuchungen zur Menschensohn Christologie im Johannesevangelium. Göttingen: Vandenhoeck & Ruprecht, 1957. [Untersuch. Menschensohn Christol.]
Schütz, Roland. "Zum ersten Teil des Johannesevangeliums." ZNW 8 (1907):243-55.
Schwartz, Eduard. "Aporien im vierten Evangelium." In Königlichen Gesellschaft der Wissenschaften zu Göttingen. Philologisch Historische Klasse. Nachrichten. Berlin: 1907, pp. 324-72; 1908, pp. 115-88, 497-560. ["Aporien"]
Schweitzer, Albert. Von Reimarus zu Wrede. Tübingen: Mohr, 1906. ET: The Quest of the Historical Jesus. London: Black, 1910. [Quest]
Schweizer, Alexander. Das Evangelium Johannis nach seinem inneren Werte und seiner Bedeutung für das Leben Jesu kritisch untersucht. Leipzig: Weidmann, 1841. [Evang. Joh.]
-----. "Das Johannesevangelium." Protestantische Kirchenzeitung für das evangelische Deutschland 11 (1864):362-63. ["Johannesev."]
Schweizer, Eduard. Ego Eimi: Die religionsgeschichtliche Herkunst und theologische Bedeutung der johanneischen Bildreden,

zugleich ein Beitrag zur Quellenfrage des vierten Evangeliums. (FRLANT, N.F.,38) Göttingen: Vandenhoeck & Ruprecht, 1939. 2. Aufl., 1965. [Ego Eimi]

Scott, Ernest Findley. The Fourth Gospel: Its Purpose and Theology. Edinburgh: Clark, 1906. 2d ed., 1908.

Shorter, M. "The Position of Chapter VI in the Fourth Gospel." ExpT 84 (1973):181-83.

Smalley, Stephen S. "Diversity and Development in John." NTS 17 (1970/71):276-92.

Smend, Friedrich. "Die Behandlung alttestamentlicher Zitate als Ausgangspunkt der Quellenscheidung im 4. Evangelium." ZNW 24 (1925):147-50.

Smith, Dwight Moody, Jr. The Composition and Order of the Fourth Gospel: Bultmann's Literary Theory. (Yale Publications in Religion, 10) New Haven: Yale University Press, 1965. [Composition and Order]

-----. "John 12:12ff. and the Question of John's Use of the Synoptics." JBL 82 (1963):58-64.

Soltau, Wilhelm. Das vierte Evangelium in seiner Entstehungsgeschichte dargelegt. (Sitzungsberichte der Heidelberger Akademie der Wissenschaften. Philosophisch-historische Klasse, Band 7, 6 Abh.) Heidelberg: 1916.

-----. "Die Reden des vierten Evangeliums." ZNW 17 (1916): 49-60.

Sparks, Hedley Frederick Davis. "St. John's Knowledge of Matthew." JTS, N.S., 3 (1952):58-61.

Spitta, Friedrich. Das Johannes-Evangelium als Quelle der Geschichte Jesu. Göttingen: Vandenhoeck & Ruprecht, 1910. [Joh.-Evang.]

-----. Zur Geschichte und Literatur des Urchristentums. Band 1. Göttingen: Vandenhoeck & Ruprecht, 1893. [Geschichte und Lit.]

Stanton, Vincent Henry. The Gospels as Historical Documents. 3 vols. Cambridge: University Press, 1903-1920.

Strachan, Robert Harvey. The Fourth Evangelist: Dramatist or Historian? London: Hodder & Stoughton, 1925. [Fourth Evang.]

-----. "Is the Fourth Gospel a Literary Unity?" ExpT 27 (1915/16):22-26, 232-37, 280, 330-33.

-----. The Fourth Gospel: Its Significance and Environment. London: SCM Press, 1917. 3d ed., 1941. [Fourth Gospel, 3d ed.]

Strathmann, Hermann. Das Evangelium nach Johannes. 7. Aufl. (Neues Testament Deutsch, 4) Göttingen: Vandenhoeck & Ruprecht, 1954.
Strauss, David Friedrich. Das Leben Jesu. 2 vols. Tübingen: Osiander'sche Buchhandlung, 1835-36. ET of 4. Aufl.: The Life of Jesus Critically Examined. London: Chapman, 1846.
Strayer, P. M. "Transpositions of Text in St. John's Gospel." JTS 2 (1901):137-39.
Streeter, Burnett Hillman. The Four Gospels. London: Macmillan, 1924. [Four Gospels]
-----. The Fourth Gospel: A Study of Origins. London: Macmillan, 1926.
Teeple, Howard Merle. "The Greek Article with Personal Names in the Synoptic Gospels." NTS 19 (1972/73):302-17. ["G. Article"]
-----. "Methodology in Source Analysis of the Fourth Gospel." JBL 81 (1962):279-82. ["Methodology"]
-----. "The Oral Tradition that Never Existed." JBL 89 (1970):56-68. ["Oral Tradition"]
Temple, Sydney. "A Key to the Composition of the Fourth Gospel." JBL 80 (1961):220-32. ["Key"]
-----. "The Two Signs in the Fourth Gospel." JBL 81 (1962): 169-74.
-----. "The Two Traditions of the Last Supper, Betrayal, and Arrest." NTS 7 (1960/61):77-85.
Thompson, James Matthew. "The Composition of the Fourth Gospel." Exp., 8th series 11 (1916):34-46.
-----. "An Experiment in Translation." Exp., 8th series 16 (1918):117-25.
-----. "Is John xxi an Appendix?" Exp., 8th series 10 (1915): 199-47.
-----. "Some Editorial Elements in the Fourth Gospel." Exp., 8th series 14 (1917):214-31. ["Editorial Elements"]
-----. "The Structure of the Fourth Gospel." Exp., 8th series 10 (1915):512-26.
Tobler, J. T. "Über den Ursprung des vierten Evangeliums." ZWT 3 (1860);169-203.
Turner, Eric Gardiner. Greek Papyri: An Introduction. Princeton: Princeton University Press, 1968.
Unnik, Willem Cornelius van. Newly Discovered Gnostic Writings. Tr. from original Dutch ed., 1958. (SBT, 30) Naperville:

Allenson, 1960. [Gnostic Writings]

Völter, D. "Grundlage und Überarbeitung im Evangelium des Johannes." Teyler's Teologische Tijdschrift (1900):447-93; (1911):57-107.

Watkins, Henry William. Modern Criticism Considered in Its Relation to the Fourth Gospel. London: Murry, 1890. [Modern Criticism]

Wead, David W. The Literary Devices in John's Gospel. (Theologische Dissertationen, 4) Basel: Reinhardt, 1970.

Weiss, Bernhard. Das Johannesevangelium als einheitliches Werk: Geschichtlich erklärt. Berlin: Trowitzsch, 1912. [Johannesev.]

Weiss, Johannes. "Literaturgeschichte des Neuen Testaments." (RGG, 3) 1. Aufl. Tübingen: Mohr, 1912.

Weisse, Christian Hermann. Die Evangelienfrage in ihrem gegenwärtigen Stadium. Leipzig: Breitkopf und Härtel, 1856. [Evangelienfrage]

-----. Die evangelische Geschichte kritisch und philosophisch bearbeitet. 2 vols. Leipzig: Breitkopf und Härtel, 1838. [evang. Geschichte]

Wellhausen, Julius. Erweiterungen und Änderungen im vierte Evangelium. Berlin: Reimer, 1907. [Erweiterungen]

-----. Das Evangelium Johannis. Berlin: Reimer, 1908. [Evang. Joh.]

Wendland, Paul. Die urchristlichen Literaturformen. (Lietzmann, Handbuch zum N.T., I, 3) Tübingen: Radermacher, 1912.

Wendt, Hans Hinrich. Das Johannesevangelium. Göttingen: Vandenhoeck & Ruprecht, 1900. ET: The Gospel according to St. John. Edinburgh: Clark, 1902. [Gospel St. John]

-----. Die Schichten im vierten Evangelium. Göttingen: Vandenhoeck & Ruprecht, 1911.

Wetter, Gillis Petersson. "Der Sohn Gottes." Eine Untersuchung über den Character und die Tendenz des Johannes-Evangeliums. (FRLANT, N.F., 9) Göttingen: Vandenhoeck & Ruprecht, 1916.

Wilkens, Wilhelm. Die Entstehungsgeschichte des vierten Evangeliums. Zollikon: Evangelischer Verlag, 1958. [Entstehungsgeschichte]

-----. Zeichen und Werken: Ein Beitrag zur Theologie des vierten Evangeliums in Erzählungs- und Redestoff. (ATANT, 55) Zürich: Zwingli Verlag, 1969.

Willemse, J. Het vierde evangelie. Een onderzoek naar

zinnsstructuur. Hilversum-Antwerp: Paul Brand, 1965.

Williams, Francis E. "Fourth Gospel and Synoptic Tradition: Two Johannine Passages." *JBL* 86 (1967):311-19. ["Fourth G. and Synopt. Trad."]

Wilson, W. G. "The Original Text of the Fourth Gospel: Some Objective Evidence against the Theory of Page Displacements." *JTS* 50 (1949):59-60. ["Original Text"]

Windisch, Hans. "Der johanneische Erzählungsstil." In *Eucharisterion: Studien zur Religion und Literatur des Alten und Neuen Testaments; Herman Gunkel zum 60. Geburtstage*, pp. 174-213. (FRLANT, 36, 2. Teil) Göttingen: Vandenhoeck & Ruprecht, 1923. ["joh. Erzählungsstil"]

-----. *Johannes und die Synoptiker*. Leipzig: Hinrichs, 1926. [*Joh. und Synopt.*]

Wolfson, Harry. *Philo.* 2 vols. Cambridge: Harvard University Press, 1947.

Zahn, Theodor. "Das Evangelium des Johannes unter den Händen seiner neuesten Kritiker." *Neue Kirchliche Zeitschrift* 22 (1911):28-58, 83-115. ["Evang. Joh."]

Zimmermann, Hellmuth. "Lk und die johanneische Tradition." *TSK* 76 (1903):586-605.

LATER ADDITIONS to the list above:

Broome. Edwin C., Jr. "The Sources of the Fourth Gospel." *JBL* 63 (1944):107-21.

Clarkson, Mary E. "Underneath the Last Discourse." *ATR* 33 (1951):12-17.

Cullmann, Oscar. "Der johanneische Gebrauch doppeldeutiger Ausdrücke als Schlüssel zum Verständnis des vierten Evangeliums." *TZ* 4 (1948):360-72.

Hönig, Wilhelm. "Die Construktion des vierten Evangeliums." *ZWT* 14 (1871):535-66.

Holtzmann, H. [not H. J.] "Unordnungen und Umordnungen im vierten Evangelium." *ZNW* 3 (1902):50-60.

Lohmeyer, Ernst. "Über Aufbau und Gliederung des vierten Evangeliums." *ZNW* 27 (1928):11-36.

Muilenburg, James. "Literary Form in the Fourth Gospel." *JBL* 51 (1932):40-53.

Schneider, Johannes. "Zur Frage der Komposition von Joh 6, 27-58 (59) . . ." In *In Memoriam Ernst Lohmeyer*, W. Schmauch, ed., pp. 132-42. Stuttgart: Evangelisches Verlagswerk, 1951.

AUTHOR INDEX